ROSE LOWDER
BOUQUETS

EDITED BY
SCOTT HAMMEN

Eyewash
Books

ISBN: 978-2-9582044-6-4

❀ Created with Vellum

CONTENTS

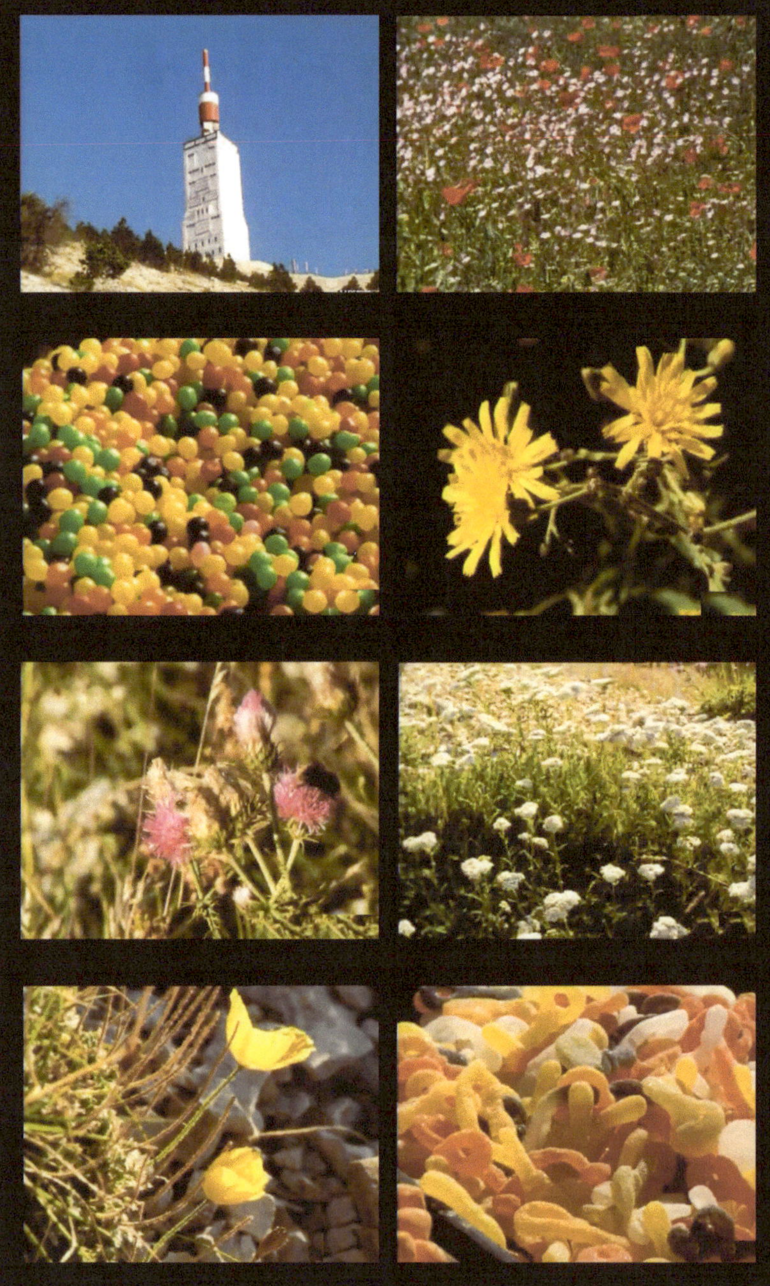

EDITOR'S NOTE

The critical essays in the first section of this book are presented in the chronological order of their first publication, and are intended to suggest, particularly for those unfamiliar with Rose Lowder's work, reasons to be interested in the following section, a catalogue raisonné of her *Bouquets* with details and comments on each. The final section collects a number of articles by Lowder herself, most originally published in French and translated here by the editor.

For the most part, Lowder wrote in response to specific inquiries about how her *Bouquets* series were made and similar questions recurred in each inquiry. So her responses inevitably contain some repetitive elements. Though this repetition may seem unnecessary, it also serves as a testament to the consistency of a remarkable artistic vision.

While Lowder began the *Bouquets* series near the beginning of her life-time of filmmaking, the earliest *Bouquets* were not her first attempts at composing films frame-by-frame. Before *Bouquet 1* (1994) came *Parcelle, Rue des Teinturiers, Champ Provençal* and *Retour d'un repère* (all 1979), composed entirely in the camera and shot continuously in a single place.

Lowder then went on to explore temporality in a different way in the series *Scènes de la vie française* (1985-1986). She explained that "images filmed from the same angle at different moments were woven by printing in a way that mixed the appearance of the same scene at different seasons."[1]

Then, in 1989, an exposure error while shooting her film *Impromptu* led her to run the same roll of film through her camera a third time.

> I realized that, since my camera could go both forwards and backwards, by rewinding the roll of film I could position images at any place in the roll, regardless of when it was shot, as long as I could devise a system to identify the exact place in the roll where frames had already been exposed and where they had not.[2]

The discovery eventually led to the first one-minute *Bouquet* which, interspersed between her longer films, became a decades-long chronicle of her explorations of visual perception. The second series (*Bouquets 21-30*) added another dimension - the artist's ecological convictions. All subsequent *Bouquets* were to be place-specific, focussed on organic farms and ecology centers devoted to environmental causes.

That this book is devoted exclusively to the *Bouquets* series is not meant to suggest that the other films Lowder was making in parallel are less important. It is simply because the *Bouquets* provide an ideal port of entry into her unique and beautiful world.

Scott Hammen
Paris, February 2023

PART 1 : CRITICAL VIEWS

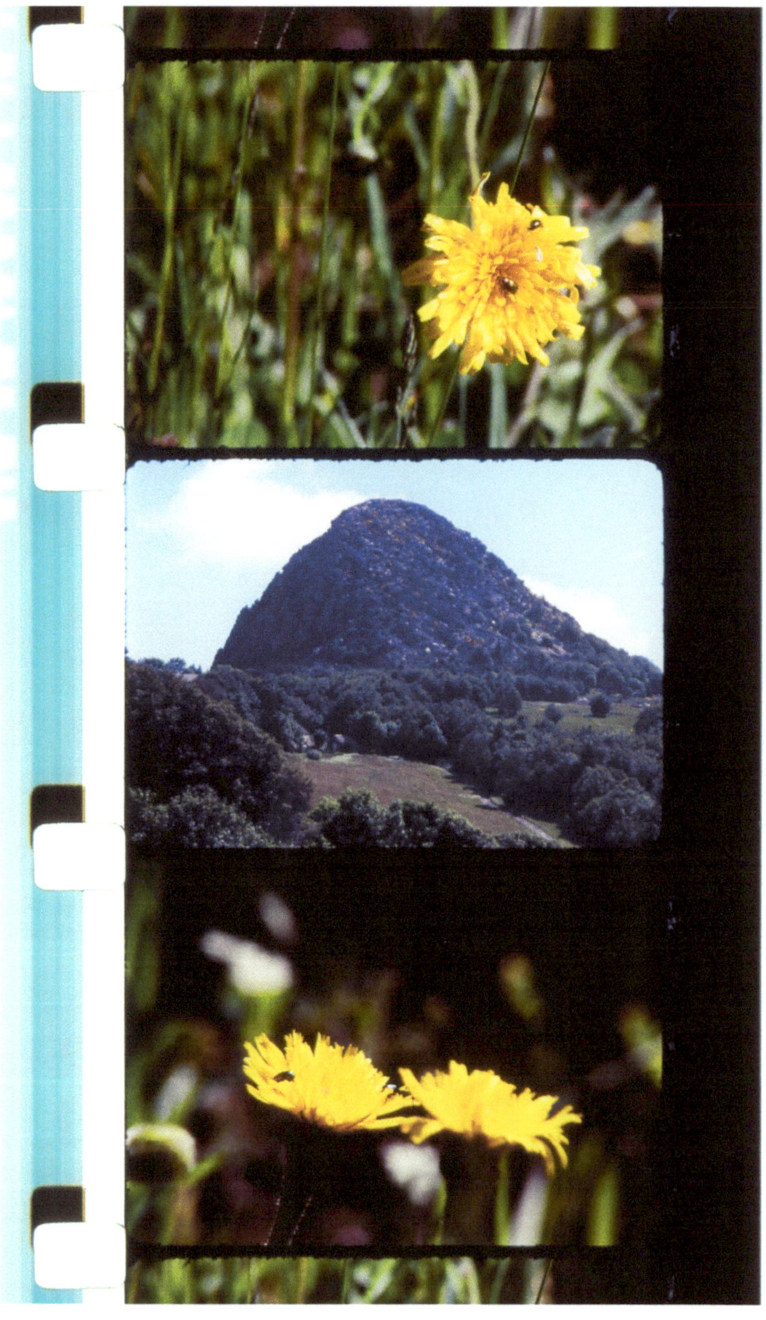

Bouquet 35 (2016)

TOWARD AN ECOLOGICAL CINEMA

SCOTT MACDONALD

By the time Rose Lowder bought her own 16mm camera, she had spent years working with loops of 16mm film, trying to determine whether the smallest unit of film structure was the single frame - as the Austrian Peter Kubelka had theorized[1] - concluding finally that "that's not the case at all," that in fact "pieces from different frames can make up what you're seeing on the screen."[2] Lowder's researches into the microcosmic units of cinema continued after 1977, once she was shooting her own imagery (for those early experiments she had used various film leaders and had worked directly on strips of clear celluloid: punching holes through frames, scratching or drawing lines along the filmstrip). While some of her earliest films use relatively long, continuous shots, others involved a painstaking process of recording imagery a single frame at a time, refocusing from one focus point to another in a single framed space, according to precisely organized "scores." This approach came to fruition in a triad of films, each of which focuses on a different kind of garden.

For *Rue des Teinturiers* (1979), Lowder set up her camera to look out the balcony window of the second story of her house in Avignon, through her tiny balcony garden, at the Rue des Teinturiers across the way.[3]

Over a period of months, she recorded this space, using a range of focus points so that, in some instances, elements of the street are in focus through the blur of nearby leaves, while at others, the leaves are clear and the distant street is a blur. Of course, because the focus point changes in virtually every frame, the resulting experience creates a continual retinal collage that suggests the perceptual immensity of even the tiniest space and the myriad intersections between Lowder's cinematic plan, the activities on an Avignon street, and the various changes in light, breeze, color - some of them predictable, others outside of Lowder's control - occurring in the balcony garden. In a sense, the little garden and Lowder's camera provide an analogy: each becomes a medium between Lowder's inner world (her domestic space, her plan for the film) and the space of the world outside: just as Lowder organized the garden to provide a tiny but effective "screen" between the busy street and her private space, the finished film is meant to screen out (if the reader can forgive the pun), at least for a moment, the usual commerce of film narrative and conventional exploitation of space.

Much the same procedure was used to make *Retour d'un repère* (1979), in which Lowder explores a portion of a public park in Avignon; and for *Champ Provençal* (1979), for which she filmed a peach tree in a Provençal orchard on three separate occasions (April 1, April 16, and June 24). In all three instances, Lowder uses her painstaking, even obsessive, procedure to expand what for most filmmakers - and especially commercial directors - would be a minimal bit of setting into a substantial film experience.[4] Beginning with *Les Tournesols* (1982), however, Lowder began to shift her tactics. *Les Tournesols* is a brief (3 minutes) film of a field of sunflowers, photographed from a wide variety of focus points within the camera's field of vision. While the film certainly maintains its gaze on a single scene for far longer than any commercial film would, Lowder's single framing of the field seems to energize the field, condensing the subtle movements of the sunflowers that occurred during a period of hours into a comparatively brief cinematic moment. That the film's energizing of the field seems particularly reminiscent of van Gogh's sunflower paintings, which were painted in nearby Arles, was not Lowder's conscious intent: "I didn't go out to make a Van Gogh film, and never imagined that I had, because the brush strokes of Van Gogh ... are so far removed from the kind of work I had to do to make the film."[5]

In the years after *Les Tournesols*, Lowder's "minimalism" became less and less an attempt to reveal the complexity of tiny local spaces by expanding them cinematically and more and more an attempt to explore what might be accomplished by condensing events that took place over the period of a day into a single, limited duration of film. Whereas the early films often explore the deep space of a single composition, recent films explore time more fully than space. In *Impromptu* (1980) Lowder focuses on three trees and a field of poppies, each location filmed on a different day in a different way and strung together to make the finished film: "In the case of the first tree in *Impromptu* (a tree in a courtyard in Avignon), I just exposed one frame, left the next one black, exposed the next, left the next one black. Then I wound the film back to exactly the same place ... and then... exposed the second, fourth, sixth frames."[6] In the resulting imagery of the tree, the space remains constant, but the time is reconstructed so that during any one second we see twelve frames filmed during one sustained moment during the day, interspersed with twelve frames filmed at a later time during the same day; and because various natural factors - the light, the breeze, the shadows are continuously undergoing more or less dramatic changes of their own, the resulting intensification of time within the space of the frame causes the tree to shimmer and quiver; it is as if the time-condensed imagery of the tree reveals the remarkable but normally invisible energy of photosynthesis. When Lowder concludes this first roll with a few seconds of normal motion, the normal motion looks as mysterious and surprising as the intensely worked passage that precedes it. Subsequent passages of *Impromptu* focus on a lime tree in an orchard near Avignon, a field of red poppies, and a peach orchard; in each instance, Lowder energizes a limited space by condensing and reorganizing the hours it took to make the imagery into the brief, seemingly continuous durations of the finished film.

Lowder's urge to explore the spaces and times of life in and around Avignon, and especially to condense experience into minimal cinematic durations, culminated in *Bouquets 1-10*, ten one-minute mini-films, made during 1994 and 1995. Even more than the earlier films, the *Bouquets* are meant to provide a cinematic model for ecological awareness: for Lowder, the relationship between her filmmaking and commercial filmmaking is analogous to that between organic farming and industrial farming:

MACDONALD: But do you see your concentration in your films as a kind of cine-politics? You eat organically; you don't own a refrigerator. Is your decision to work frame-by-frame a kind of environmental statement?

LOWDER: In opposition to big budget TV or cinema footage, yes. A developed society doesn't have to be a wasteful society. Take the example of organic farming. To survive today in France, an organic farmer has to be much more technically knowledgeable than an industrial scale farmer. The traditional farmer will be comparatively uneducated on the whole and will have technological sales representatives come along and tell him what to do, and when to do it. To reduce the number of people working on a farm, you need a tremendous amount of heavy equipment. You depopulate the countryside; you do very little manual work; and you produce a tremendous amount of food - too much, so much you have to throw some of it away (the government pays you to throw it away so that the prices stay up). Now if you look at the organic farmer, besides having to have more education, he or she will have to do more manual work. The field will need to be dug up by hand, or by more gentle machines, three or four times. The organic system requires that people are brought back to work on the land. Actually, in organic farming, there are more pieces of machinery, but smaller, more precise, and designed to accomplish particular tasks.

As an artist - to come back to your question - it's the same choice. You can work in a very precise way and make very particular decisions about everything you do. When I worked in the industry, we sometimes had a sixty-to-one shooting ratio. I worked in one television company where I was throwing away sacks and sacks of stuff every day. In the industry, the only things that count are the ones you sell...

I don't propose that things change all at once - that would be unecological - but hopefully things could change in an ecological direction by gradually moving toward a world that is more in the interests of everyone.[7]

The idea of digging up a field by hand, more than once, describes Lowder's procedure in a variety of her films, especially in *Impromptu* and in sections of *Bouquets 1-10*, where our field of vision is created by Lowder's planting - on our retinas - images made by moving along the furrow of the film and exposing individual frames to light, several times. The unusually high energy of the landscapes in *Impromptu* is analogous to the high energy achieved by an organic diet.

Like Lowder's earlier films, *Bouquets* is arranged formally, like a carefully planned formal garden. Each *Bouquet* is exactly one minute long, and is separated from the *Bouquet* that follows by six seconds of dark leader punctuated by a single frame of a single flower in close-up.[8] Each *Bouquet* begins with the title, spelled out one letter at a time, and ends with "Rose Lowder" and a completion date, spelled out a single letter or number at a time. In any particular *Bouquet*, Lowder explores a range of visual possibilities of working one frame at a time, sometimes creating effects familiar from *Impromptu*, *Les Tournesols*, and other earlier films, sometimes creating powerful, strobelike flicker effects.

Whereas earlier Lowder films tend to arrange successive frames that have a clear compositional relationship to one another, gaps between successive frames in *Bouquets* are often so considerable that viewers tend to be seeing several kinds of spaces simultaneously: one triad of successive frames in *Bouquet 10* (1995), for example, reveals a close-up of a yellow *Lactuca perennis*, followed by a long shot of the artificial lake near the French Alps created by the Serre-Ponçon dam on the Durance River (completed in 1960, the dam flooded two villages, leaving only a hilltop church in the center of the frame - above water level), followed by a close-up of a yellow *Hieracium*. Another triad (in *Bouquet 7*) reveals a Provençal skyscape, a close-up of a tiny waterfall, and a tree in a courtyard. Lowder's consistent interplay among multiple spaces has the opposite effect of her articulation of multiple focus points in *Rue des Teinturiers*: the earlier film expands a minimal physical space into an expanded cinematic space; each *Bouquet* condenses a considerable number of small, medium, and large spaces into a single, tiny, multi-layered cinematic experience.

Not only do particular moments in individual *Bouquets* sometimes create "retinal bouquets" - more literally, when successive frames reveal a succession of different flowers, and always figuratively, since Lowder is almost always gathering the "flowers" of the physically beautiful region in which she lives - but the series of mini-films, as the title suggests, is conceived as a bouquet: a bouquet of *Bouquets*. Like a conventional bouquet of flowers, this one is designed not just for a single look but to be savored over a period of time. Certainly the visual density and the distinctive visual design of each individual *Bouquet* (*Bouquets 1-10* is silent) demands multiple viewings - the way an individual flower can sustain attention to its particulars. And the cluster of films involves so many different images of so many different places, presented in so many ways, that few viewers can summon the energy necessary to see the entirety of what Lowder has done during any single viewing. Fortunately, this cinematic bouquet has a life span considerably longer than a real bouquet - although, as Lowder's title also implies, each *Bouquet* she has presented us with is fragile, not only in the obvious sense that our eyes and memories can't hold onto its complex imagery for long, but also in the sense that like all objects in the material world, any particular film (and especially every color film) is subject to decay the moment it leaves its creator's hands. *Bouquets 1-10* requires that we gather our (cinematic) rosebuds while we may.

FLOWER POWER

MICHAEL SICINSKI

"Ah, yes! Rose Lowder! " This is the response when the name of the French experimental filmmaker comes up in conversation among the avant-garde cognoscenti, the recognition that Lowder is not only a major master of our time but a kind of inevitability, one of the essential pillars of cinema as a material art form. And yet, her work isn't as widely written about or addressed in canonical surveys, compared with comparable figures of her generation, with comparable levels of achievement. It seems that Lowder is taken as a given, part of the overall landscape of the experimental film universe, an axiom. No one makes films like hers, but there are dozens of films for which Lowder is the only logical point of comparison. Her *Bouquets* series has become her best known set of films (arguably the works that cemented her reputation), but they are but one small part of an oeuvre that dates back to the 1970s.

The *Bouquets* films, like almost all of Lowder's films, are characterized by a rapid-fire perceptual workout generated by frame-by-frame photography. She exposes her scenes at alternating increments, introducing a vibration or alternation between two distinct positions or, in many cases, subjects, thereby depriving cinema of its standard capacity to replicate "normal" vision. This natural look, we might call it, is replaced with a tense, heightened dialecticism, which electrifies that which might otherwise be mistaken for being inert. Although the *Bouquets* (and other Lowder films) contain all sorts of images drawn from in and around Lowder's home in provincial France, the image which has become her standard recognition baseline (a kind of cine-avatar, if you will) is the flower, either in isolation or dispersed across gardens in color-organized beds. Lowder's flowers don't just sway in the wind. Her single-frame shifting whips the flora into a kind of molecular frenzy. Frequently, another view - a hillside, a home, even an animal - will intersect with this flower motion, its dominant melody allowing the unexpected content to function as counterpoint.

Earlier works didn't plant themselves in the garden at all. For instance, 1986's *Scènes de la vie française: La Ciotat* alternates between two distinct times in a single place, the fishing docks, each separate timeframe demarcated with a color code. Her film shot in Avignon from the same series (also 1986) focuses on trees and a picnic area in a park. Nevertheless, the *Bouquets* have proven so successful partly because of their combination of potency and brevity. They are each exactly one minute long, usually shown in groups, and so it becomes possible to discern exactly how Lowder can maintain the same essential format and re-invent it each time, a kind of seriality without the crushing burden of old-style structuralism. Every *Bouquet* starts with the same title "card," the letters B-O-U-Q-U-E-T flashing in block letters, frame-by-frame, followed by the number of the film. (The films end with the filmmaker's name popping up in the same font, followed by the date.) While the earliest works in the series tended to zero in much more intently on flowers and plant life, with other elements (such as barns or pastures) serving as the contrapuntal backdrops, *Bouquets 11-20*, completed between 2005 and 2009, were filmed at places Lowder terms "ecological sites" throughout France, Italy and Switzerland. As is evident from the films themselves, Lowder is providing much more space within this set of *Bouquets* to the material between the flowers, and much of it is surprising. We take actual pauses to see cows, goats, and farm cats moving through the farmscapes and gardens, claiming them as their own even as Lowder's trademark frame-by-frame (re)animation allows the plants and flowers to "reclaim" the earth for themselves.

This, in a sense, could speak to a dialectical view of ecology and the Green movement's insistence that human engagement with nature be a role of stewardship rather than dominion. When one looks at the earlier Lowder films, there is an energy almost verging on anger, as though "pretty" flowers were demanding their say in an image-world that had relegated them to the status of brute matter. (Capitalism only considers the natural inasmuch as it functions as a "resource" - what Heidegger called "standing reserve." But even Marx wrote of the natural world as inert matter, waiting to be transformed by human labor.) Now, in *11-20*, there is a commensurate adequacy of the camera gaze to multiple perspectives on the environment, the nervous vibration coexisting with a placid, even loving look of protection. Lowder's *Bouquets* are not only jostling us out of our habitual assumptions regarding the passivity of the world before our gaze. They are also enframing that world in order to remind us of just how much it contains that is beautiful and singular, and vital to save.

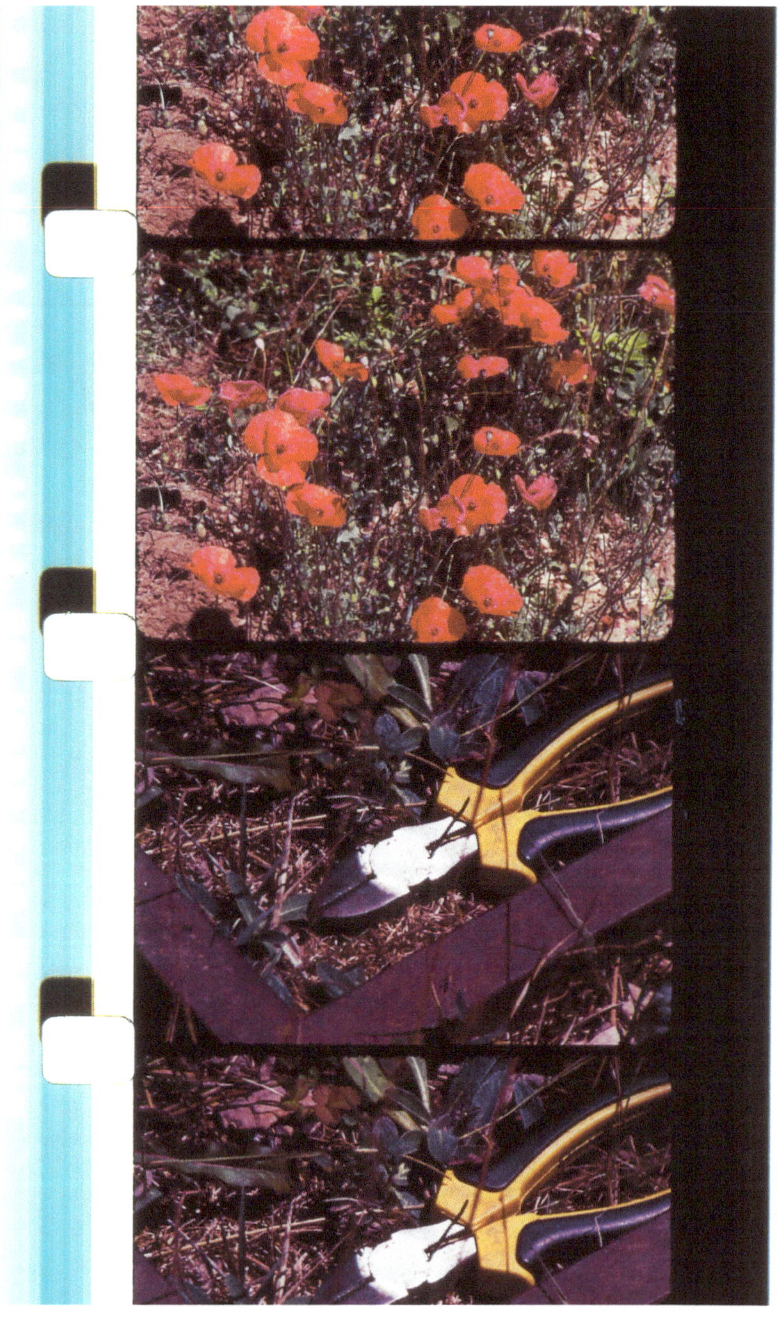

Bouquet 32 (2015)

A FILMIC EXPLORATION BY MEANS OF BOTANICAL IMAGERY: NOTES ON ROSE LOWDER

ENRICO CAMPORESI

I'd never been on a farm and am not even sure which are begonias, dahlias, or petunias. Plants, like algebra, have a habit of looking alike and being different, or looking different and being alike; consequently mathematics and botany confuse me.

– Elenore Smith Bowen

When looking at what can be considered the canon of so-called experimental film one suddenly realizes that there is a segment of this production devoted to botanical imagery. The presence of this imagery functions as the catalyst of a distinction between the filmmakers involved in this common exploration; even if one can trace links between this shared concern for the subject the approaches are extremely varied. As a starting point one could argue that the interest in botanical imagery among different artists might be due to a shared desire to deal with established pictorial genres, most notably still-lives and landscapes; but this too seems inaccurate.

. . .

If one looks at the work of Marie Menken (*Glimpse of the Garden*, 1957), Stan Brakhage (*Mothlight*, 1963; *The Garden of Earthly Delights*, 1981), or Kurt Kren (*3/60 Bäume im Herbst*, 1960; *37/78 Tree Again*, 1978) - to name just a few artists who deal with the subject at hand in those specific films - the difference among pictorial representations is startling. For instance, Menken constructs her *Glimpse of the Garden* on close-ups and dynamic hand-held camera movements. Brakhage deals with botanical elements in a manner directly based on the collage technique, gluing flowers and plants onto the clear film strip. Kren works rhythmically with short cuts and a fast in-camera editing style. The case considered in this article - the film work of Rose Lowder - is particularly interesting because of the artist's commitment, made explicit through an entire series of films with botanical imagery. The aim of this article then is an inquiry into this subject with an attempt to point out the different uses and functions that plants and flowers embody in some of her major works.

Cameraless film

Before examining the subject directly, it is worth noting that Rose Lowder's cinematic experiments (starting around 1976) began even before she was able to shoot film with a camera. It can also be useful to recall here that before making "experimental" films Lowder trained as a painter and sculptor in artist studios and art schools (in Lima at The Art Center, La Escuela de Bellas Artes, and in London at Regent Street Polytechnic, Chelsea School of Art). Her training in the visual arts was pursued in parallel with working as an editor in the film and television industry. This dual aspect of her biography proves to be crucial when dealing with her film work since it is possible to find both pictorial concerns and an in-depth knowledge of the filmic apparatus.

. . .

Her first works (which are grouped together in a sort of anthology and distributed under the literal title *Loops* – an evident reference to the film strip) seem to deal directly with film material. Furthermore, not only are they entirely abstract (or more accurately, not at all figurative) but they do not rely on any image obtained photographically. These loops are composed of transparent 16mm film leader in which Lowder made holes using a paper-punch in addition to using an ink marker to trace lines on it.

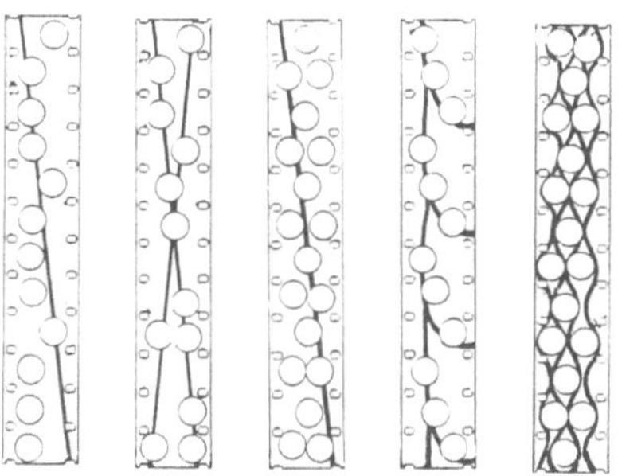

Fig. 1: Studies for the *Loops* films (from Lowder 1987, p. 283).

These first attempts to deal with film reveal at least two major things about Lowder's work. It is clear that the photographically-obtained image (and consequently questions of composition, light, etc.) is secondary in her production, being entirely absent in these works. Also, these experiments underline something that will become even more central in her subsequent work. The loops she created around the second half of the 1970s make visible the dual nature of film; that is to say they point out that what lies on the film strip does not correspond to what is shown on the screen by the means of projection.[1]

The first of these issues discussed above is also expressed by the filmmaker herself in a text published almost 20 years after these first experiments (on the occasion of a program on experimental film and

color curated by Philippe-Alain Michaud at the Louvre Auditorium).
Tracing the history of cinema in concise yet accurate terms, Lowder
explains the following:

> [w]hile the cinematographic tradition has been built upon two types of
> movement - that of the camera and that of filmed reality - it is the
> concern for the very mechanism of the filmic apparatus that makes
> manifest the inherent possibilities in the arrangement of individual
> frames and the movement of the film strip.[2]

Therefore, as clearly stated by the filmmaker, it is not so much the
camera nor the "filmed reality" that opened up new possibilities for
cinematographic movement but rather those possibilities were themselves already inscribed in the mechanics of the apparatus - in the film
strip, the projector, the shutter, etc.[3] When Lowder began producing
her own images - that is to say, when she bought her first 16mm
camera in 1977 - those questions where not put aside but rather
shifted slightly towards another direction with the introduction of
some aspects of composition that interacted with the already well-
defined formal concerns mentioned above.

Now that the crucial importance of the film apparatus has been
established there is another important point to be made. The loops
that Lowder worked on at the beginning of her career seem to embody
an implicit critique and mark a theoretical difference with one of the
major orientations in experimental film of the period. Although one
can trace some similarities with the realm of so-called "structural film"
(due to the interest in the essential components of the film medium)
there is at least one notable difference with this sphere of production.[4]
To make a comparison it is possible to see that in one of the most
precise formulations of the poetics of structural film delivered by Peter

Kubelka, which refers to "metrical film" with respect to his own production, there is at least one element that clashes with Lowder's first works. At the core of Kubelka's formulation is one key assumption: that of the primary role of the frame in film composition. Kubelka argues that the single frame is the smallest unit of film structure, thus the essential articulation of cinema takes place "not between shots, but between frames," in opposition to standard conceptions of narrative cinema.[5] Whereas for Lowder, as she clearly stated years later in an interview with Scott MacDonald, even Kubelka's position seems to fall short of the truth:

> [a]s these experiments demonstrate, pieces of different frames can make up what you're seeing on the screen. In other words, you can construct an image on the screen with bits from different frames. You can change very slightly parts of frames or several frames - change the color, the thickness of the lines, whatever, and a completely different thing happens.[6]

The frame and its supposed central role is challenged from Lowder's earliest work; it is as if the filmmaker wanted to decompose - down to its most minute parts - what is generally taken for granted as the smallest unit in film. However, this research did not stop when Lowder started shooting with her camera. On the contrary, it found a new configuration in the figurative style of her later films while keeping continuity with her early works and also ambiguously shifting back and forth between modes of abstraction.

First lesson in botany (towards abstraction)

It is at this point that it becomes possible to detect the presence of botanical elements, most notably in Lowder's work from 1979 entitled

Rue des Teinturiers. In this film the camera is set up on the tiny balcony which, as the title indicates, faces the rue des Teinturiers at the back of the filmmaker's house in Avignon. Through the window one can see the street below but there are plants located on the balcony that interfere with the vision of the observer. Most notably, leaves of laurel always appear as a screen (in its etymological sense), blocking the view.

The method applied by Lowder is meant to complicate this relationship between figure and background. Over a period of several months the filmmaker recorded this space, alternately focusing on the plant and the background. Since the focus changes virtually in every single frame the distinction between figure and background tends to disappear, giving birth to a certain composite image of the two elements.[7] Through this peculiar device the whole field of vision appears to widen and the process is even more astounding since it is carried out from an extremely narrow point of view. Furthermore, the whole scene is subject to infinite changes that perpetually overlap. Not only does the focus change, constantly mixing the laurel tree with the background scene, but the whole image is continually subjected to a metamorphosis due to the inevitable multitude of mutations in light, colors, and movement. Because some elements are beyond the control of the filmmaker (cars and people strolling down the street) the changes are often extremely unpredictable. In this dialectic between outer and inner space an entire theory of perception is challenged - namely the canonical distinction between figure and ground that can be traced back to Gestalt psychology.

As Lowder explains:

> [i]t seemed to me that if you wanted to create, not reality - that's not interesting at all; you might just as well see reality - but if you want to make a work of film art that is as rich as what one is used to in reality,

you have to enrich the film image somehow. One way is to continually focus on slightly different focus points that allow you to see around the corners of things just a bit. In certain scenes in *Rue des Teinturiers,* you'll notice that at some points you can actually see through the flowering laurel tree trunk in the middle of the balcony. You are seeing behind it as well, because one of the focus points is the trunk itself, and still another is in front of the trunk. Because I use all these focus points over and over, you see multiple things in the same space, which in reality is physically impossible.[8]

Therefore film, through a simple shift of focus - although in the production process itself it was not that simple, since it had to be done for every frame - can offer a different path towards perception. The relationship between figure (the laurel tree) and the background (the street scene) creates a dynamic unity made possible by the image projected on the screen. As is the case in the *Loops* films what you see on the screen is in fact not what is printed on the film strip. Indeed the extremely rapid alternation of single frames produces a projected image that cannot be found in the regular succession of frames as observed on the 16mm strip.

What then is the role of the plant in this case? It is clear that the laurel tree was not chosen for its iconographic qualities, nor does it recall any pictorial genre; it functions instead in a twofold manner. At first it embodies the role of an obstacle to vision; the view from the balcony is closed by its presence. Yet as we have seen it is also through this presence that the dialectic between the domestic space and the outer landscape is articulated by the means of a technical device (the change of focus). The laurel tree stands as a threshold of perception, something that can be penetrated by the gaze of the spectator but also something on which the very same gaze can focus.[9] Furthermore, due to the long period over which the film was shot, the living nature of the laurel plant is highlighted and acts as a prism for the reflection of the overall changes. The light that hits its leaves and the wind that shakes them alert the spectator to the singular condensation of time made possible by the frame-by-frame filming technique. So one could argue that in a way the cinematographic apparatus (the camera, the strip of film, and its continuous movement) does not clash with the natural element (nor the botanical one) but rather that it is an instrument for stressing its presence and opening a broader exchange between the daily rhythm of nature and the filmic, mechanical element.

Another film that Lowder made during the same year (1979) offers a similar example although not dealing at all with botanic imagery. The object in *Couleurs mécaniques* is at first difficult to recognize. The whole pattern of the film, composed of colorful lights spinning in different directions, appears to be almost entirely abstract. Gradually one is able to understand where these lights come from: the element that produces this light show is a carousel, but the camera's point of view focusing only on narrow portions of it allows the viewer to catch a fugitive glimpse of the entire structure. What can we find here that is so close to the nature of *Rue des Teinturiers*? Something essential lies in the title - *Couleurs mécaniques*, (Mechanical Colors) - which is in fact a direct reference to Fernand Léger and Dudley Murphy's avant-garde classic *Ballet mécanique* (1924), though the fact that the title is plural shifts the meaning considerably. As the film-maker herself points out the key difference between Léger and Murphy's film and *Couleurs mécaniques* is due to the fact that the avant-garde of the 1920s was fascinated by the machine itself. On the contrary Lowder in *Couleurs mécaniques* aims precisely to use the workings of the machine in an opposite way - she wants to use them in order "to free the objects' colors for another visual purpose".[10] In a similar manner to *Rue des Teinturiers* then, where the mechanical aspects of filmmaking are indeed linked to the botanic element displayed in the film, here the machine-originated colors are meant to lose their link to the technical apparatus and are freed from it, propelled towards abstraction.

It is not surprising that during this same period, just some time before all the aforementioned works from 1979, Lowder created an entirely abstract film. *Parcelle* (1979) stands apart in her production, since although it is true that the *Loops* films are abstract they can hardly be considered a finished work. On the contrary *Parcelle* is a fully-accomplished work of abstract film. The film introduces a geometric frame into a sequence of pure color ones: a small colored square positioned in the middle of the frame alternating with a circle of the same size. As Nicky Hamlyn points out the size of the object is crucial: "[i]t is just big enough for the viewer to distinguish between the circle and square, but not so big that the alternations between the circles or square are gross or dramatic, or threaten to overwhelm the background color field."[11] The whole rhythm of the film is based on the alternations between the colors of the background and those of the figures and their two shapes (circle and square).

Hence, we again encounter two major elements discussed earlier. One is a concern for challenging the laws of perception through the filmic apparatus. *Parcelle* functions in a manner similar to *Rue des Teinturiers*, where one can experience the simultaneous view of figure and ground (the laurel tree and the street scene). In the abstract film the border between figure and ground is constantly shifting thanks to an extended use of the "flicker" effect.[12]

The second aspect coincides with an idea that can be traced back to Lowder's first attempts at filmmaking: the strong belief that the frame is not the minimal unit of film. The frame itself can be split within its boundaries as the small circle and square rapidly alternating at its centre demonstrate. This idea which seems to remain crucial to the filmmaker's work will be subjected to another original variation in a work that she made some years after *Parcelle,* in which we once again find the presence of a botanical element.

From flowers to ornament

Les Tournesols (1982) not only stands out as a key work in Lowder's filmography but also indicates a theoretical turning point in her career. The subject of this three-minute film is a field of sunflowers framed to exclude the horizon.[13] The quasi-pictorial image is under tension as a result of the same device used in *Rue des Teinturiers* but with a remarkable shift that is coherent with the spatial and framing restrictions. The field is photographed with a large number of different focal points so that the uniform pattern is constantly moving. *Les Tournesols* proceeds through spatial and temporal condensation.[14] As MacDonald describes it:

> Lowder's single framing of the field seems to energize the field, condensing the subtle movements of the sunflowers that occurred during a period of hours into a comparatively brief cinematic moment.[15]

It is also worth evoking the tactical shift operated by the filmmaker in the use of botanical imagery. Whereas in *Rue des Teinturiers* the laurel tree functioned mainly as a threshold to test a theory of perception (and to dialectically challenge the distinction between figure and ground) here the sunflower field is chosen because of its inherent capacity to introduce movement within the borders of the frame. By focusing alternately on different points within the shot the overall pattern becomes dynamic and in doing so produces a series of motifs that modulate the image. Thanks to the singular in-camera editing

technique this movement is not abrupt but rather continuous. As
Lowder states:

> You're focusing on successively different flowers all over the field, and
> together they all look in focus. But when the images were shot, parts
> of every frame were out of focus.[16]

The peculiar pattern that comes out is therefore produced by the
simultaneous presence of two components: the natural element (sub-
mitted as such to a whole series of chance events: breeze, light, etc.)
and the rigorous formal structure in which it is contained.

With the *Bouquets 1-10* series (1994-1995), one of her most celebrated
works, Lowder's method of composition becomes increasingly
complex and articulated. The series consists of ten films shot in the
south of France as well as elsewhere.[17] As the title indicates the
subject matter is mostly (but not exclusively) flowers. Each of the
Bouquets is a one-minute long film strip - which is to say they are
composed of 1,440 frames each. Each of the films is shot frame-by-
frame but in non-chronological order and according to a careful plan,
following something of a musical score. On this point Lowder notes:

> The work is similar to that of a musician. I fix my sheets securely to
> the tripod, or put stones or my foot on them if nothing else will do,
> and then play my instrument, the camera as best I can. The reality
> filmed shares, with the grid-like charts to be filled-in, the function of a
> score. The difficult execution interpreting within the given constraints
> demands the same concentration as the careful attention a musician
> gives to the beginnings and endings of first and last notes (frames) of a
> movement in a piece of music.[18]

.   .   .

The formal organization thus moves towards a certain abstract quality (like a musical score) although the medium used for its expression is photographic reality. This conflict between the rigorous procedural structure and the uncontrolled reality which is recorded stands at the core of the *Bouquets* series and is the extreme conclusion of a process towards abstraction that began with *Les Tournesols*. Lowder uses the filmic apparatus to distil pure visual motifs out of the landscapes she carefully explores, freed from the mere photographic recording of reality. By means of the frame-by-frame filming technique the rapid alternation of one image with a different one creates a vibrant surface animated by an overlapping of abstract motifs. As Michaud recently pointed out, discussing Lowder's *Bouquets*:

> [w]hen film is imagined as projection phenomenon, it is freed from its frame, spreads out in space and multiplies. At the same time, the projection of colored surfaces takes on an ornamental density, negating the fictitious depth that opens up on the screen, and asserting its artificial aspect. The stylised figures now only have a compositional or formal value. The spatial treatment concludes in an interplay of colored motifs and lines that connect, break up, overlap or counter each other. The illusionist realism of film that aspires to create stable representations of the transitory appearance of things is countered by the deliberate schematism of ornamental images that suggest a different way of occupying the surface. Ornamental order is not the order of the narrative, but of composition: rather than attempting to imitate the real, it seeks to transform it into a motif.[19]

In this way the flowers that make up *Bouquets* seem to enter into the realm of the ornamental. They are used to form a fleeting composition that appears in a flash and rapidly dissolves, as with fireworks (to appropriate the metaphor proposed by Michaud). Their formal qualities (color and shape) are then exploited to produce this unstable pattern that can be shown on the screen by means of projection but that cannot be found on the film strip.

Throughout her filmography Lowder has established different ways of dealing with botanical imagery, using it either as a theoretical tool for an inquiry into perception (as in the early part of her artistic production) or as a means of producing ornamental motifs. However, there is coherence in her gradual progression from one approach to another because in each case botanical imagery is framed in a rigorous manner. Ultimately the botanical elements displayed in her films do not appear as elements appropriated from reality but rather as a catalyst for the filmic apparatus itself. When looking at the fleeting motifs that recur in the *Bouquets* one can feel disoriented. The composition lasts for an extremely short length of time and the surface constantly changes, invaded by a new motif, while at the same time entangled with the surrounding elements.

In her anthropological novel *Return to Laughter* (1954) Elenore Smith Bowen described a sense of confusion precisely in regards to plants which, like algebra, "have a habit of looking alike and being different, or looking different and being alike."[20] One could ask what she would have thought of Lowder's films, where the almost mathematical composition constantly frames and organizes the botanical element. I would argue that while perhaps coupled with the sense of confusion described in those lines she would also have experienced a deep aesthetic astonishment.

It is worth mentioning that the very same passage from Bowen's novel was quoted by Claude Lévi-Strauss in the first chapter of his *The Savage Mind*, titled *The Science of the Concrete*. This chapter is devoted to the methods of acquiring knowledge which differs from scientific thought. When Lowder collects and gathers flowers and plants for her *Bouquets* she is not producing taxonomies or anything of the sort. Rather, by making her rigorous filmmaking practice collide with botanical imagery, she is demonstrating the aesthetic achievements of a *science of the concrete,* a science whose axes are the profound knowledge of film and its mechanical apparatus, and the experienced gaze of the botanical connoisseur.

Acknowledgements

This text was first published in *NECSUS – European Journal of Media Studies* 3, Spring 2013. I subsequently revised it, integrating most notably a couple of remarks by Rose Lowder, for its publication in *OEI* 69-70, "On Film," edited by Martin Grennberger and Daniel A. Swarthnas, 2015. This second version is the one reprinted in the present volume.

My research was carried out at Light Cone, which distributes Rose Lowder's films, and at Centre Pompidou, where Alexis Constantin helped me to examine the 16mm prints held in the museum's collection. Oliver Lee Wootton and Noah Teichner attentively read the first draft, giving me invaluable help on the subtleties of the English language.

Bibliography

Cartwright, L. and Gidal, P. "Rose Lowder's Composed Recurrence," *Millennium Film Journal* 16-17-18, Autumn-Winter 1986-87: 176-179.

English, W. "Three Aspects of French Experimental Film. Interviews with yann beauvais and Rose Lowder and Alain-Alcide Sudre," *Millennium Film Journal* 23-24, Winter 1990-1991: 102-116.

Gidal, P. *Materialist Film.* New York-London: Routledge, 1989.

Hamlyn, N. *Film Art Phenomena.* London: British Film Institute, 2003.

Kubelka, P. "The Theory of Metrical Film" in *The Avant-garde film: A Reader of Theory and Criticism* edited by P. Adams Sitney. New York: Anthology Film Archives, 1978.

Lévi-Strauss, C. *The Savage Mind* translated by J. Weightman and D. Weightman. Oxford: Oxford University Press, 1996 (orig. in 1962).

Lowder, R. *Le film expérimental en tant qu'instrument de recherche visuelle. Contribution des cinéastes expérimentaux à une démarche exploratoire.* PhD dissertation, Université Paris X Nanterre, 1987.

______. "Propos sur la couleur en partant des Bouquets" in *Poétique de la couleur. Anthologie* edited by N. Brenez and M. McKane. Paris: Auditorium du Louvre-Institut de l'image, 1995.

______. "Leaving the Artist's Studio Behind or How to make Bouquets out of Flowers and Film", Cantrills Filmnotes 85-86, June 1997: 55-58.

______. "Du pictural au filmique : l'imprévu, l'inattendu, l'inconnu" in *L'image en mouvement. 25 ans d'activité pour la défense du cinéma comme art visuel* edited by R. Lowder and A. Sudre. Avignon: Archives du film expérimental d'Avignon, 2002, pp. 71-76.

______. "Le cinéma comme art plastique" in *Le septième art. Le cinéma parmi les arts* edited by J. Aumont. Paris: Léo Scheer, 2003, pp. 191-196.

______. "De l'enregistrement comme moyen de composition de l'image", *Pratiques* 14, Autumn 2003: 44-54.

MacDonald, S. *A critical cinema 3: Interviews with independent filmmakers.* Berkeley-Los Angeles: University of California Press, 1998.

______. *The garden in the machine: A field guide to independent films about place.* Berkeley-Los Angeles: University of California Press, 2001.

Michaud, P. *Sketches. Histoire de l'art, cinéma.* Paris: Kargo & l'Éclat, 2006.

______. "Conjuration, Imitation" in *Noches eléctricas/Electric nights. Arte y pirotecnia/Art & pyrotechnics* edited by P. Michaud, B. Weil, and L. Le Bon. Gijón: LABoral, 2011.

Sitney, P. Adams "Structural Film", *Film Culture* 47, 1969: 1-9.

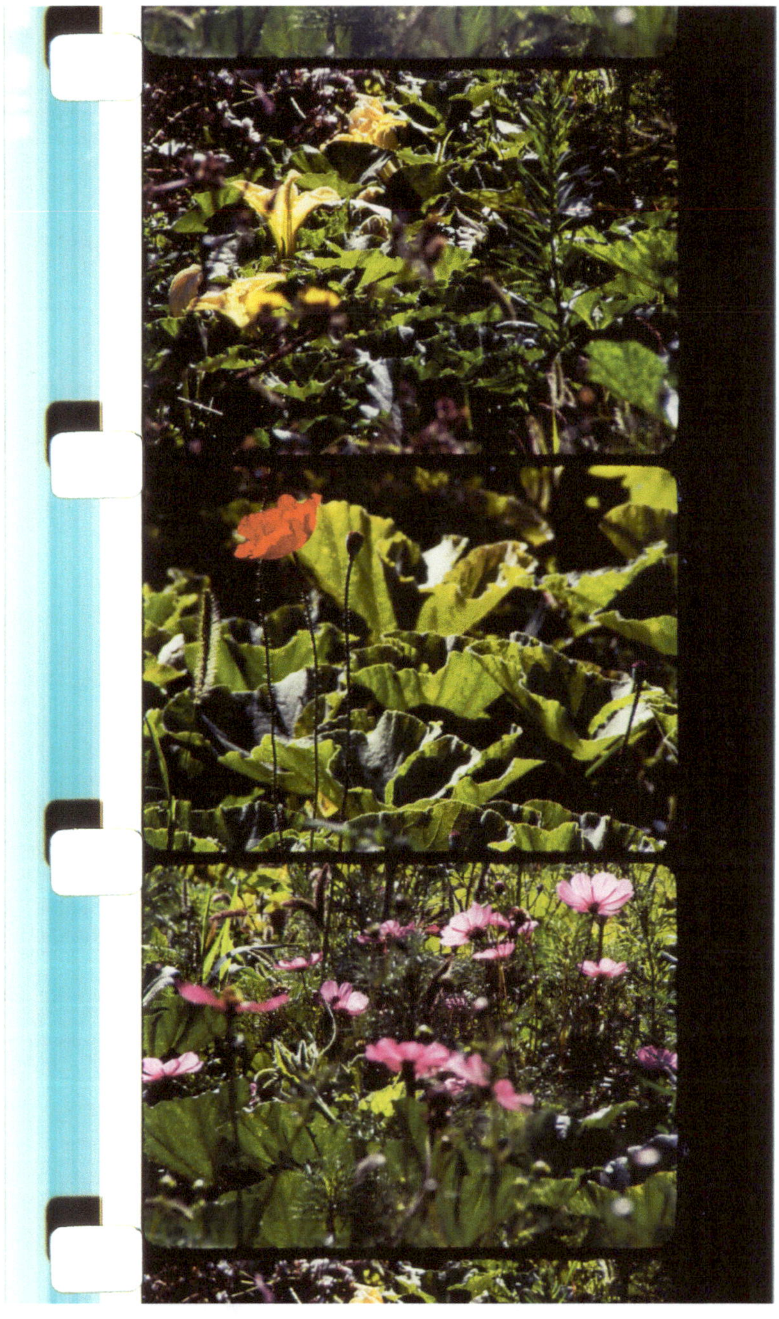

Bouquet 36 (2016)

PERCEPTUAL-IMAGINATIVE SPACE AND THE BEAUTIFUL ECOLOGIES OF ROSE LOWDER'S BOUQUETS

SARAH COOPER

Throughout her *Bouquets* series, which she began in 1994, experimental filmmaker Rose Lowder has turned increasingly to the portrayal of specific subjects in ecological places, with flowers as her central point of focus. She notes that her love of flora has led people to ask her whether there are not more important things to do today than to make films about flowers, reporting that she would answer them with a question: "are there really more important things?"[1] Emphasizing the dependency of bees on flowers and the essential link in the food chain they provide, she affirms how such a subject is not only relevant for her as a filmmaker but also vital to life. In keeping with this, the production of the *Bouquets* is rooted in a concern for the environment. *Bouquets 1-10* (1994-5) were made from 16mm film stock left over from other projects that Lowder did not want to go to waste - an economy of means key to her ecological principles. She used the stock to film anything that she found interesting in a place that she was just passing through, and predominantly it was the flowers in those places that caught her eye. Lowder added to these initial films with two further series: *Bouquets 21-30* (2001-5) and *Bouquets 11-20* (2005-9).[2] There is a seasonal unity to all three series (they are filmed in spring or summer), and each film is roughly a minute in length (1,440 frames), made in-camera and not edited after it has been shot. In the latter two series the images are from organic farms and ecological gardens, mainly in France but also neighboring countries of Switzerland and Italy. Made in this way relatively close to home, Lowder's work has a low carbon footprint, and she lives by these standards too, buying and eating local produce, and mindful of sustainability wherever possible.[3]

In spite of their name, then, Lowder's *Bouquets* are not the filmic equivalent of the eponymous floral arrangements that are an everyday part of the global mass-market cut flower industry. Rather, they stand apart from mainstream commercial culture as experimental works on perception that attend to wild or organically grown flowers still in their soil. Yet these flowers filmed in situ reach out from the environments in which they grow into the realm of aesthetics: as such, Lowder's bouquets of images open onto an appreciation of beauty that stretches from nature into art and has a long historical lineage. The *Bouquets* constitute an assortment of images configured in such a way that the spectator's involvement is essential to their making, their beauty a function of perceptual production in conjunction with the film apparatus. Lowder's experiments with perception forge in turn a hitherto unexplored connection to imagination that proves crucial to understanding how beauty entwines with ecological commitment - both her own and that which might be stirred in viewers upon watching her films. In this article, I bring imagination explicitly into discussion of her experiments with visual perception as I trace the creation of a perceptual-imaginative space from her early work onwards, attending to questions of beauty and balance that inform the ecologies of her *Bouquets*.

Forming Perceptual-Imaginative Space

Born in Miraflores, near Lima, with a fine art background acquired through her studies first in Peru and then London from the early 1950s to the mid-1960s, Lowder began her career in the film industry working as an editor in London and Paris from the mid-1960s to the early 1970s, before turning to concentrate on her own experimental practice from her home in Avignon in the south of France.[4] In her doctoral thesis, nominally supervised by Jean Rouch and completed in 1987, Lowder makes the point that it is only by setting aside intentions that are either purely expressive or aesthetic that experimental film can explore the perception of the sensible world.[5] Fittingly, she began her experimental film work on visual perception without a camera, punching holes in pieces of 16mm filmstrip and drawing lines on them directly with a marker pen, captivated by the difference between what could be seen on the strip and what then appeared on screen when the strip was run through a projector. These *Boucles* (1976–7) served as her starting point for advancing further experiments with perception, now using a camera and filming a range of subjects. Before I address the perceptual explorations of Lowder's *Bouquets*, it is useful first to consider an early work that paved the way towards the series, since it enables us to glimpse the emergence of a relation to imagination that will be important throughout my ensuing discussion.

Rue des Teinturiers (1979) is one of Lowder's earliest films made with a camera and is her first treatment of a vegetal subject. She set up her camera on her small balcony on rue des Teinturiers in Avignon in order to shoot the foliage of a laurel on the balcony and the street behind it over a period of six months, alternating between focusing on plant and street, figure and background.[6] When projected, the film bears some similarity to structural film form as defined by P. Adams Sitney with reference to US films of the 1960s, due to the persistent vibrating or flickering effect generated by filmmaking and projection.[7] The quivering quality was to dominate many of her other films, including the *Bouquets* series, and in Lowder's practice it comes from the fact that she filmed one frame at a time on her 16mm film stock and changed the focus for each frame. The camera is entirely static throughout the filming process, but when the images are projected, the changes of focus seen in swift succession generate the rapid movements that give rise to a composite image of the filmed elements, such that there is no superimposition but rather individual frames mixing instead. When speaking of a later film, *Les Tournesols* (1982), Lowder describes how the viewer's perceptual mechanism contributes to this effect: "Due to the varying time-lengths our perceptual system needs to treat different types of visual stimulus, parts of images situated on separate frames are seen, under certain circumstances, depending on the graphic and plastic features of the successive frames, to appear simultaneously or as overlapping each other on the screen."[8] For Lowder the smallest unit of film is smaller than the frame. The effects of perception in response to her films lead to the mind creating more than is visible frame-by-frame in a more complex manner than was discernible in her initial, camera-less *Boucles*. On the strip of *Rue des Teinturiers* there are clearly discernible individual images but when run through the projector, the film stock coupled with the perceptual mechanism of the spectator gives rise to a viewing experience of a visual palimpsest. The effect of filming and projecting the plant and the street in this manner means that shots of the plant give way to shots of the street and, at times, albeit momentarily, viewers see through the plant to its other side whereas in ordinary perception this would, of course, be impossible since what is behind the plant would have to be imagined instead.

As Lowder notes in her doctoral thesis, one of the aims of *Rue des Teinturiers* was to use the filmic apparatus to gain access to elements present in reality that would otherwise have remained imperceptible.[9] Her reference points in her research into perception are many and varied, with visual perception of movement and colour forming a main area of enquiry supported by scholarly research on the topic published in the early 1970s.[10] Her experimentation with perception recalls the philosophical explorations of early twentieth-century phenomenologists, too. Lowder's filming of the laurel and the street reveals that it is necessary ordinarily to move around three-dimensional objects in space and time in order to perceive them and what lies behind them, as both Jean-Paul Sartre and Maurice Merleau-Ponty would concur in their now-classic work. In the work of Sartre and Merleau-Ponty, differing elaborations of the phenomenology of perception in the visible world broach nonetheless a relation to what cannot be seen, and a cube is one of the emblematic objects for their observations.[11] For Sartre, the perception of a cube, like other objects, signifies "the necessity of making a tour of objects, of waiting, as Bergson said, until the 'sugar dissolves.'"[12] For Merleau-Ponty, it is by conceiving of his body as a mobile object that he is able to interpret perception and construct the cube whose sides are not visible to him without moving around it.[13] For Lowder, it is the camera that permits access to an eventual vision of what is normally invisible at specific moments in time from fixed vantage points but without moving around what it films. Through the intricate filming of the laurel, followed by the combined effects of projection and spectatorial perception, Lowder enables viewers to see multiple things in the same space and to see through solids - here the laurel - to what lies beyond them. The space mapped from the perceptible to the imperceptible relies on a point of contact established with what can normally only be imagined from a given standpoint. It is not that Lowder activates imagining in the sense that spectators conjure mental images of what is not there.[14] Rather, the spatial structure is that of both perception and imagination, due to the impossible perspectives created on the basis of what is seen.

Lowder's filming of the laurel on her balcony is necessarily more restricted in spatial terms than the filming of her *Bouquets* will be as she roams across many different sites. Moreover, between *Rue des Teinturiers* and the later series, Lowder will also make other films that explore perception and that feature flowers and blossoms in more expansive spaces, from peach blossom in an orchard (*Champ Provençal*, 1979) through to sunflowers in a field (*Les Tournesols* and *Les Tournesols colorés*, 1982-3). The presence of flowers heralds the arrival of beauty in abundance, and the very filmic vision that gave rise to perceiving what could normally only be imagined beyond ordinary sightlines can now invite reflection on its pleasures in the light of an array of colourful, quivering petals. The floral images call for the spatial discussion of perception and imagination to be opened out to broader historical associations formed between imagination, pleasure and beauty - in nature and art - but these will lead back eventually to the connection between the geometrical cuboid shape in the twentieth-century phenomenologists' reflections and Lowder's perceptual-imaginative space.

There may not be much that links the differing reflections of the twentieth-century phenomenologists on perceiving and imagining to the eighteenth-century philosopher Joseph Addison's talk of imagination, but the insistence on a link to vision is something they share, especially in the case of Merleau-Ponty. In his late text "Eye and Mind," Merleau-Ponty asserts that imagining "borrows from vision and employs means we owe to it."[15] Addison focuses more specifically on what he terms the pleasures of the imagination, but insists that they proceed from sight. He positions imagination between sense and understanding, saying that its pleasures derive principally from seeing what is "great, uncommon, or beautiful."[16] These pleasures divide into two categories: primary pleasures that are from objects before the eyes and secondary pleasures from objects that are not actually before the eyes but called up by memories or visions of absent or fictitious things.[17] The play of absence and presence characteristic of much imaginative activity as described through the ages inheres within that play of the invisible and visible also evident in Merleau-Ponty's attention to the cube, in so far as something that is not before the eyes is brought forth in a manner that owes something to vision. The reason why Addison is of particular interest here as I turn to consider Lowder's filmed flowers is not just that he lauded the pleasures of the imagination prompted by beauty, but that he was writing on imagination in relation to beauty at a turning point in the eighteenth century just before other philosophers - most notably Edmund Burke and Immanuel Kant - would introduce a distinction between the beautiful and the sublime. Whereas beauty stimulates the pleasures of the imagination in unalloyed fashion in Addison's work, imagination was to be overwhelmed by the sublime.

When Kant writes in an early series of reflections on the distinction between the feeling of the beautiful and the sublime, a natural scene that may have been spoken about as all of a piece by Addison in terms of the pleasures of the imagination is now divided: "Lofty oaks and lonely shadows in sacred groves are sublime, flowerbeds, low hedges, and trees trimmed into figures are beautiful."[18] In the later *Critique of Judgment,* and from the magnitude of the mathematical sublime to the might of the dynamic sublime, Kant affirms a bond that will abide thereafter between the feeling of the sublime and the imagination's inadequacy.[19] The aesthetic power of judging the beautiful refers the imagination in its free play to understanding, whereas in judging a thing sublime it refers the imagination to reason.[20] In the former, imagination and understanding are in accordance; in the latter, imagination and reason are in conflict.[21] There is thus an agitation to the mind in presenting the sublime in nature, but in an aesthetic judgement of the beautiful in nature the mind is in restful contemplation.[22] Although the beautiful was never intentionally downgraded to a secondary position through discussion of the sublime, the influence of the distinction led to a hierarchy in the attention paid to each in years to come such that in the late twentieth century, as cultural scholar Elaine Scarry notes, talk of beauty waned in the Humanities to be replaced by a fascination with the sublime.[23] Alongside beauty, imagination is also displaced when the sublime is privileged. The magnitude and might that the imagination was faced with determined its adequacy.[24] To turn now to Lowder's *Bouquets,* the proportions of her flowers will loom as large on screen as mountains at times, and the quivering dissonance of the images will seem to agitate rather than encourage contemplation; as Guinevere Narraway notes, Lowder's films do not appear to generate the harmony of Kant's conception of the beautiful in nature, Naturschöne.[25] But they still maintain a link to the beautiful in which Addison, Burke, and Kant found pleasure in their earlier historical context, in nature and in art, albeit in defamiliarized form. Contemplative harmony may be challenged in the form of her films but a different kind of balance is achieved in the process, which is crucial to her ecological vision. Furthermore, the distinctive perceptual-imaginative space already formed in *Rue des Teinturiers* expands in the *Bouquets* to suggest that there is more to this filmic encounter with floral beauty than meets the eye.

Just Beautiful Bouquets?

Whenever I have presented conference papers on Lowder's *Bouquets* or had conversations about her films, people have commented most frequently on how beautiful her work is, even as they note the challenge of viewing its vibration and flicker. Were appreciation of her filmed flowers to stop at an aesthetic judgement, the environmental import of the work would risk getting lost. Some might say that this does not matter, but thinking back to the ecological principles that inform their production as well as her lifestyle beyond her filmmaking, a response to these films that cuts off responsibility to the environments in which they were made seems a distortion of her practice. An appreciation of the beauty of her filmed flowers can, however, lead viewers towards rather than away from ecological commitment. This move is founded in the specificity of Lowder's treatment of perceptual imaginative space, and Scarry clears the path for us to understand and make such a journey.

Following her observation that the Humanities shifted their interest to the sublime in the late 1990s, Scarry notes that the Sciences, in contrast, still featured discussion of "beautiful" solutions to problems and "pretty" theories.[26] Scarry's overriding interest in this work that originally took the form of her 1997-98 Tanner Lectures on Human Values is in how beauty might lead to justice. She cites two friends who respond to her research question, summarizing their observations with the assumption that they both share: "beautiful things give rise to the notion of distribution, to a lifesaving reciprocity, to fairness not just in the sense of loveliness of aspect but in the sense of 'a symmetry of everyone's relation to one another.'"[27] The beauty of the scientific subjects that seek truth is connected to a sense of fairness that spans definitions of the beautiful and the just. For Scarry, equality and symmetry of measure - what for classical philosophers was epitomized in the shape of the sphere but that I suggest could also encompass the cube - lead from geometrical shapes into the realm of justice. Even though we seem to have travelled some distance from the cube of the phenomenologists, it is by re-establishing a connection to matters of geometry and equal measure that it is possible to move from the beautiful to the just in ecological terms, indebted to that perceptual-imaginative spatial bond that Lowder first lays bare in *Rue des Teinturiers*. By expanding the human-centered relationship of "a symmetry of everyone's relation to one another" so that it becomes one in which the human and other forms of life entwine, Lowder's *Bouquets* create symmetries that lead from beauty to a just relationship with the environment.

Beauty, for Scarry, invites and even requires acts of replication - it inspires a desire to bring copies of itself into being, inciting a gamut of activities from human reproduction to artistic creation.[28] While Lowder's *Bouquets* are non-mimetic versions of the reality of the flowers that she perceives with the naked eye prior to filming, they still bear the trace of their inspiration. These are painstakingly crafted works, and experimental film scholar Enrico Camporesi notes indeed how Lowder's exploration of botanical imagery is also a means of producing ornamental motifs.[29] Indebted to the plein air tradition of leaving the studio and going out into nature, and possessing a color palette sensibility that she attributes to her childhood in Peru, Lowder's is a painterly inheritance and she speaks of an effect akin to pointillism in relation to her *Bouquets*.[30] The beauty of her *Bouquets* pertains, however, to both the floral source and the experimentation that results from the camera and spectator's perceptual systems working with one another to process the films. For Scarry, "Beauty seems to place requirements on us for attending to the aliveness or (in the case of objects) quasi-aliveness of our world, and for entering into its protection."[31] As Lowder places her filmed flowers in the field of human regard, she engages in the activity that beauty assists us with, according to Scarry - addressing injustice by requiring of us "constant perceptual acuity."[32] Scholarship on Lowder's work has noted the importance of her perceptual explorations with regard to her botanical subject matter. Both Scott MacDonald and Guinevere Narraway have connected Lowder's ecological ethic to what MacDonald terms elsewhere in relation to eco-cinema "a retraining of perception" that engages the viewer in seeing the world differently.[33] The need to alter perception is recognized more widely within contemporary eco-philosophy. In her work with philosopher Michael Marder on the vegetal world, feminist philosopher Luce Irigaray argues that a change in perception is necessary in order to be able to approach coexistence with plants in a meaningful way.[34] It is through further exploration of perceptual-imaginative space that Lowder broaches this question of coexistence in her *Bouquets*.

As with the filming of *Rue des Teinturiers*, the *Bouquets* reveal perceptual-imaginative spatial palimpsests, which allow viewers to see through solid entities to their other side, but they also grant access to something filmed in another place at a different time. In the intervening period between *Rue des Teinturiers* and the making of the first *Bouquets*, Lowder had attempted to reduce the degree of vibration apparent in the earlier work and also to combine this with other techniques. Her way of working was similar to the approach she used in a couple of prior films, *Impromptu* (1989) and *Quiproquo* (1992), both of which involved several passes of the same roll through the camera with different frames exposed each time (both are sound films, too). This repeated passing of the roll through the camera also characterizes her *Bouquets*, but the main difference when she came to make the later series was that she was no longer weaving together images that were identically framed. The *Bouquets* intermingle shots of different places within the same general area, rather than comprising shots of exactly the same place at different times (there are also occasional frames that are shot normally and some blank frames). More freely than in *Rue des*

Teinturiers, the filmed subjects construct the space that ordinary perception from the same standpoint could not ever achieve simultaneously, and an imagined space formed through intricate perceptual observation emerges through the layered images on the basis of Lowder's constantly shifting and creative engagement with the environments she films.

With the exception of *Bouquets 6* and *8* in the first series, which do not feature any flora, flowers return persistently within the perceptual field. In *Bouquet 1*, for example, filmed at Mont Ventoux in Provence, in which shots from the base of the mountain intermingle with shots at the summit where people could buy sweets among other things, running water appears over flowers, as do landscapes over water, and flowers over cars and people. In *Bouquet 13*, filmed on an organic farm and agro-ecological site in Aujac in the Gard, shots of a butterfly and other insects, along with vegetables, intermesh with people working on the land, interspersed with and overlaid by flowers. Animals make regular appearances throughout the series, for example a cat and then a donkey in *Bouquet 21*, filmed at the same farm in Aujac in the Gard through a haze of yellow flowers, in which farm workers and visitors also interweave throughout. And *Bouquet 22*, filmed in the pastures of the mountainous Grand Perron des Encombres, features images of the snow-streaked peaks, of buildings, of a children's play area, of people young and old, all of which mesh with the flowers. Human dominion is challenged as relationships with other forms of life - flowers most notably - come to the fore in a practice where visual perception frequently meets its limits.

To recall the equality and symmetry of measure that allowed me to link Scarry's association of beauty and the just to the perceptual-imaginative space of Lowder's early films by means of the philosophers' cube, it is the balance that Lowder achieves between the different aspects of her *Bouquets* that is important here, making people part of the picture alongside myriad other forms of life. The flowers assert their shimmering beauty, de-centering the human and thereby making people a less pivotal aspect of the filmed environments that viewers perceive. In this, Lowder's work is in tune with other philosophers who travel more explicitly the route that Scarry is interested in mapping from beauty to being just. Indeed, for moral philosopher Iris Murdoch, the experience of beauty involves an experience of "unselfing" that links perception to a sense of justice. For Murdoch, experiencing beauty in the enjoyment of nature and art, as well as in intellectual disciplines, prompts an ability "to forget self, to be realistic, to perceive justly."[35] The beauty of nature that prompts perceiving justly involves imagining, too, as Murdoch affirms: "We use our imagination not to escape the world but to join it."[36] Murdoch's example as she introduces the experience of unselfing is a scene from nature. She describes looking out of the window one day and seeing a kestrel, a sight which distracted her from brooding thoughts and cleared her mind of selfish care to the point that she declares "[t]here is nothing now but kestrel."[37] Building upon this example, she includes in the experience of unselfing "delight in flowers;"[38] and taking her observations into the realm of art, she talks of its genesis and enjoyment as "a thing totally opposed to selfish obsession."[39] Looking out of the window at a kestrel or taking delight in flowers may be close to the activity of the filmmaker who first scopes out her subjects in the environment prior to filming, but they are clearly different perceptual experiences from watching one of Lowder's films, in which the effect on natural perception of the apparatus is part of a broader experience.[40] Yet through the perceptual-imaginative space of her films Lowder reconnects creatively with a world that has the human in it but is not dominated by it. She is thus attuned to the work of unselfing that involves perceiving justly, and she attunes viewers of the *Bouquets* to this, too.

The fairness that pointed to loveliness of aspect as well as justice for Scarry in the journey that began with beauty joins here not only with her sense of perceptual acuity but also with the retraining of perception noted by MacDonald with reference to eco-cinema and with the alteration of perception that Irigaray calls for in her eco-philosophy. Fairness has an additional sense pertinent to this discussion, though, having stood historically as a marker of the female and the feminine. The sexual and gendered resonance of this term has long aided cultural associations between beauty, women and flowers to be passed off as natural and has placed a frequent barrier between women and the sense of fairness that is connected with justice.[41] Wherever reference to Mother Nature has served to essentialize the relationship between nature and the maternal-feminine, the feminine risks being eclipsed in culture, and while her survival in the latter domain is crucial, the networks of relations built beyond human reproduction are just as important. Lowder's work relates to the replication of beauty that Scarry talks about, but by remaining with and foregrounding the flowers, she sets herself apart from the sole replication of human beauty by means of reproduction. Lowder's enmeshing of different species in the environments she films may not have the stridency of feminist theorist Donna Haraway's call to "Make Kin Not Babies," but her work has tacit affinities with this feminist ecological drive.[42] As Irigaray notes, the Western tradition has focused too much on the fruits rather than the flowers, on the bearing of the fruits of carnal love rather than the flowering of lovers.[43] For Lowder, to linger on the flowers while also bringing in other occupants of the ecological sites she films is to reach beyond the fruits of human relationships alone, and to make kin of all kinds. The symmetry of relations or balance between different forms of life is not about making everyone or everything like everything else but is, as Irigaray notes, vital to coexisting in difference, the first dwelling for which, when humans relate to the vegetal world, is the silence of a wordless encounter.[44]

Lowder's commitment to filming in 16mm in silence in these films - even though a function of much experimental filmmaking that has no explicit ecological connection - ensures nonetheless that the *Bouquets* correspond with such vegetal silence. Irigaray observes that, in the Western tradition, silence has been left to nature and to women assimilated to nature, and she seeks to reinvest it with a positive value while undoing the essentialist assimilation of women to nature.[45] Like Merleau-Ponty, Irigaray is interested in looking beyond what is visible to the eye, and while she follows him into invisible spaces, she has always paid more attention to the darkness of the starting point in life - initial contact with a mother's body in utero through touch and hearing - carrying this forwards and never forgetting this founding relation. For Irigaray in her earlier work the very operation necessary to bring the maternal-feminine into language "requires passage through the night, a light that remains in obscurity,"[46] and she notes the importance of the voice for introducing sexuate difference. Lowder's *Bouquets* may not engage this vocal connection but they do embed the presence of the director's name and film title in fragmented form at the start of each bouquet of images, establishing a tacit connection to the female filmmaker, while involving her in the transformed world of her films, the letters of "BOUQUETS" and of the proper name "ROSE", also a flower, broken up and strewn like petals among the imaged flowers at the beginning or end of each film. Moreover, as a result of their seasonal unity, Lowder's films exude intense warmth and are flooded with light. The darkness into which one needs to venture, following Irigaray, thus seems initially to bear a less literal relation to Lowder's films than the silence. But attention to what cannot be perceived in the light is crucial to appreciate the life of plants, which grow above and below ground, and wherever there is a point of acknowledgment of obscurity in Lowder's *Bouquets*, viewers come into contact with this too. The flicker within the brightness of the films introduces this at regular intervals: the photo encounters the phyto between light and darkness - a condition of film, of course, but also the possibility of meeting flowers on their own terms. The connection to perceptual-imaginative space that I have been concerned with throughout serves this purpose too.

Indeed, thinking about an encounter with this obscurity in terms of an experience of what is never normally perceived from a given perspective - the experience of perceiving-imagining the entirety of the cube from one vantage point - the abiding importance of that initial figuration of perceptual-imaginative space can be invested now with a link to coexisting in difference. Lowder's ecologies constitute a way of being with the vegetal embedded in how she films her *Bouquets*, still in tune with Scarry's interest in fairness (loveliness of aspect/equality and symmetry of measure) that connected beauty to the just, but now bringing with it a de-essentialized link to the feminine, too. Lowder's exquisitely woven images are a privileged artistic site in which the concerns of aesthetics and moral philosophy meet those of eco-philosophy, with everything stemming from flowers in their habitat. Her ever-burgeoning *Bouquets* give rise to a distinctive encounter with the beauty of each individual film, which is never *juste un bouquet* but *un bouquet juste*.

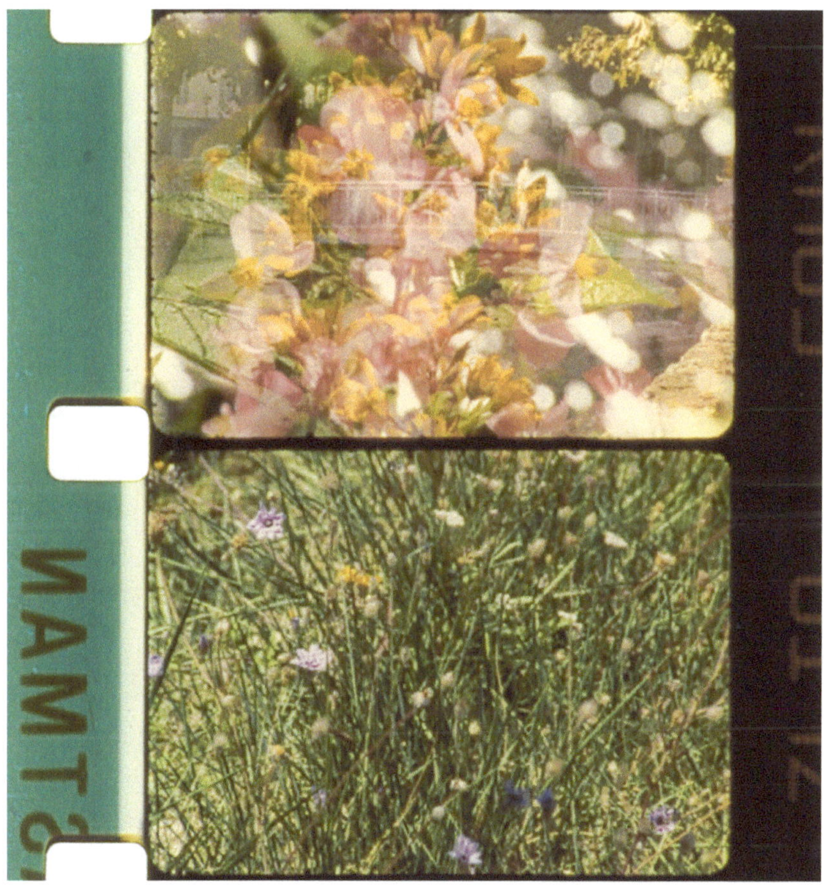

Bouquet 3 (1995)

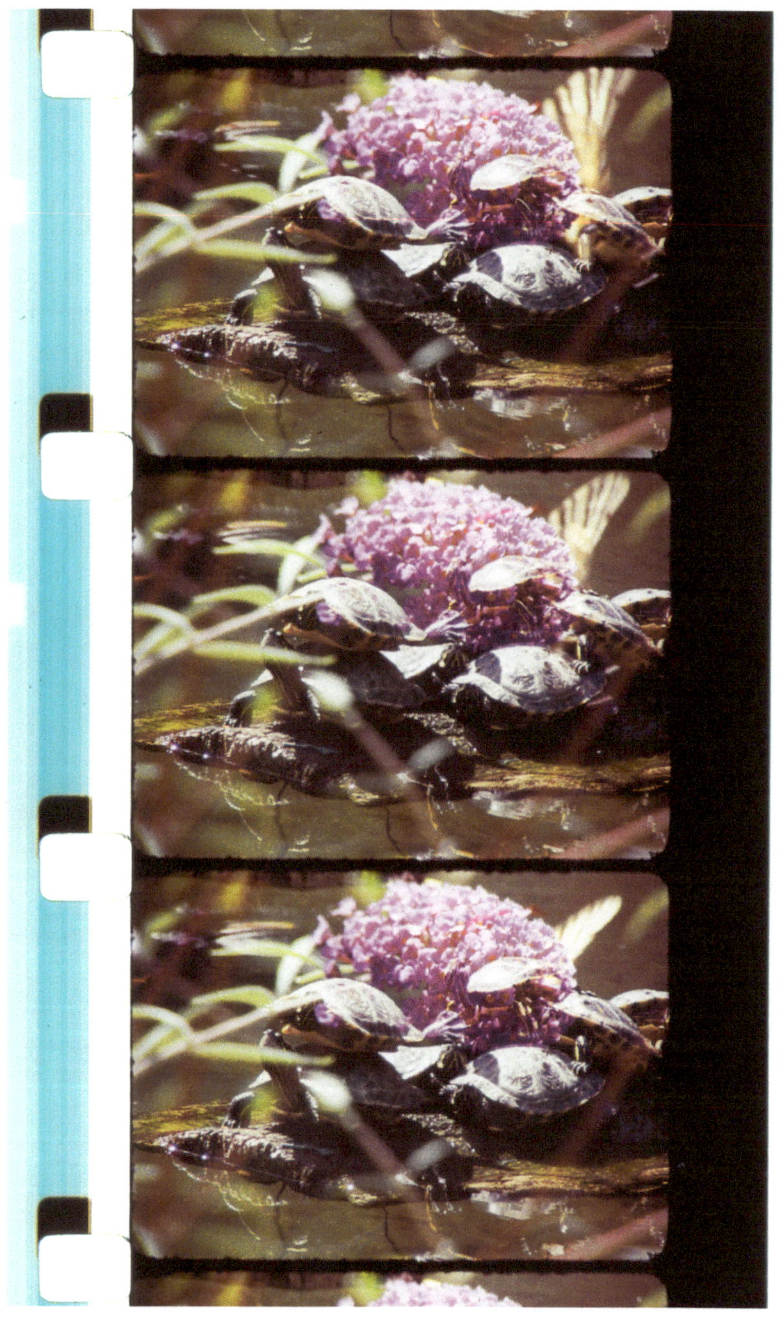

Bouquet 34 (2015)

THE BOUQUET NOTEBOOKS

TARA MERENDA NELSON

I was first exposed to Rose Lowder's films in 2003, while attending monthly screenings at a microcinema called *Jefferson Presents* that showed experimental films in Pittsburgh, Pennsylvania. The regular audience for *Jefferson Presents* was a lively handful of artists, musicians, filmmakers and experimental film enthusiasts who eagerly gathered in a small, unheated gallery to sit on metal chairs and watch an hour or two of flicker films. We were a participatory group, and cheers or jeers from the audience were to be expected at every screening.

But when a Rose Lowder film was shown, the room was inevitably silent (as are most of her films) as the audience became fully engrossed in an intense visual encounter with the screen. Red poppies danced in sunny fields traversed by sailboats gliding on shimmering blue seas; bustling city streets in summer intertwined with empty urban plazas in autumn; peach trees trembled between morning light and evening shade; time and space collided in a field of sunflowers. Sequences of images blended into powerful rhythmic patterns, drawing our attention to each frame of film and its contribution to the structure of the overarching composition, culminating in an experience of visual consciousness that was stunningly profound. We were speechless.

Not much was known about Rose Lowder in our small circle of artists, and each of us had our own theory about how she created such perceptually engaging work. After screenings we would gather outside the gallery to smoke cigarettes and argue our theories on how Lowder made her films, attempting to reconcile our experience of seeing the film with our understanding of the process of filmmaking. I recall scrutinizing one of the *Bouquet* films over a light table, hoping to find a clue that would help reveal the secret formula for creating such compelling work. But instead of the secret, I found only a paradox: the film on the light table was both exactly what I had seen and nothing at all like what I had experienced.

As part of my thesis work at the Massachusetts College of Art and Design in 2011, I invited Lowder to the United States for a lecture and screening tour of Boston, Chicago, Milwaukee and New York. While in Boston she gave a lecture on her unique approach to working with 16mm film as a tool for perceptual experimentation, and showed excerpts from her hand drawn film notebooks to help illustrate her methods. These images were intended as visual aids for purposes of the lecture, and Lowder quickly moved through the slides mentioning that she had brought some copies of the pages with her for those who may have wanted to hear more about them after the talk. I don't think she was quite prepared for the large crowd that gathered around afterwards to look at the notebooks, eager to have a closer look at the complex compositions that could decode her creative process. What they found instead was another level of complexity; a visual score which pointed to an iterative process that combined logic, mathematics, language, music and poetry. Furthermore, each page could stand alone as a brilliant graphic composition, masterfully drawn by the hand of an artist who had spent decades refining an aesthetic that was completely her own.

Lowder has explained that each rendering found in the notebooks is transcribed from film to paper *after* the film is shot, serving as both a record of the process and an illustration of the resulting structure of each film. By transcribing the films this way, she is able to create a frame-by-frame record in order to directly examine the results of the experiment. This is significant, as the *Bouquets* films in particular are shot somewhat spontaneously. Though each environment has been painstakingly researched and selected, the precise subject and structure of each film is created in response to the environmental conditions of the moment. Lowder keeps meticulous records as she shoots in order to keep track of her progress; recording each shot into a notebook allows for a deeper reading of the results. But it is the film itself that reveals the "success" of the perceptual experiment.

Since being introduced to these documents in 2011, I gradually came to understand how the notebooks are vital to understanding the phenomenology of Lowder's films, and provide a key to comprehending how her work integrates the creative process with the scientific method. My ambition became to explore these extraordinary links between the notebooks and the films in a book of my own. The result was a paper edition of the notebooks for *Bouquets 11-20: Notebooks by Rose Lowder*.[1]

The book reproduced complete records from Lowder's notebooks of ten films (*Bouquets 11-20*), each consisting of exactly 1,440 frames, broken into 24-frame segments on three stacked lines of graph paper, ten segments per page, six pages per film. Each film is briefly introduced by Lowder through a short memoir on the location in which the film was shot. *Bouquets 11-20: Notebooks by Rose Lowder* can be read in many ways: as documentation of decisions made by a filmmaker; as precise notations of the elements included in each film; and as graphic representations of the visible elements within each frame along with an account of events that took place outside of it. For the reader, the relationship between the notebooks and the films they describe is both direct and incidental: one may appreciate the films without the notebooks and the notebooks without the films. But their publication

50

in an ebook format that included links to video transfers of *Bouquets 11-20* offered the opportunity to appreciate both. Readers may "follow along" with the transcription as they watch the film.

While the images found in the notebooks are derived from a film, they are themselves unique works of art, masterpieces of dynamic visual code transposed into a language of color, pattern, symbol, line, and sequence. Each page is a distillation of a whole into its parts, revealing the complex nature of each distinct unit and the intrinsic connection of each unit to its source. They are notations, memoirs, and reminiscences made by an artist as she deconstructs her own creative process and creates a new body of work at the same time. These notebooks are fascinating, complicated records of scientific inquiry, while also being profoundly beautiful works of visual poetry. They are time on paper.

I have poured over Rose Lowder's notebooks for more than a decade, and although I can say that I am able to translate them to some degree, they continue to leave me speechless.

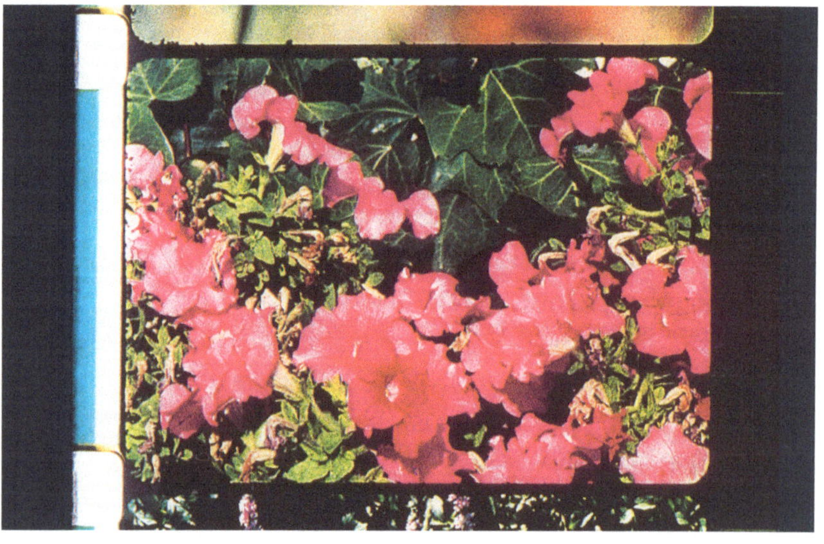

Bouquet 3 (1995)

ROSE LOWDER, SINGLE FRAME WORKER

ELENA DUQUE

Discarding the prejudices that separate "serious" filmmaking from animation, and bringing together imageless flicker films and films that celebrate intermittence without renouncing the figurative possibilities of the image, one can retrace a whole genealogy of single frame workers.

Single frame workers: the word "workers" is crucial here because it is important to highlight the patience and labor involved in this form of creation. Only a few seconds of film can involve several hours of work and effort. When discussing experimental filmmakers, who usually work alone, one can imagine this meticulous and solitary endeavor almost as a meditative act (or, less charitably, a coping mechanism for Obsessive Compulsive Disorder), as it requires a high level of concentration and a systematic way of moving one's body. A lot of the work of these filmmakers is seldom seen outside certain specialized cinema circuits since their films are usually only a few minutes long. Their oeuvre is built of small units that need to be considered as a whole to fully understand and appreciate their magnificence but these qualities are often obscured by the deceptive beauty or wit of the films when they are considered separately.

In this genealogy of single frame workers there is a family line to which Rose Lowder belongs: those who dismantle cinema into its basic unit, the frame, in order to highlight the intermittency and the involvement of the mechanical apparatus in the creation of a moving image that in no way resembles what we see with our naked eyes in the world. This is the ultimate "pure cinema" - to use the expression of Henri Chomette[1] - a cinema that humbly refuses to be a replica of reality, even when capturing reality was the first step in the fabrication of its magical potion. Rose Lowder's work both comprises and distills many decades of achievements and, at the same time, displays a unique way of working and some highly developed visual ideas related to painting, color, perception, and other phenomena. And the ultimate product of this distillation is her *Bouquets*, series - brief bursts of intensive single frame experiments.

An Invented Genealogy

But let's be more specific about this "family line" to which Rose Lowder belongs. We can think about Robert Breer as a father (but not a patriarch, as his carefree attitude is proportionally inverse to his achievements). In 1954, Breer made an experiment that would be determinant in his career and in this story we are trying to tell. As he himself explained,

> I exposed six feet of film one frame at a time, as usual in animation, but with this important difference: each image was as unlike the preceding one as possible. The result was 240 distinctly different optical sensations packed into 10 seconds of vision.[2]

The result of this procedure was a challenge to perception, a discovery that Breer summed up in this way:

> Whereas the usual intention in animation has been to represent natural movement and to do this by gradual modification of forms

permitting the eye to blend them into fluid motion. I began treating the single images as individual sensations to be experienced separately, more in counterpoint than in harmony.

I find myself combining freely very disparate images and finally using continuous motion simply as a means to connect up the various fixed images. This technique tends to destroy dramatic development in the usual sense and a new continuity emerges in the form of a very dense and compact texture. When pushed to extremes the resulting vibration brings about an almost static image on the screen.[3]

We can extend the affirmation applied to animation to all cinema in general, but beyond this, this idea of setting a counterpoint of single images, and using continuous motion as a way of connecting these images is certainly key in Lowder's work. Lowder attended some of the screenings at the Better Books bookshop in the 1960s, prior to the founding of the London Filmmaker's Coop in 1966, where she was able to see some of Breer's films. Besides the single frame ideas that sprang from this, she began to think about the timing and persistence of the frames according to the contents of the image, how there are images that, even if their presence on the screen is equivalent to others (one frame, for instance) seem to remain in our eyes and to neutralize others. The thought of the frame and what it depicts as a whole is also present in Robert Breer's work, as he explained to Scott MacDonald, in his ambition to give presence to every corner of the image and not only to a "subject" in the middle of a "background," as usually occurs in both live action and animation. This is a conception that can be linked to his background as an abstract painter. He noted, talking about this subject-background system, character (actor or cartoon) that we follow on the screen that "it sets up a constant visual hierarchy that to me is impoverished. I want every square inch of the screen potentially active, alive - the whole damned screen."[4]

There is yet another single-frame-worker wonder for the eyes that links Lowder and Breer: the superimpositions generated by juxta-posing frames - one action every other frame, and with another subject in the frames in between. Breer did this when he began using rotoscopy (an animation technique that consists of tracing live action frames one by one), interspersing, for instance, an aerographed index card with an index card tracing the flight of a gull in *Gulls and Buoys* (1972), generating in this way a pulsating sort of superimposition in which the action on the gull "cartoon" is a continuous movement agitated by the flicker of the interspersed frames. This would become the core of Rose Lowder's *Bouquets*, in which she recorded a sort of time-lapse on every other frame of the filmstrip, leaving "blank" frames in between them, and then later on intercalating another time-lapse by means of her rewinding technique, filling up the blank frames.

Here we can digress a little bit to consider yet another group of single frame workers, the "Time-Lapsers," who record nature for different purposes, but are also inspired by painting. I am referring to the English cinematic landscapists William Raban and Chris Welsby. Concerned with weather, the changing light and other matters, they share with Lowder this spirit, derived from Gainsborough, Constable and then the French Impressionists, of portraying people inhabiting nature while at the same time rendering its colors and light qualities. Cinema permitted the concerns of time and movement to be introduced into these traditional painting motifs and they also relate to the time-lapse techniques used in Gary Beidler's *Hand Held Day* (1970), which holds a mirror in front of a landscape, reminding us of the frame of a painting or a postcard.

A different take on time-lapse can be found in films such as *Go Go Go* (1962) by Marie Menken or *Coney* (1975) by Frank and Caroline Mouris. Although they are more focused on transmitting the energy of a vibrant surrounding, one can imagine a link between the Mourises and Lowder through the rapid-fire collage images in *Frank Film* (1973), images that seem to pile themselves up in our eyes as the flowers in the *Bouquets* do.

Another side to these shared ideas about interspersing frames is the understanding of how colors are mixed by the eye from a painter's point of view. Having both in mind - how the paint pigments are combined and what the results of this operation are - one can consider from this point of view the mixtures "prepared" by the eye and brain when different colors are shown in a rapid alternation of changing frames. Keeping the sequence of movements stable in the frame but alternating colors, Breer made films such as *69* (1968). He talked in an unpublished manuscript from 1957 about how to mix colors:

> Take red and green genuine oil paint and mix them together to get gray. Make red dots and green dots dance together on the canvas for an impressionist grey. Now take a red and green and mix them in the camera, red after green, for 72 frames to have three seconds of red and green mixed. It is not grey.[5]

This sort of blending/not-blending also interested Paul Sharits in films such as *Declarative Mode* (1976). Lowder, on the other hand, seems to be much more interested in the persistence of the qualities of each individual color than in their fusion. According to Lowder:

> If we compare this to a physical superimposition, the interest of this way of proceeding resides in the qualitative interval/difference in the perception of juxtaposed colors and motifs that the time-space organi-zation of this mode of image interweaving induces. By means of the choice of association of colors and configurations, the tones can be more intense and the movements more dynamic than they would be by superimposing images in the same film strip.[6]

The Flickerists

Of course there is also a link between Lowder's work and the so-called flicker films of Peter Kubelka, Tony Conrad and Paul Sharits.

Besides the obvious interest in what the flicker generates in the eyes and minds of the audience, there are some other metric concerns here related to the working processes of these flicker-siblings: counting single frames, establishing patterns and rhythms with them, and drawing diagrams to manage it all. In particular, Lowder shares with Kubelka and Sharits the awareness of the physical filmstrip: what the material looks like per se (and how this very thing can turn into a work of art by itself), and the change produced by the projection of the film. We can think about the filmstrip displays devised by Kubelka - his *Monument Film* (2012) that was exposed on opposite walls, *Arnulf Rainer* (1960) and its anthesis *Antiphon* (2012) and by Sharits (his *Frozen Film Frames,* 1976). And even though Lowder does not show her films this way, she is obviously concerned about the appearance of the filmstrip as you look at it with the naked eye, without the use of a projector, and its divergence from the projected image. She prints and hands out postcards of her films with clusters of three consecutive frames each, highlighting this way the contrast between frames, almost in an educational way for the audience to understand how they are made. So, even though the frames are not exhibited in any kind of boastful way, the filmstrip as a work of art in itself and as a way of reflection on cinema mechanisms are also ideas present in her work.

Lowder works by editing mostly in camera, so her diagrams are in part scores, in part mnemonic tools. She also drew diagrams for her *Bouquet* films as a way of keeping track of what was being shot in every roll. So that her meticulous interspersing technique could work, she had to rewind an exact number of frames so she could precisely fill the blank frames in between. For instance, the image of boats sailing in the sea, or of a flower. In films such as *Arnulf Rainer* (1960) and *The Flicker* (1966), which are films completely devoid of images and colors - the diagrams are made beforehand, as a way of organizing the film according to a pattern. In Kubelka's case, he used black and transparent leader (according to P. Adams Sitney[7]). His intention was to work with the basic units of cinema: the single frame, the light and the darkness (and also sound and silence). He planned different combinations of these elements mathematically.

Conrad, on the other hand, actually shot with a camera frame-by-frame, getting the black simply by covering up the camera lens, and the white by shooting a white piece of paper on a wall. He made a sort of score for the first sequence that he then printed several times, cut and spliced together in different arrangements (he made more than 500 splices). In his case, the idea was to transfer musical ideas to cinema (something that was also in Kubelka's mind), as well as to experiment with the effects of the cinema apparatus on the body and the psyche of the audience (he wanted them "to lose themselves"[8]).

These perceptual interests are also present in Paul Sharits' flicker films, though he moved from the intention of psychologically and physically effecting the audience (even with the intention of replicating the sensation of an epileptic seizure) to purely materialistic concerns. In any case, it is interesting to contemplate in this instance the afterimage effects, especially in the films in which he combines the flat color fields with single frames of human figures (such as *T,O,U,C,H,I,N,G*, 1968). By creating sequences of similar but divergent images that blend into each other, he creates a sort of multifaceted image maintaining some of the basic shapes on screen (the face, the evolving square), the same way as Breer in *66* (1966), *69* (1968), *70* (1970) and *77* (1977). There is also a sort of continuation of these endeavors combining photographic and painted images in works of the French filmmaker Jean-Michel Bouhours such as in his *Sécan-ciel* (1979).

There are other explorations of flicker effects on perception through abstract graphic imagery in Robert Russett's films such as *Neuron* (1972), almost a scientific approach to optical phenomena. As he explains:

By using the single-frame technique, certain kinds of strobing perceptual phenomena can be mechanically diagrammed in time to produce unusual filmic color structures. These structures have their own synthetic quality - a luminous appearance - which cannot be produced in other art forms. In *Neuron* I basically used two techniques to achieve these effects: (1) color afterimage, an illusion produced from animated black-and-white patterns, and (2) optical color mixture, a form of temporal pointillism.[9]

As a "Flickerist", Rose Lowder has accomplished a highly complex modulation of her motifs throughout the whole *Bouquet* series that goes beyond the theoretical premises of absolutes of these predecessors. In each *Bouquet,* one can experience how a motif blends with another if there are some similarities in color and texture, while in another section one of the images clearly dominates and crushes the other. Arrangements of three different elements converge punctuated by black frames, creating rich compositions by the interweaving of these pulsating images. Frames full of flowers construct a pattern that occupies the whole frame imprinting this pattern in the next image, seemingly painting over it. Rapid movements seem to apply brush strokes to the adjacent static takes. The textures of the world, in Lowder's work, deeply rooted in nature, create a new dimension apart from the flicker works cited above, working instead with flat color fields and graphic images or nearly graphic photographs. And it is important to highlight how the figurative elements, with the single frame treatment, seem to approach abstraction, attaining its figurative qualities, as contradictory as that may sound. The world never loses its meaning despite how rigorously formal the treatment applied to it might be.

In this particular sense, one can draw a parallel between Lowder's work and that of a younger single frame worker, Jodie Mack, who also uses humble real world materials to create highly ambitious flicker films. Rooted in down-to-earth elements (in Lowder's case, flowers, animals, fields, food, and in Mack's textiles and flowers as well) they remain tied to the human essence of labor and its meaning, extracting from supposedly mundane subjects (subjects related historically and socially to women) highly sophisticated moving images composed frame-by-frame.

These works also share ecological concerns: Lowder's "ecological" *Bouquets* made on organic farms, and Mack's *Wasteland* series that especially echoes Lowder's work in the use of frozen flowers in films such as *Wasteland No. 2: Hardy, Hearty* (2019) and *Wasteland No. 3: Moons, Sons* (2021), and in the interweaving technique (in this case created on the animation stand) of two elements, as it usually occurs in the *Bouquets*, in films such as *Wasteland No. 1: Ardent, Verdant* (2017), where she intersperses computer motherboards and poppies.

The Camera as Ally and Accomplice

There are yet still other single frame workers that we can associate with Rose Lowder's work who share some of her concerns and working methods. One of the fields of exploration of Lowder's early work is the single frame work associated with the optical properties of the camera. That is to say, how drastic variations of focus between one frame and the next can produce strange and vibrant depth effects when projected. *Rue des Teinturiers* (1979) is an early example of this, in which light variations also play a key role. In that film she shot the view from the window of her house in Avignon over a six-month period, changing the focus in every frame, using different combinations of focusing distances at different frame cadences, also varying the diaphragm opening of the camera (and incorporating the variation introduced by the different light of different moments of the day). This strategy is used also in *Les Tournesols* (1982), changing the focus every frame to a different flower in a sunflower field.

This idea can be compared to Ernie Gehr's experiments in films such as *Wait* (1968) - the change in the exposure time of every frame using the same scene as its "canvas" - and *Serene Velocity* (1970), in which he applies focal length variations from frame to frame. An idea that also comprises the time-lapse side of Lowder's work, *Serene Velocity* was shot during a whole night in a hallway at Binghamton University, from dusk to dawn. After some tests, Gehr decided to introduce his variations in sequences of 4 frames each, projected at 16 frames per second (while Lowder usually, though not always, works in a ratio of 1 frame per variation). So, in both cases, the optical possibilities of the camera were a fundamental part of this perceptual experience crafted frame by frame. There is also a beautiful idea expressed by Gehr in an interview with Scott MacDonald about "activating the screen plane" beyond the figure-background relationship (following Breer's inclinations):

> I became increasingly interested in an exploration of the intervals between frames, in activating the screen plane frame to frame more dynamically than I had done previously, as well as in the idea of a composition taking place in time.[10]

Yet another single frame worker comes to mind when thinking about these strategies related to Lowder's *Bouquets*. This is the Austrian film-maker Kurt Kren, especially in his work related to trees: *3/60 Baume in Herbst* (1960) and, more specifically, *37/78 Tree Again* (1978), which is a sort of time-lapse shot of the Vermont countryside about which the punk band Really Red sings: "Frame to frame on celluloid, Kurt Kren came from Austria." [11].This film relates to *Impromptu* (1989), a film that preceded the *Bouquets* and that forged the technique used by Lowder for them. Not only are they similar iconographically (since they both depict trees from the distance, in a landscapist fashion), but also in the quick alternation of contrasting lights from different times of the day and weather conditions, quicker and vibrant in Lowder's film. Also there is a similarity in the technique: as Stefan Grissemann explains about Kren's film:

> To create three and a half minutes of cinema Kren shot for 50 days, repeatedly rewinding the film according to a precise score that allowed him to shoot on portions of previously unexposed frames on film, seamlessly inserting "delayed" images.[12]

This also evokes a beautiful idea present in superimpositions, which is that of merging different moments in time through the physical and optical qualities of film.

. . .

Discontinuous Continuity

Besides the "broken stroboscopic continuity" mentioned above in reference to Lowder and Breer, there are other single frame workers that apply this sort of idea in different ways to their films. That is, establishing some elements of continuity from frame to frame, but disturbing this continuity by different methods that differentiate one frame from the other. In Lowder, this is something that arises especially in those films where there are elements moving in a clear trajectory inside the frame. For instance, in a couple of maritime *Bouquets*, such as *Bouquet 6* and *Bouquet 8*, where there are boats moving, people swimming and windsurfing. There is a line of continuity in each alternate frame, which "jumps" thanks to Lowder's intercalating strategy.

Though mainly using still photographs and paintings, Jean-Michel Bouhours's films contain in a very intelligent way this sort of discontinuous continuity idea, linking similar yet disparate frames that compose a sort of pulsating flickering movement. In films such as *Rythmes 76* (1976), an allusion to Hans Richter's *Rhythmus 21*, *Chronoma* (1977), *Sécan-ciel* (1979) or *Vagues à Collioure* (1991), his strategy is to use as a starting point a still photography, usually in black and white, that he then traces a number of times in different celluloid sheets with gouache, every time changing the colors, or highlighting a part of the frame in different variations. Then he shoots the sequence several times adding some variations, using the same elements repeatedly which, nevertheless, produces very different sequences according to the number of frames he shoots of every picture, the different order and alternation, the use of black frames in between (some of these procedures come from the work of musicians such as Steve Reich, Philip Glass, Terry Riley and La Monte Young), and the displacement of the images in every frame, generating in this way different sort of movements from contrasting frames. The picture remains, fixing in this way a common denominator in every sequence and providing a sort of continuity, broken by the flicker produced by the change of colors and compositions and the displacements.

The field of rotoscopy, in the tradition of Breer, also brings some examples of this discontinuous continuity. For instance, in Jeff Scher's works such as *Milk of Amnesia* (1992), in which he rotoscopes following a given action of a character, but drastically changes the colors and drawing line patterns, introducing different background papers and including collage elements. The result is a brilliant, pulsing and flickering film that, nevertheless, respects the sometimes serene timing of the rotoscoped scenes.

We have discussed how this idea can be applied using different strategies including drawing and painting, but in this single frame workers family we can also include the work of Japanese filmmaker Tomonary Nishikawa, specially his *Sketch Films* (2005-2007) and *Market Street* (2005). In these films, he shoots his surroundings in the city of San Francisco frame by frame. He keeps the image stable from one frame to the next in a geometric composition formed by the lines randomly found in the street - for example, a diagonal line that divides the frame in two. In this way, he fires off rapid frames that shake our eyes, but there is an animation produced by the continuity of the geometric element, that may also involve creating a movement. There is another layer to this which consists of transforming the urban landscape into abstraction, just keeping the pure lines of it using sometimes odd framings. As in Lowder's work, the framing is conceived according to a single frame technique applied repeatedly and, again, there is a stroboscopic disturbance to the continuity of the movement that nevertheless retains the essential idea of continuity of movement.

Jodie Mack's work also can relate to discontinuous continuity. She uses this technique by shooting similar elements, one in every frame, as the patterns of different pieces of fabric (flowers, paisley, etc) according to an animation technique called "replacement animation" that is also used by filmmakers such as Paul Bush. It consists of taking a single image of an object, for instance, and then replacing this object in the next frame with another one of similar shape (either of the same size, bigger or smaller), and so on. By using similar but different elements (for instance, chairs, scissors, fruit or shoes in Bush's *Furniture Poetry*, 2000), a continuity is created that generates objects or patterns that seem to morph before our eyes, creating in this way a continuity composed of disparate elements.

Single Frame Workers, Unite!

As we can see, Lowder and all her like-minded single frame colleagues are linked by a very particular school of thought (sometimes a form of intuition): an obsession with the basic principle of cinema - the action that the projector extracts from a succession of single still images - and how to make the most of it. Cinema, in their hands, is not a mere medium of reproduction, but one of creation of unique moving images, inherent in the constitutive elements of its technology. They have created a body of films that resemble nothing but themselves, even when they are related in all the ways described above. There is an indescribable rush, which is the one of seeing for the first time what happens when all these still frames are projected, how they look when they are set in motion. All the effort put into the arduous single frame work is worth it, a hallucinatory stroboscopic pleasure, the pulsating euphoria infused in our bodies by the flickering screen, the otherworldly sensation of seeing something new.

The finest single frame workers can find themselves united, rallied by Rose Lowder's *Bouquets*, one of the greatest expressions of this particular way of thinking and filming.

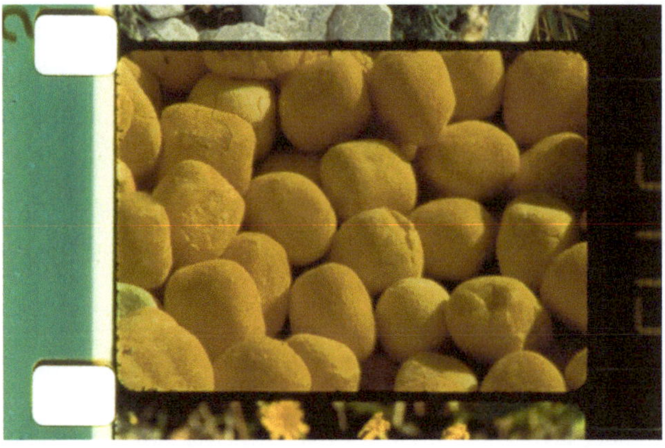

Bouquet 9 (1995)

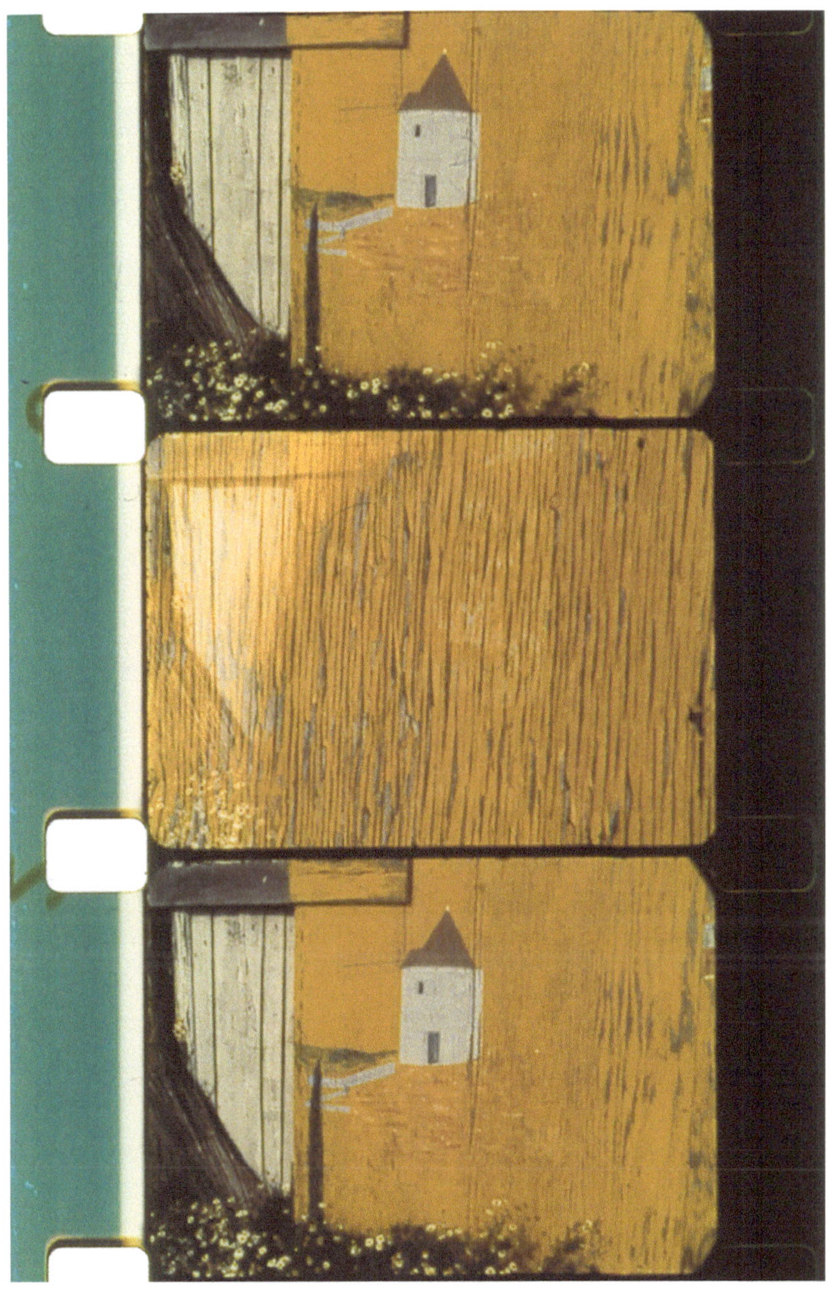

Bouquet 4 (1994)

PART 2 : A CATALOGUE RAISONNÉ

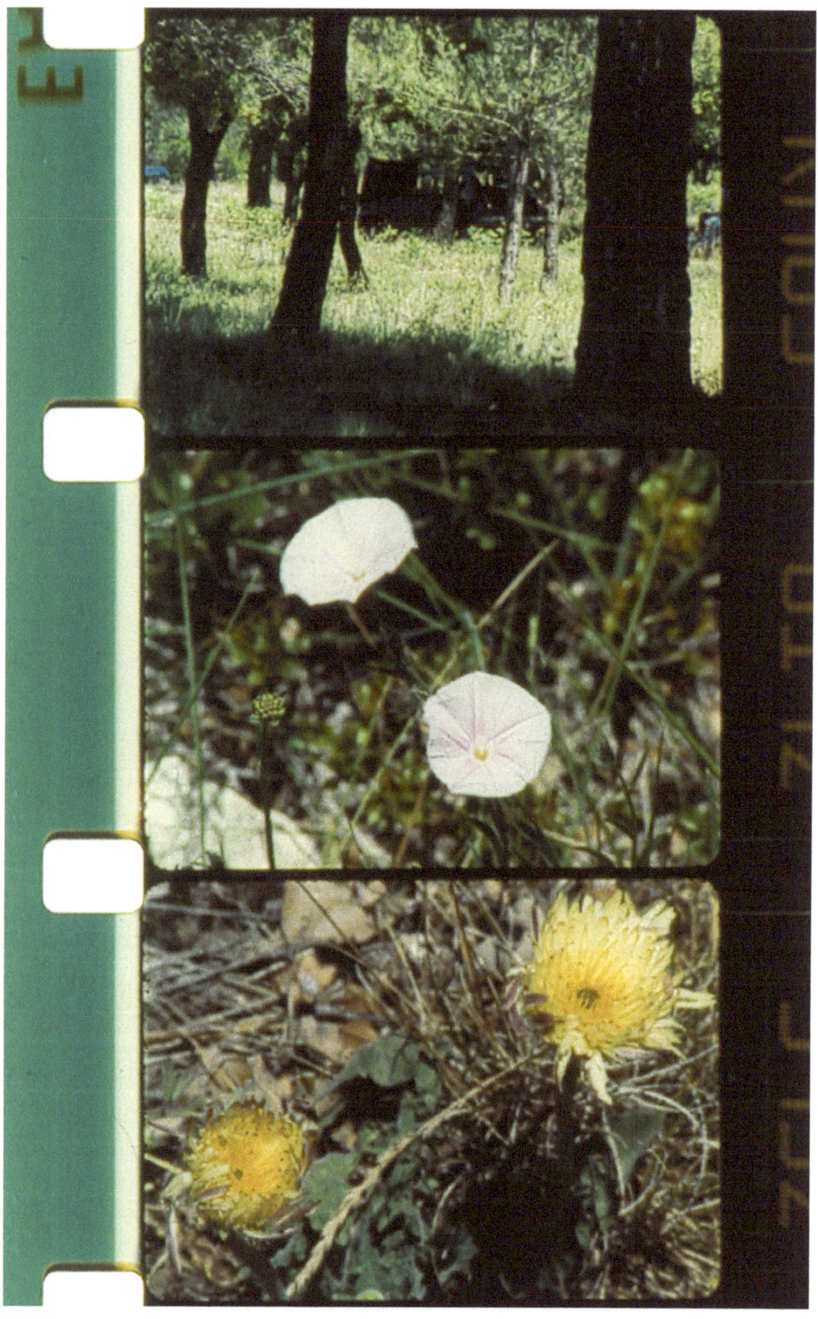

Bouquet 5 (1995)

AN INTRODUCTION BY ROSE LOWDER

The *Bouquets* series started off because I realized that after I had filmed a roll for a specific film I often had a little bit left over at the end. I also frequently saw a particular place where I wanted to shoot but that didn't need a long film to do what I thought was possible there.

So the first ten *Bouquets* were filmed in places that I happened to pass by and thought were interesting for different reasons. I developed the technique begun in *Quiproquo* (1992) and *Impromptu* (1989): several passes of the same roll through the camera with different frames exposed on each pass. But the difference here was that I was no longer weaving together images which were framed identically each time.

For example, in the first *Bouquet,* there are scenes of the Mont Ventoux, activities at the base of the mountain and then also the summit at an altitude of 1912 meters and tourists buying candy or whatever they sell there. So this *Bouquet* shows different scenes from roughly the same location mixed together. I was not intermingling shots of exactly the same place at different times but shots of different places within the same general area.

There are also scenes in the series shot in the Camargue area where I found lots of flowers and a place with quite elaborately painted summer houses on the beach - one has a painting depicting a bull-fighter and a bull by a windmill with its door and a typical cypress tree, all on a bright yellow background. The juxtaposed scenes in the *Bouquet* series usually have a unity of place.

The filming basically entails using the film strip as a canvas with the freedom to film frames on any part of the strip in any order, running the film through the camera as many times as needed. Thus each bouquet of flowers is also a unique bouquet of film frames. The critical thing in running the same film through the camera several times, exposing different parts of the roll at different times and in different places, is to keep track of which images have already been exposed.

Given the complexity of the filming procedure, it would have been impossible to work without noting down exactly what was being filmed. Gradually I devised a sort of system of charts to be filled in as I was shooting, indicating the number of frames that I had shot. Afterwards, I transfer into my notebooks what I've noted on the charts in pencil while filming so that I can keep the information. On the charts I note the exact number of frames that have been done so that I can go back to film on the roll knowing precisely what I have exposed previously.

I almost always shoot in late spring and summer because I can't work in cold weather - I get chilblains and it's also because the vegetation is not as good in the winter. So there's a sort of a seasonal unity to all the *Bouquets,* often based on the agricultural world. You don't do the same kind of work on a farm in winter because things don't grow and it's the same for my filmmaking.

. . .

In the subsequent *Bouquets* nearly all of the images are from ecological places. Usually, if it's an organic farm, there are a variety of things that I can film. It may be a river or people working on the farm. They may use certain kinds of equipment and grow different things. Some have been made in Switzerland, some in France, some in Italy. But within each *Bouquet* there is a unity of place for practical reasons. I don't usually mix scenes from different locations in different countries as that would involve driving long distances and I try to be as economical as possible while, at the same time, exploring a variety of things.

Nearly all the *Bouquets* are a minute long - occasionally they are a few frames more for various reasons but most of them are 1440 frames which is exactly one minute of film. You can do many, many things in one minute; 1440 images offer a lot of possibilities.

I distribute them as a group of ten but in fact some of the *Bouquets* have been shown individually or two or three at a time. Sometimes they are rented individually to be projected as a sort of punctuation between "serious" films - the cable channel Arte did that once - a few flowers between other people's "real" films!

The series was filmed in lots of different places and I had a pretty good ratio between what I filmed and what I ended up choosing to keep. But there are some rolls that weren't any good for a variety of reasons. It was very often a question of the light not having been right for what I wanted.

The second series of *Bouquets* that are numbered 21 to 30 actually came before the third in the series numbered 11 to 20 because after I had started *Bouquets 11-20*, I wasn't happy with some of them so it took longer to finish that series. Either I couldn't get to the places where I wanted to do them or the places where I did film proved unsuitable for what I wanted to do.

The basic principle was very much the same as *Bouquets 1- 10*: going to specific places and juxtaposing frames shot within that area. The difference in *Bouquets 21- 30*, and then in *Bouquets 11-20*, is that these films portray specific subjects in ecological places. Unlike *Bouquets 1-10*, they were not just shot anywhere. They are places where things are grown in a way that is not a menace to the health of the planet, unlike the refineries and power stations in *Quiproquo*. They are centered on places such as organic farms.

One particular case was a farm in Liguria in Italy. I had been invited for a seminar not far from Rimini on the Adriatic coast and I planned to take two days to drive there. So I searched to see whether there was an organic farm on the way and found this one. I stayed there for the night then went on to the Rimini area the next day. Since I particularly liked the farm I came back later to film there.

Some of the *Bouquets 11-20* were filmed before *Côté jardin* (2007) but afterwards I grouped them into a series of ten for purely practical reasons. They could be shown individually but, as a programmer, I know that it's not very cost-efficient to rent a one-minute film especially if you planned a whole screening of short films. So that was one of the reasons for my grouping the ten *Bouquets* together.

Sometimes when I went to a place, the weather did not cooperate or visually there wasn't the variety I needed but I could never tell before-hand. Sometimes in my planning I imagine a place will be magnificent,

but when I actually get there it is completely barren, no plants or flowers, or it rains every single day, and there's absolutely nothing I
can do.

When a roll comes back from the lab, I can see right away if it is any
good but I never know beforehand. Sometimes I think while I'm
filming that the situation is magnificent and then I'm very disap-
pointed with the results. Or I'll travel a long distance with my camera
to a place that I'm sure will be interesting. Then, as soon as I get
there, I see that I can't do anything and just have to go back home
again. Other times I think when I'm filming that what I am trying is
unlikely to work but when it comes back, it's fine.

What all the *Bouquets* have in common is that they are basically, as I
said, one minute of film, 1440 frames, that I do not edit in any way
after they are shot. Often one film overlaps with the making of
another. For example, *Bouquet 19* was shot at the farm where I was
staying while filming the salt gathering for *Fleur de Sel* (2010).
Usually I'm working on several films at the same time and I film
what happens to be in a place at a specific moment and when I go
back to the same place several times, it appears differently each
time.

The ten little films of *Bouquets 11-20* (1440 frames each, with the
exception of 23 frames or nearly a second more for *Bouquet 16*),
continues the work begun with the series *Bouquets 1-10* and
Bouquets 21-30. This consists of weaving in camera visual aspects of
the filmed reality in order to bring into existence specific features of
the cinematographic image, hopefully placing us on a boundary
outside the traditional roles of description or abstraction. *Bouquets 31-
40 (2014-2022)* continues, like the previous *Bouquets*, to explore
different places, which for various reasons, are ecological. For *31-40*

they are in France, in Ardèche, Alpes-de-Haute-Provence, Tarn and Vaucluse and also in Piedmont, Italy.

Editor's Note

The *Bouquets* are listed in chronological order which, as Lowder explains in her introduction, does not correspond to the numbering of the *Bouquets*. Each entry begins with the number of the *Bouquet*, the year it was filmed, and the artist's own description of its subject. It is followed by a list of the Latin (in italics), French, and English names of some - but not necessarily all - of the flowers visible in the film, and, lastly, an editor's comment.

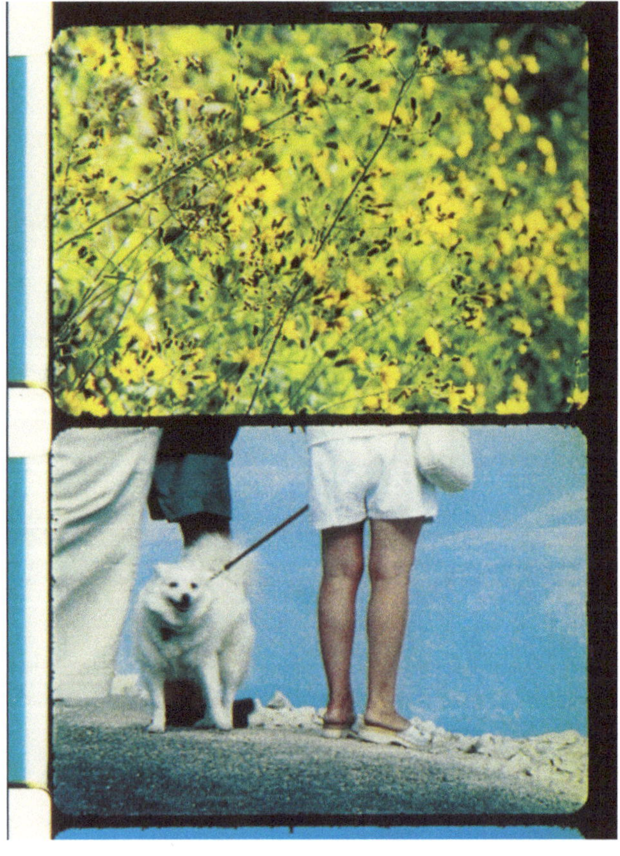

Bouquet 1 (1994)

BOUQUET 1 (1994)
MONT VENTOUX, VAUCLUSE

Filmed on the Mount Ventoux, Vaucluse, from the peak (1912 meters) to the Grozeau spring. Amongst yellow poppies and various mountain flowers, people eat their lunch, scramble or cycle up the slopes leading to the summit where they are greeted by the sale of local products: organic spelt, the local ancient form of wheat, and colored candies.

Scabiosa, Scabieuse, Scabiosa or Pincushion flower, *Rumex Acetosa*, Oseille des prés, Common sorrel, *Senecio*, Séneçon, Ragwort, *Carduus*, Chardon, Thistle, *Papaver*, Pavot, Poppy, *Epilobium*, Épilobe, Willowherb, *Silene latifolia*, Silène, White campion

A hallucinatory vision of nature - the fundamental element of the entire *Bouquet* series - is present from the start. But the first cycle includes an element that will not recur: modern society in leisure mode: sightseers, recreational cyclists attracted by the mythic status of Mont Ventoux in the history of the Tour de France, displays of colored candy, their garish artificial colors recalling the summer attire of the tourists and in counterpoint with the natural hues of wildflowers. This dichotomy is an on-going theme of the *Bouquet* series, but becomes more subtle as the later cycles focus more on farms dedicated to organic agriculture.

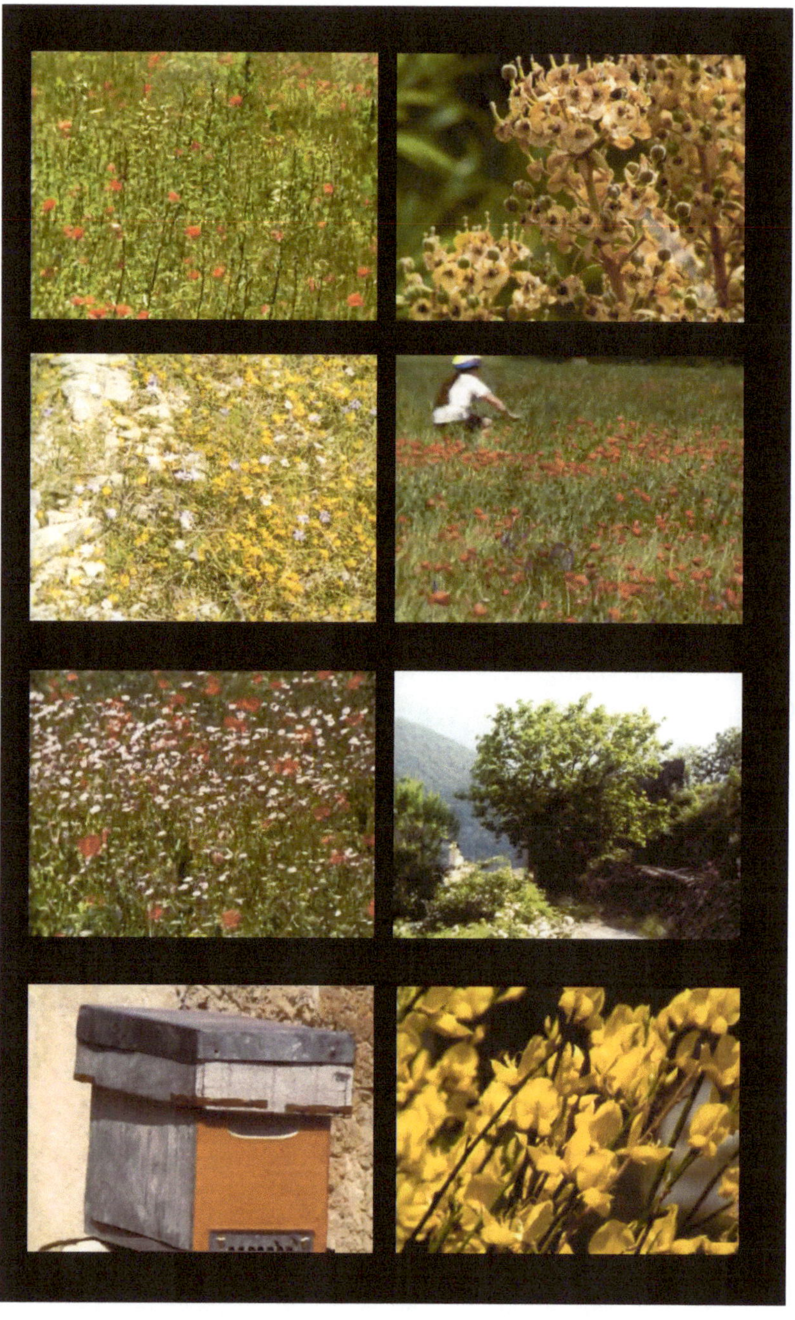

Bouquet 2 (1994)

BOUQUET 2 (1994)
BRANTES, VAUCLUSE

Filmed near the village of Brantes, amongst other things, a school cycling party passing through fields of flowers on the borders of Vaucluse and Drôme.

Sedum telephium, Orpin reprise, Orpine, *Taraxacum*, Pissenlit, Dandelion, *Genista*, Genêt, Broom, *Papaver*, Coquelicot, Poppy, *Silene latifolia*, Silène, White campion

In meadows of flowers, the force of the wind becomes explicit as the source of movement and will become a dominant one in subsequent *Bouquets*. This time the only source of human presence is the active beehive, the swarm of bees recalling that of groups of tourists in the first *Bouquet* and, though specifically recalled by the artist in her description, the school cycling party can be glimpsed in only a few single frames compared with the frequent presence of poppies.

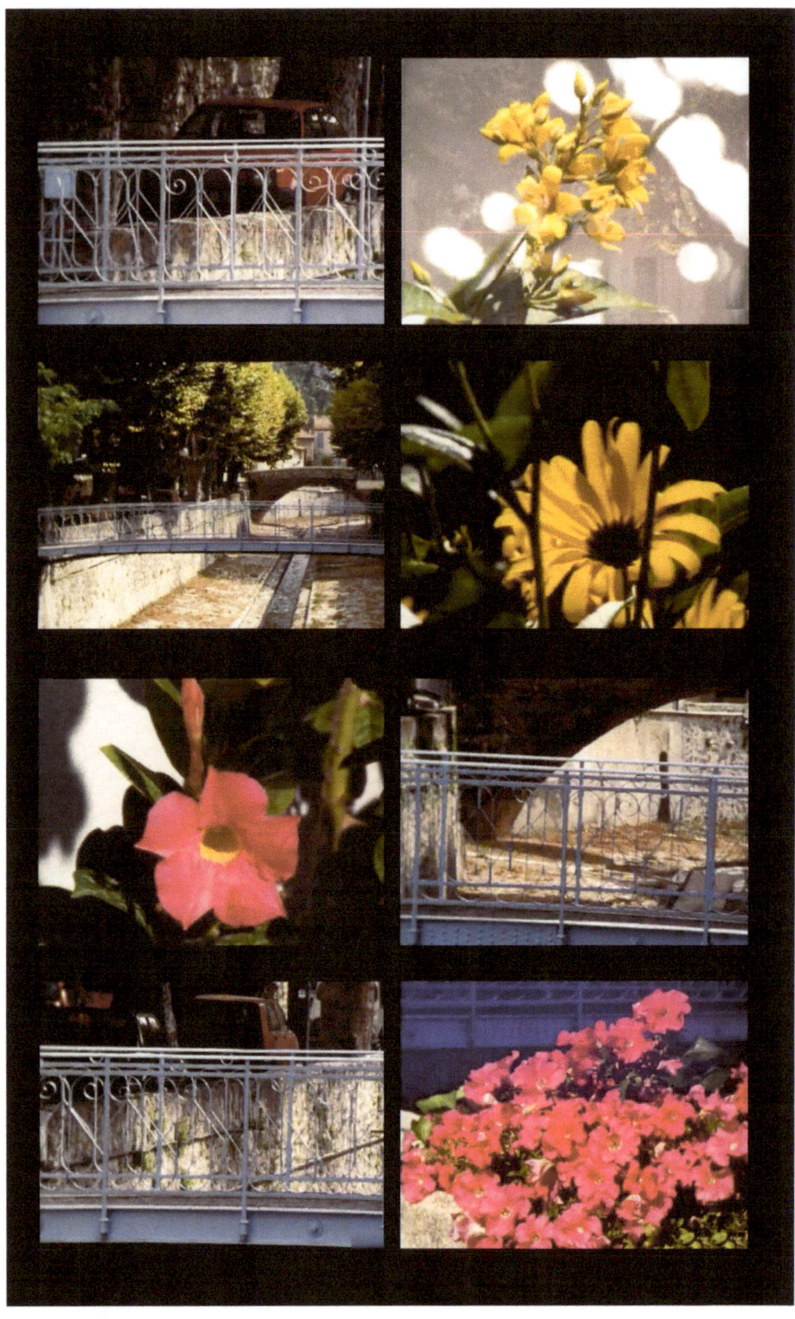

Bouquet 3 (1995)

BOUQUET 3 (1995)
ROQUEVAIRE, BOUCHES-DU-RHÔNE

Filmed on a Sunday afternoon on the banks of the Huveaune River in and on the way to the village of Roquevaire in the Bouches-du-Rhône region

Cichorium intybus, Chicorée sauvage, Common chicory, *Rudbeckia*, Rudbeckia, Black-eyed Susan, *Senecio*, Séneçon, Ragwort, *Sinapis arvensis*, Moutarde sauvage, Wild mustard, *Plantago lanceolata*, Plantain lancéolé, Ribwort plantain, *Gaillardia*, Gaillarde, Gaillardia or Blanket flower, *Petunia*, Pétunia, Petunia, *Convolvulus*, Liseron, Bindweed

The series of bridges over the Huveaune River at Roquevaire is, like the tower of Mont Ventoux in the first *Bouquet*, a unique identifying element. The specificity of the place in which it was filmed will become a consistent attribute of the *Bouquets*.

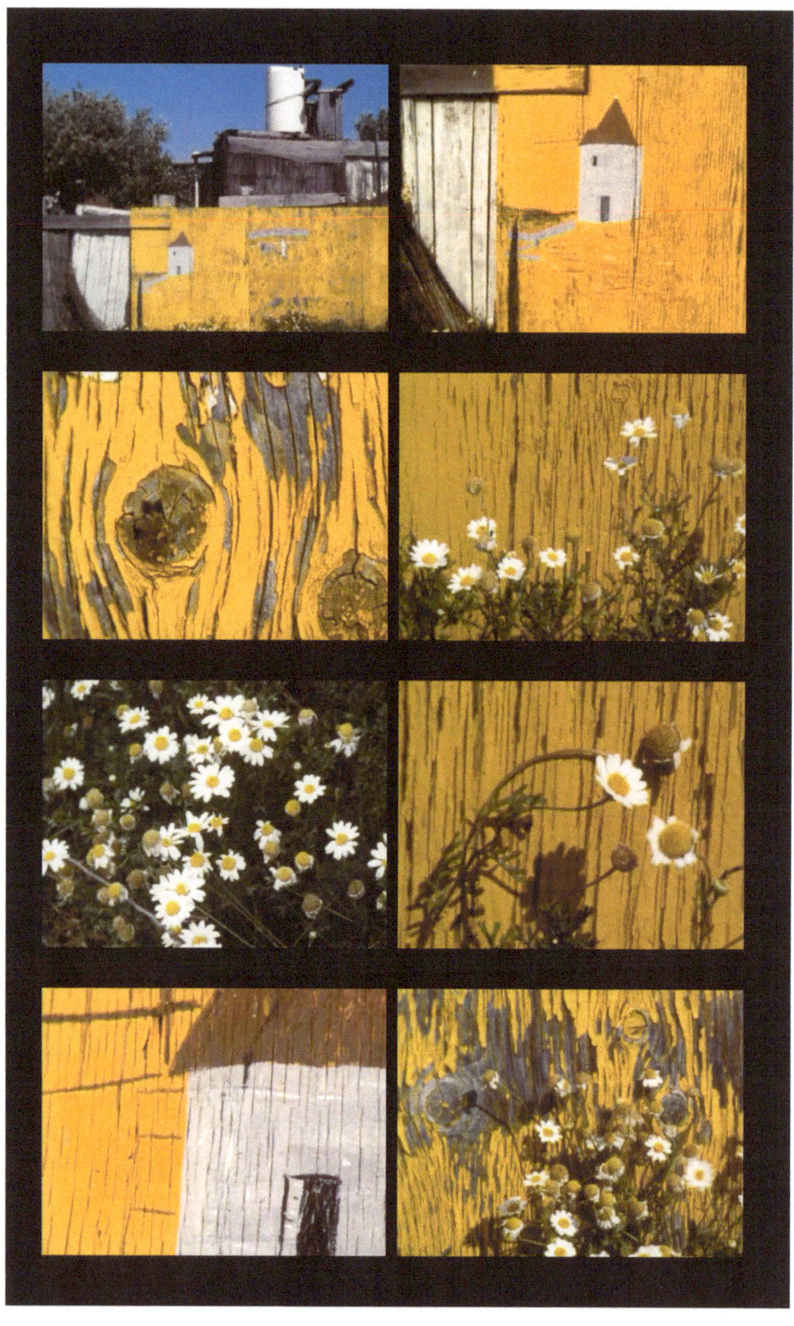

Bouquet 4 (1994)

BOUQUET 4 (1994)
BEAUDUC, CAMARGUE, BOUCHES-DU-RHÔNE

Filmed on the sands of Beauduc in the Camargue region, where people have built a small village out of bric-a-brac. One of the cabins has a Provençal scene painted on its fence: a Camargue bull is depicted in its bullring with windmill, cypress tree and bull fighter. The sea air is rapidly peeling off the paint. The local authorities are threatening to remove all the homes.

Matricaria chamomilla, Camomille sauvage, Wild chamomile

The details of a man-made artifact, the primitive painting style and weathered texture stand in juxtaposition with the white petals of daisies. In this case there is no actual intrusion of humans but a focus on what they have built, tempered by natural elements such as peeling paint. The idea of endangerment, evoked by the artist in her reference to "local authorities," will be a recurring theme but in this instance it is not nature but a trace of man-made artistry that is threatened.

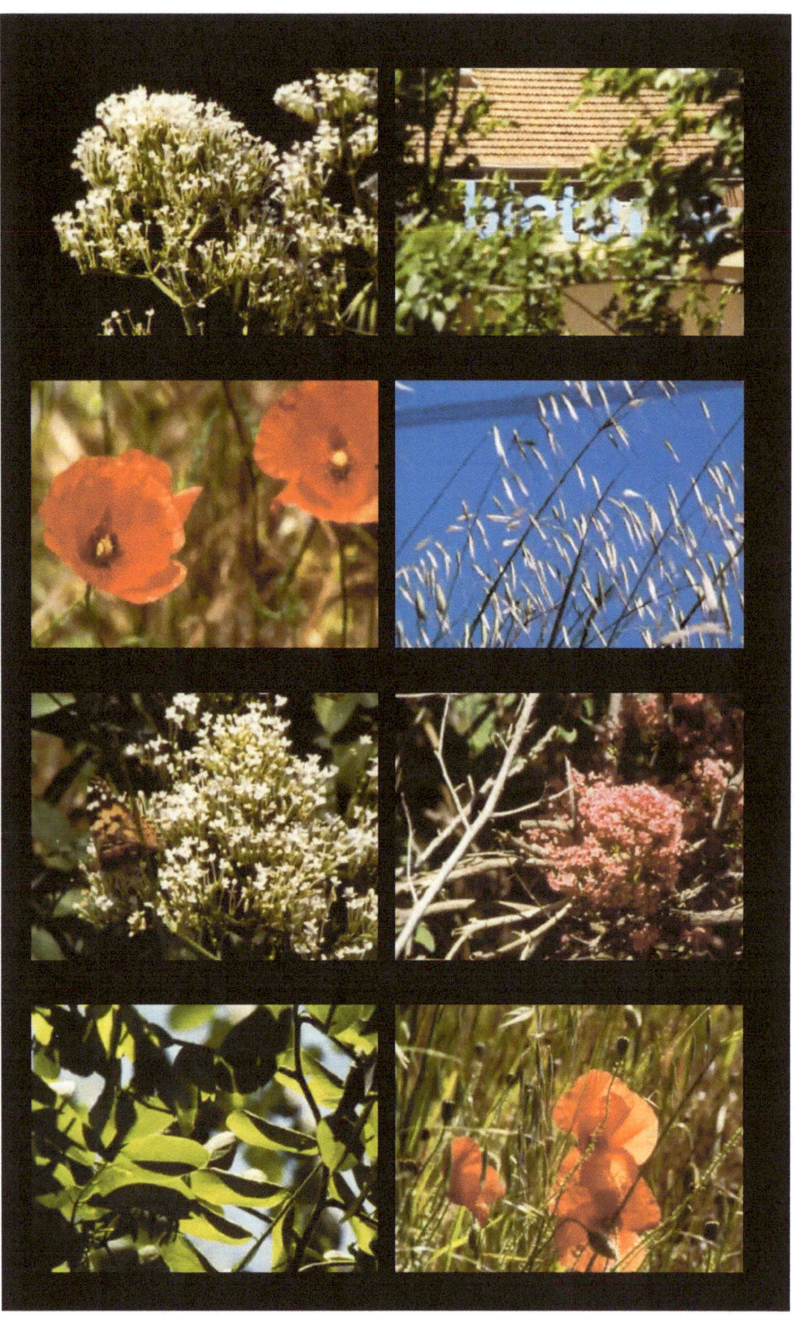

Bouquet 5 (1995)

BOUQUET 5 (1995)
TGV RAILWAY SLOPE, AVIGNON, VAUCLUSE

Filmed amongst flowers on a slope between the main Marseille to Paris railway line, just outside the ramparts of Avignon.

Papaver, Coquelicot, Poppy, *Avena fatua*, Avoine sauvage, Common wild oat, *Genista*, Genêt, Broom, *Daucus carota*, Carotte sauvage, Wild carrot

The ramparts of Avignon, an autoroute directional sign, a supermarket parking lot, a train embankment, a modern apartment block, provide a counterpoint to purely bucolic scenes. But such glimpses of urban life will become a rarity as the subsequent *Bouquets* become increasingly focussed on the realm of organic farming in remote rural settings.

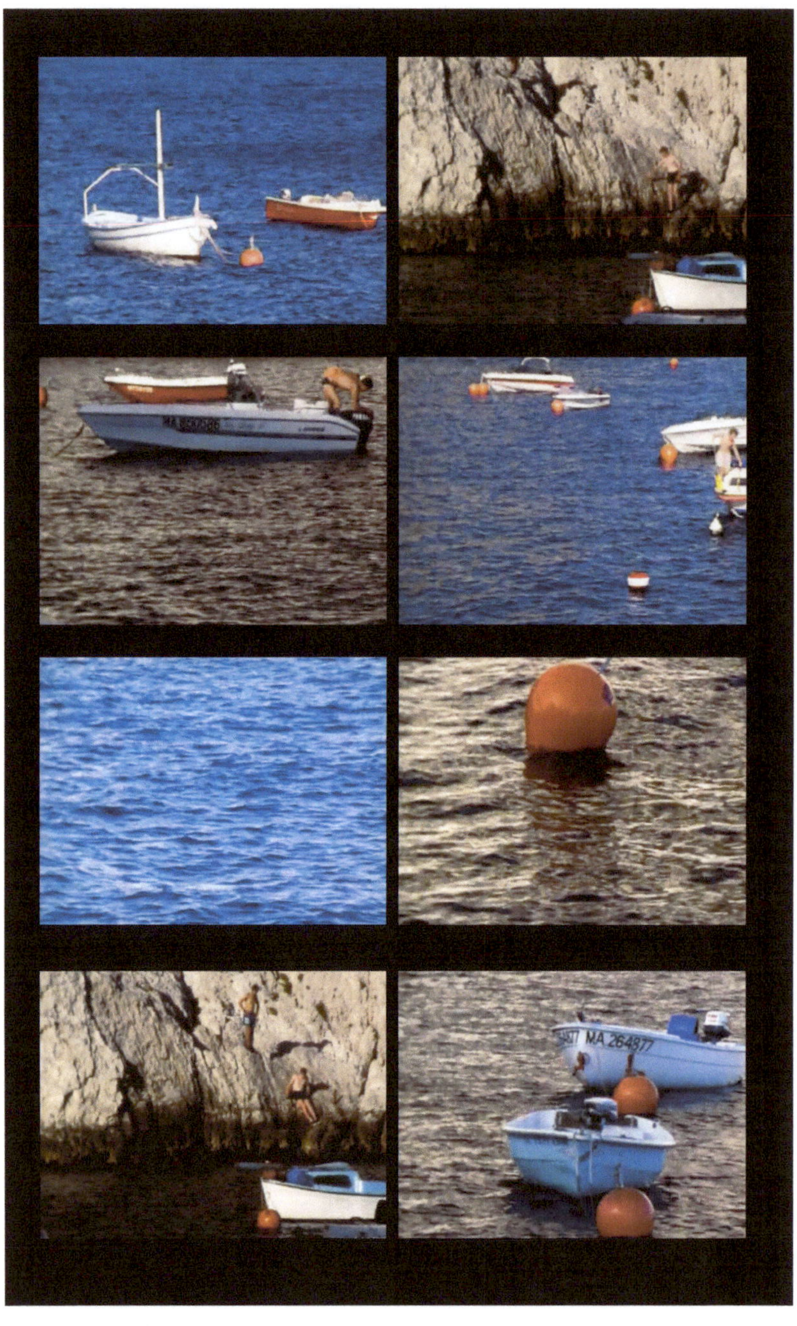

Bouquet 6 (1994)

BOUQUET 6 (1994)
LA VESSE, LE ROVE

Filmed one summer evening in La Vesse, Bouches-du-Rhône, a tiny fishing harbor on a rocky inlet near Marseille.

The captured fragments of vacation leisure time include recreational boaters and swimmers on a rocky shore - a unique instance of a *Bouquet* without flowers focussed exclusively on human activity.

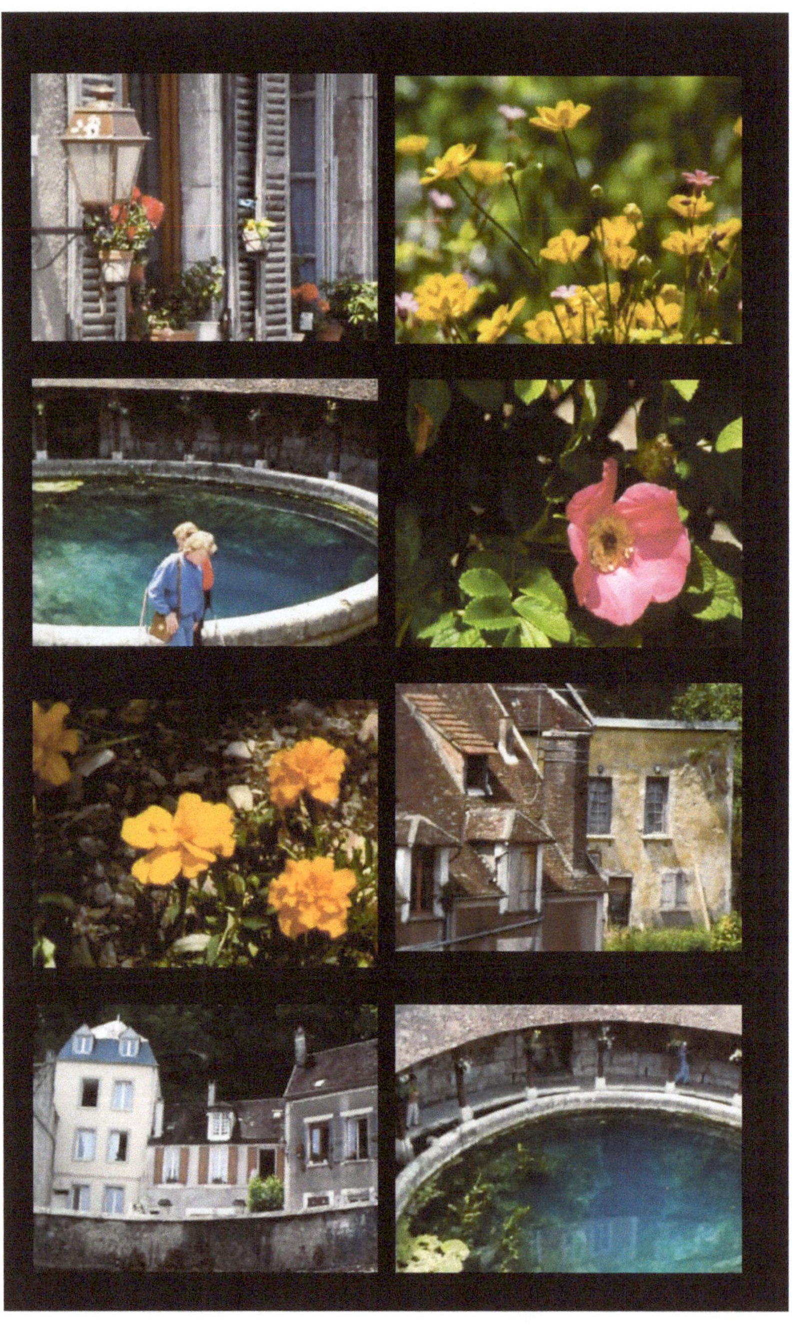

Bouquet 7 (1995)

BOUQUET 7 (1995)
LA FOSSE DIONNE, TONNERRE, YONNE

Filmed around the circular medieval washhouse built on an ancient spring, the Fosse Dionne, in the town of Tonnerre, Yonne. It is surrounded by wild flowers from abandoned terraces, plants in the St. Pierre gardens, cultivated by the disabled and the injured, which lead up to the church on the hill, flowers hanging down from pots, their reflections and others growing in or around the water's edges.

Ranunculus repens, Bouton d'or, Buttercup, *Geranium robertianum*, Herbe à Robert, Herb Robert, *Silene dioica*, Silène rose, Red campion, *Rosa canina*, Rose sauvage, Dog rose, *Vicia cracca*, Vesce cracca, Vetch, *Pelargonium*, Géranium, Geranium, *Tagetes patula*, Œillet d'Inde, French marigold

The timelessness of a tiled roof and a stone walled house around the ancient site of the Fosse Dionne contrasts with frames of a young couple whose clothes and hairstyle are clearly from the period the film was shot. A recurring juxtaposition occurs in the *Bouquets* of scenes of daily life tied to a specific time - the style of cars, clothes, commercial signs - and botanical images which could be eternal.

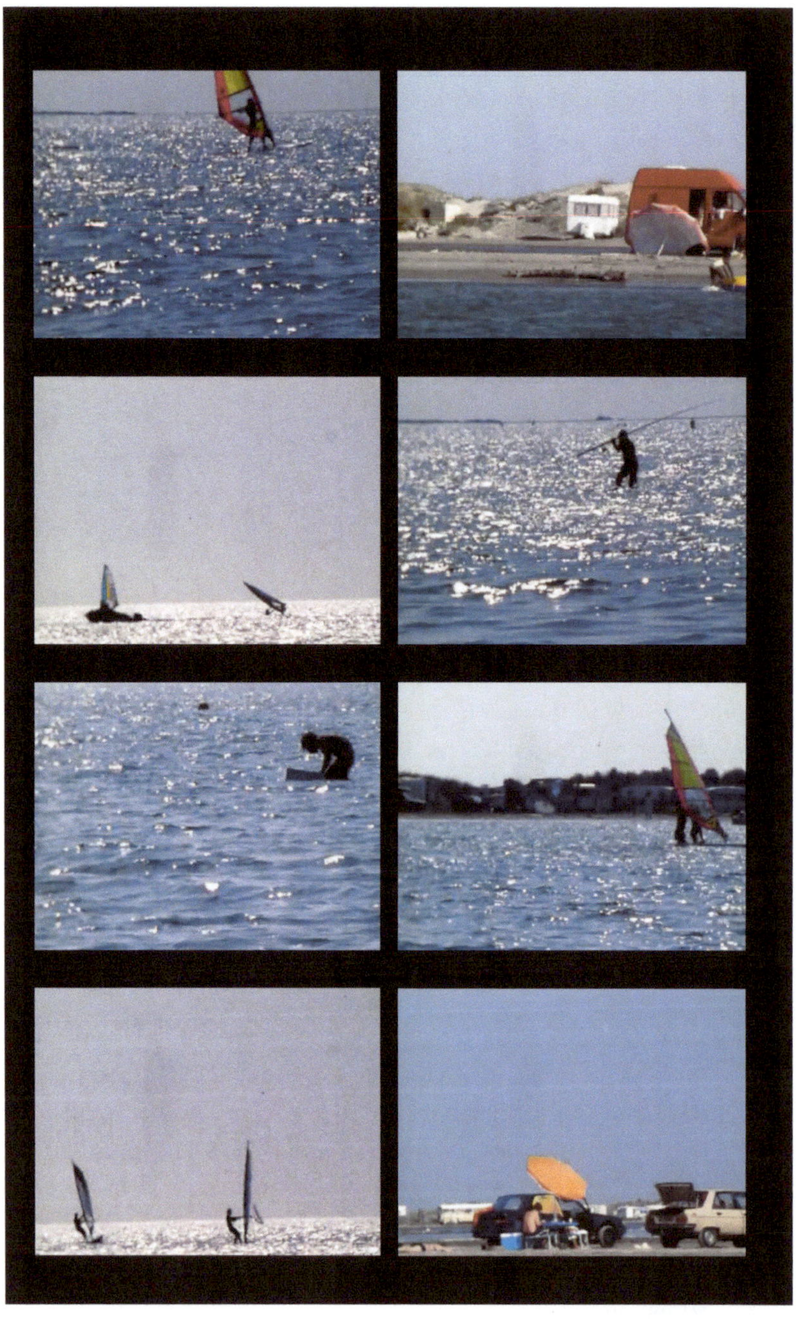

Bouquet 8 (1994)

BOUQUET 8 (1994)
PLAGE DE BEAUDUC

Filmed on the beach at Beauduc, Bouches-du-Rhône, with people sailboarding or catching shellfish.

While in general botanical images - flowers, trees, cultivated fields - tend to dominate the *Bouquet* series - some, such as *Bouquet 6* and *8*, contain none at all. *Bouquet 8* evokes the straightforward comedy of Vivian Ostrovsky's *Tatitude* (2010) as it captures the curious logic - or illogic - of people's activity on the beach. A latent humor can often be sensed in Lowder's observation of human subjects but it almost never becomes overt.

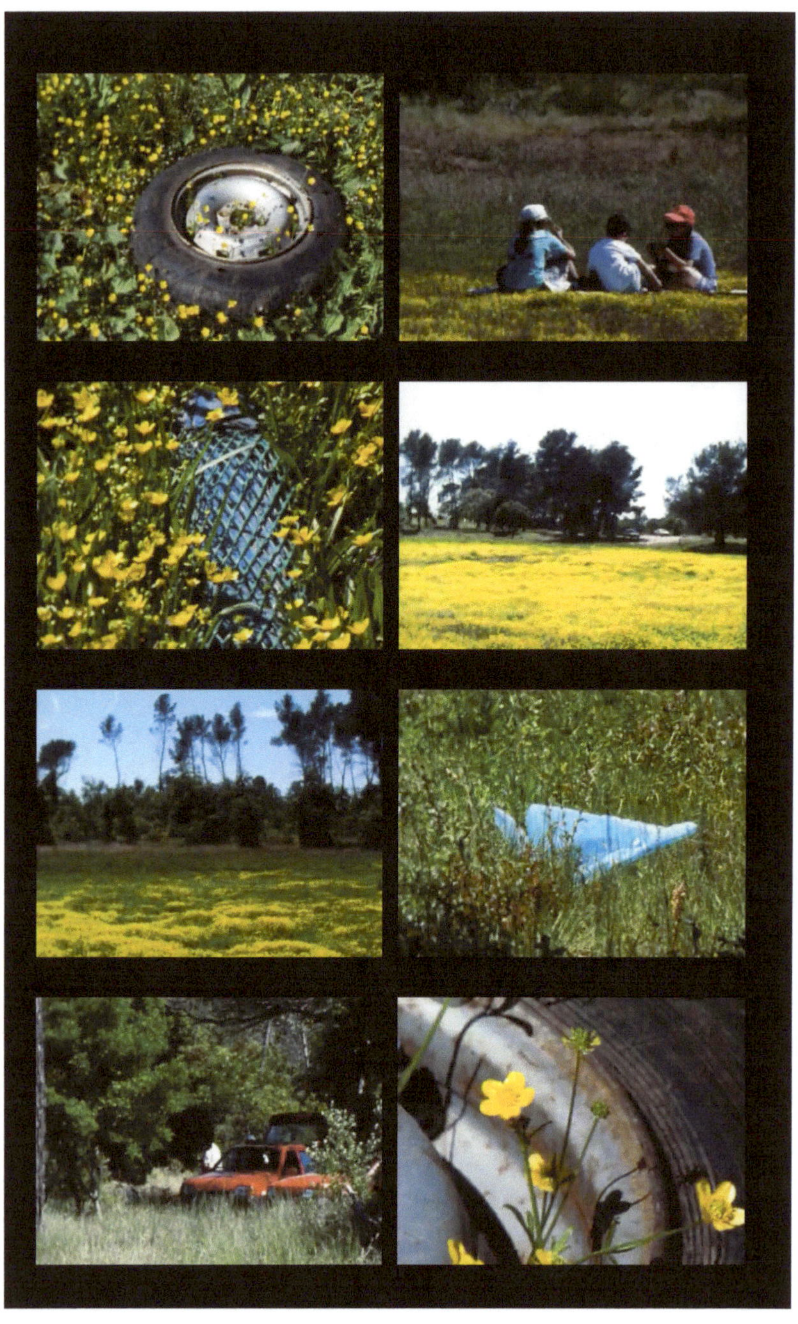

Bouquet 9 (1995)

BOUQUET 9 (1995)
ROUTE DE SIGNES, VAR

Filmed in a field of buttercups on the way to Signes, Var, with families on their Sunday outing and some of the rubbish they leave behind.

Ranunculus repens, Bouton d'or, Buttercup, *Scabiosa,* Scabieuse, Scabiosa or Pincushion flower, *Ajuga,* Bugle, Bugleweed, *Convolvulus,* Liseron, Bindweed, *Dianthus,* Œillet, Dianthus or Pink, *Trifolium,* Trèfle, Clover

The invasive colors of human activity - a red car, a blue plastic bag, the garish summer clothes of picnickers, a red baseball cap, the black of an old rubber tire and the reflective metallic silver-grey of its rim - frequently clash with the palette of botanical subjects. The detritus of modern civilization never entirely disappears even in the later "ecological" *Bouquets* - and sometimes its purely visual appeal actually seems to subvert the outward moral tone of opposition to human damage to the natural world.

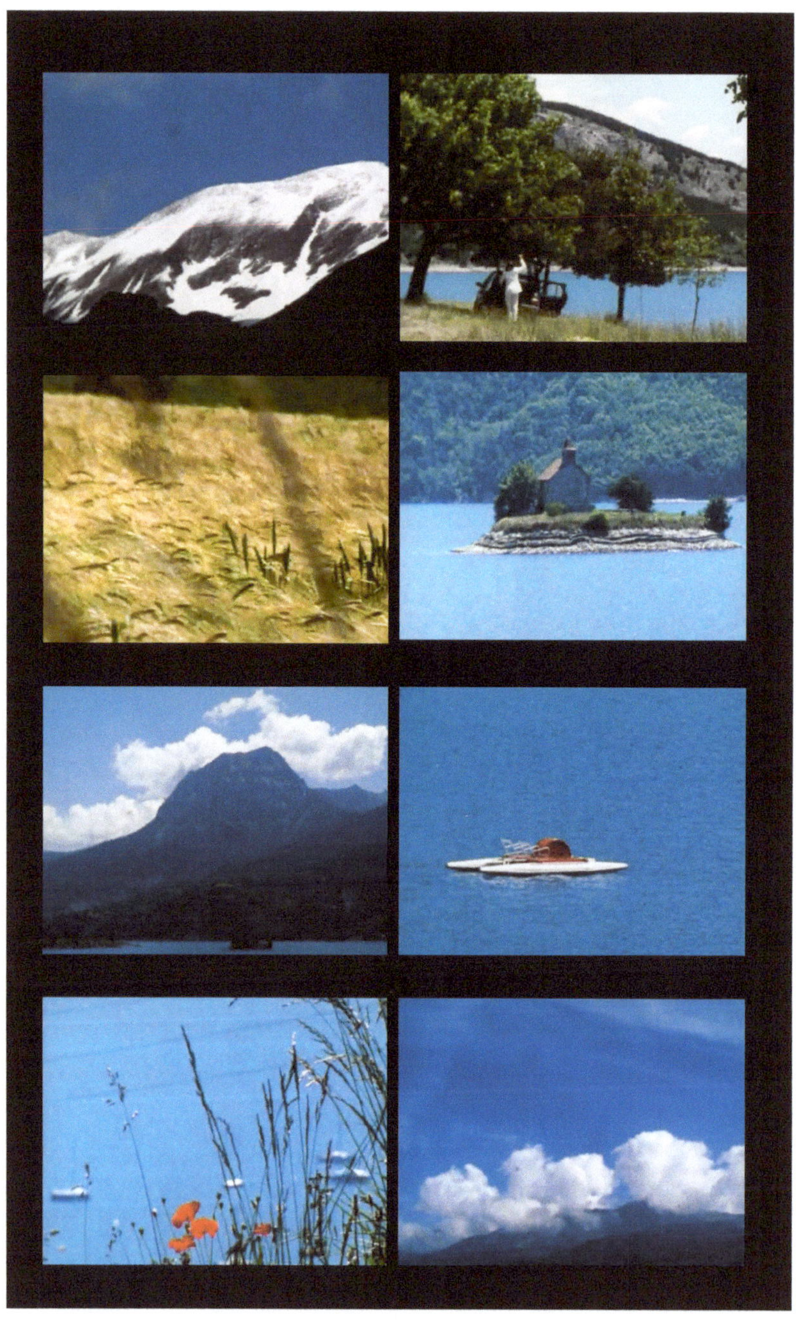

Bouquet 10 (1995)

BOUQUET 10 (1995)
AROUND LAC DE SERRE-PONÇON, HAUTES-ALPES

Filmed from the mountain slopes around St. Apollinaire overlooking lake Serre-Ponçon, Hautes-Alpes, as a flock of sheep roams the camping site and a passenger launch visits the Island of St. Michel.

Papaver, Coquelicot, Poppy, *Cyanus segetum*, Bleuet, Corn flower, *Silene latifolia*, Silène, White campion, *Senecio*, Séneçon, Ragwort, *Sonchus arvensis*, Laiteron des champs, Sow thistle, *Lotus corniculatus*, Lotier corniculé or Pied-de-poule, Bird's-foot trefoil, *Trifolium*, Trèfle, Clover, *Iberis amara*, Ibéris amer, Candytuft, *Ajuga*, Bugle, Bugleweed, *Plantago lanceolata*, Plantain lancéolé, Ribwort plantain

In a postcard view of a small lake island, boats arrive and depart punctuated by the blue and red jackets of tourists on the boat ramp. The view of pedal-boats that are actually in the same frame as a red poppy is an exception to the usual man-made/botanical juxtaposition between frames in the *Bouquets*. And the bright clothes of hikers and tour groups stand out against the green of the forest. This last of the first series of *Bouquets* marked the end of Lowder's depictions of mass tourism although she would continue to contrast the strident transient colors of human activity with the subdued eternal ones of nature.

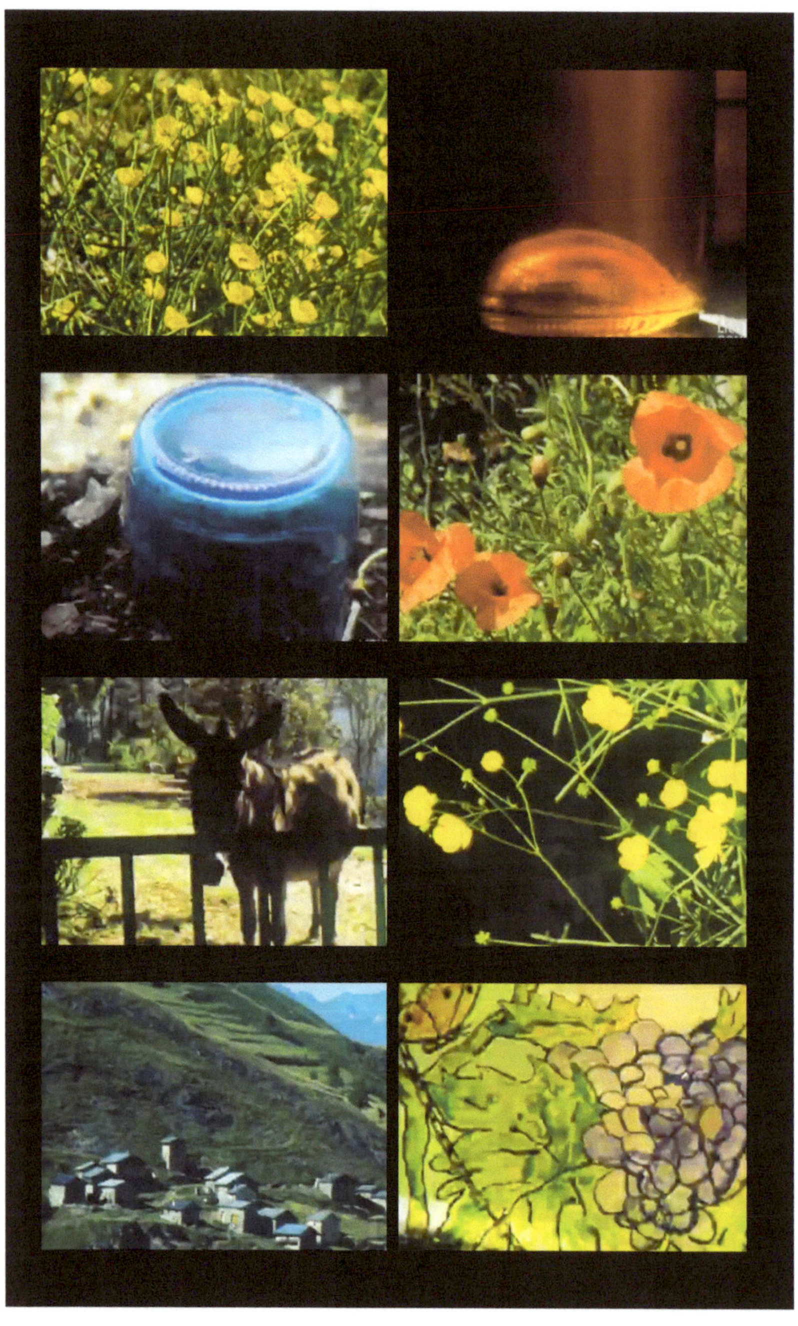

Bouquet 21 (2001)

BOUQUET 21 (2001)
LA BARAQUE, LIEU-DIT LES COUVRETTES, LOZÈRE

Filmed in a tiny paradise which took years to create, La Baraque, an organic farm situated 2 kms from Aujac, in the far corner of Gard, sandwiched between Lozère and Ardèche.

Ranunculus repens, Bouton d'or, Buttercup, *Achillea*, Achillée, Achillea or Yarrow, *Sinapis arvensis*, Moutarde sauvage, Wild mustard, *Senecio*, Séneçon, Ragwort, *Leucanthemum*, Marguerite, Daisy, *Papaver*, Coquelicot, Poppy, *Lotus corniculatus*, Lotier corniculé or Pied-de-poule, Bird's-foot trefoil

Lowder continued to celebrate man-made objects and textures but here they seem to have an integral connection to the specific place in the way the tourist activity in the previous series did not. Shafts of sunlight illuminate dishes, cups, bottles, and dishes and create floral patterns in muted green on stained glass. But the man-made objects are here not in contrast to but seamlessly interwoven with natural ones such as vibrant red poppies or goldfish in a fishpond.

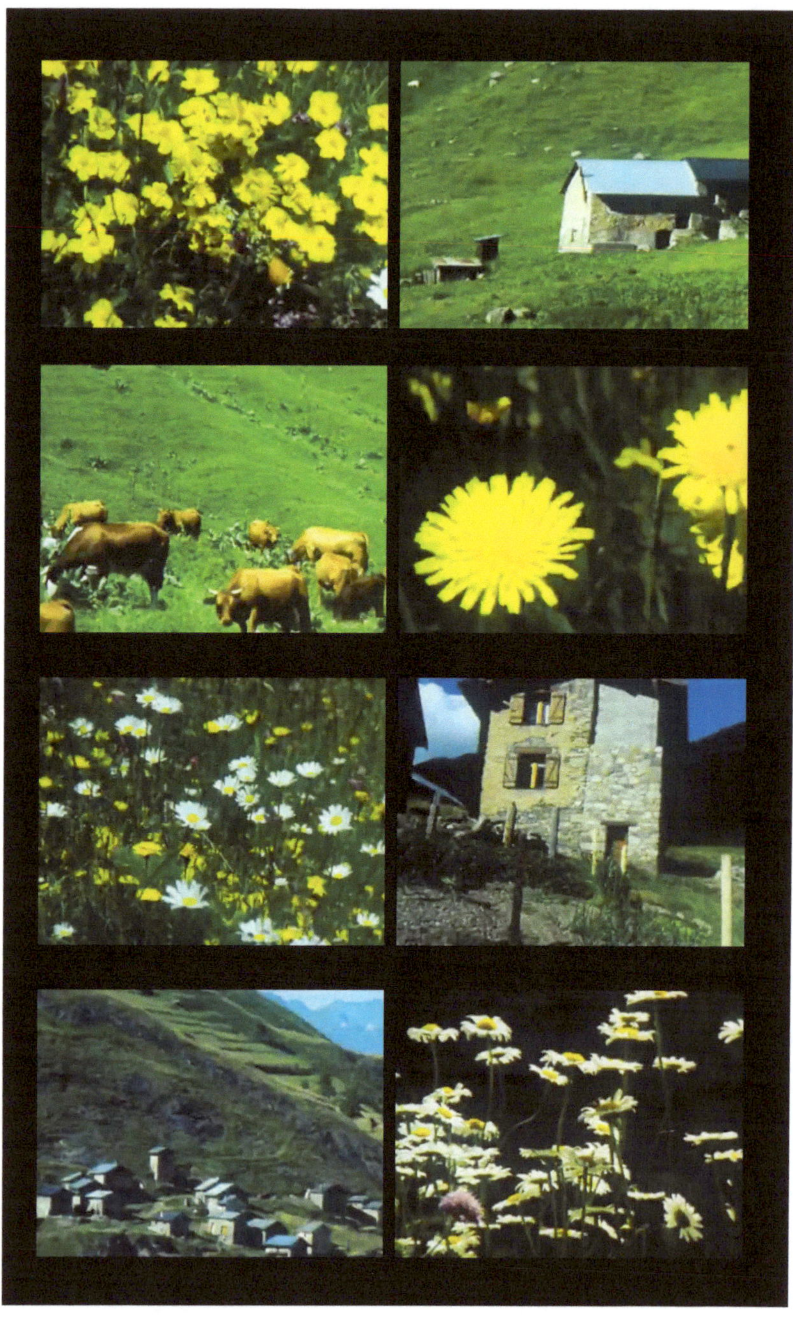

Bouquet 22 (2001)

BOUQUET 22 (2001)
BETAIX, SAVOIE

Bouquet 22 meanders over the mountain pastures near the summit of the Grand Perron des Encombres, not far from a macrobiotic centre at Bettaix, in the Belleville Valley, Savoie.

Ranunculus repens, Bouton d'or, Buttercup, *Leucanthemum,* Marguerite, Daisy, *Plantago lanceolata,* Plantain lancéolé, Ribwort plantain, *Myosotis,* Myosotis, Forget-me-not, *Silene dioica,* Silène rose, Red campion

There is a visual resemblance between the blades of snow on looming Alpine peaks and the white angular edges of wildflowers, while man-made artifacts persist as a chromatic counterpoint: the children's swing set, the massive block of yellow of a tour bus, horizontal lines of colored multi-colored synthetic rope delineating a field.

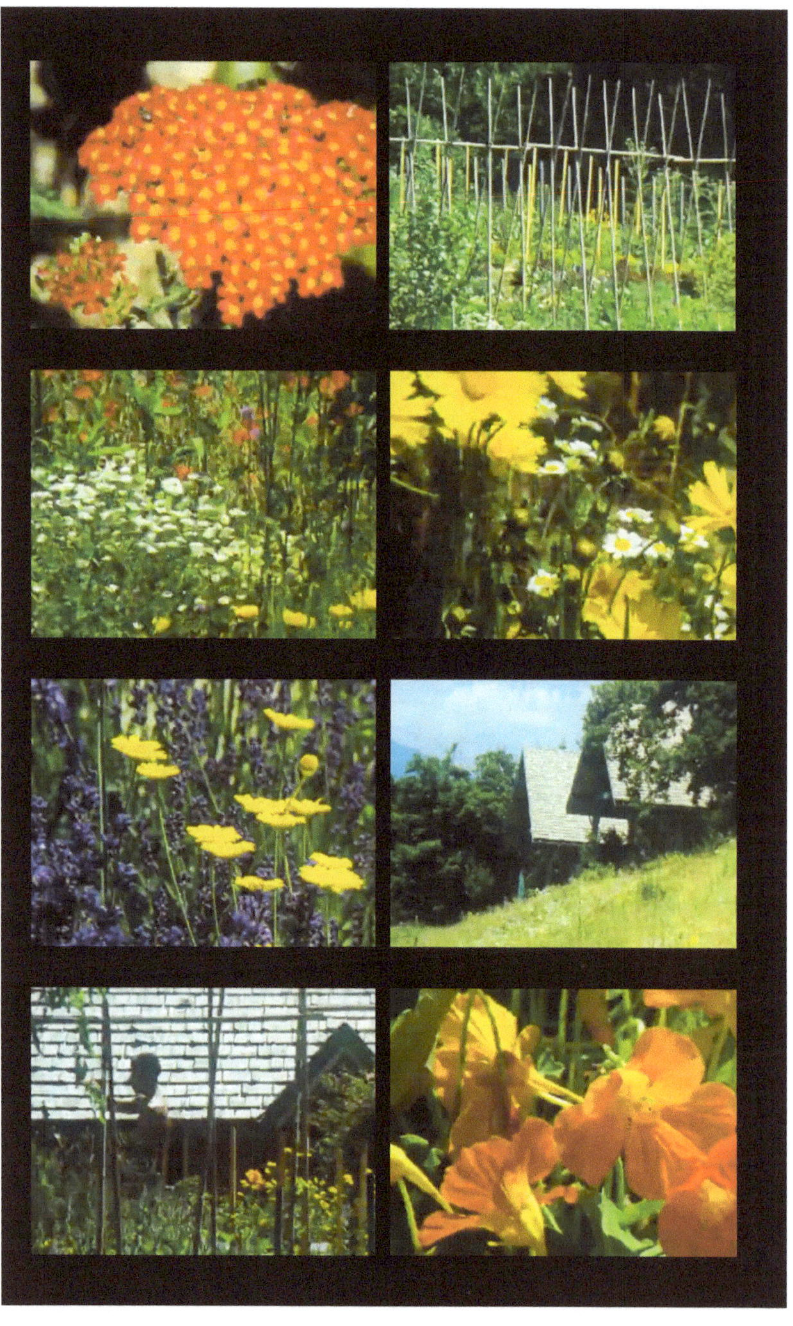

Bouquet 23 (2001)

BOUQUET 23 (2001)
TERRE VIVANTE, ISÈRE

Bouquet 23 shows Terre Vivante, a center focusing on ecological issues, located on a site of fine cultivated, or wild, flower and vegetable gardens strewn over a hillside amongst ponds. Open to the public, it organizes numerous events and publishes excellent books and a magazine.

Pilosella aurantiaca, Épervière orangée, Fox and Cubs, *Myosotis*, Myosotis, Forget-me-not, *Trifolium*, Trèfle, Clover, *Tanacetum vulgare*, Tanaisie, Tansy, *Verbena bonariensis*, Verveine de Buenos Aires, Verbena bonariensis, *Coreopsis*, Coreopsis, Coreopsis, *Borago officinalis*, Bourrache, Borage, *Salvia*, Sauge, Sage, *Papaver*, Coquelicot, Poppy

Views of modernistic structures and straw-hatted ecological pilgrims are juxtaposed with the accelerated motion of clouds. There is an interweaving, which will become increasingly more evident in the later *Bouquets,* between the natural wind-driven movement of flowers and the time-lapse rhythm created in the camera of the artist.

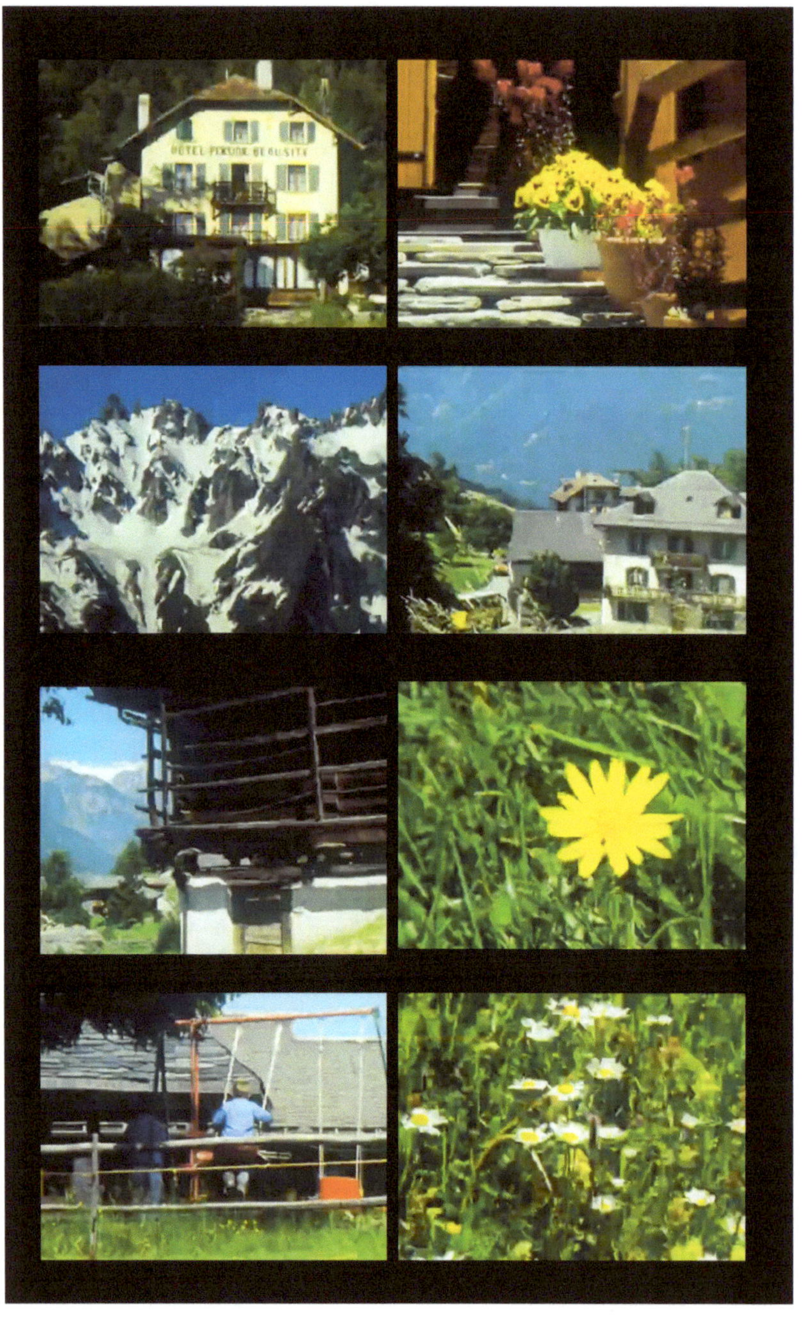

Bouquet 24 (2001)

BOUQUET 24 (2001)
BEAU-SITE, CHEMIN SUR MARTIGNY, VALAIS

Bouquet 24 was filmed in a pastoral setting around Beau-Site, an inn which provides organic meals in its preserved 1912 ambience, in Chemin-Dessus, on a mountain slope 7 kms from Martigny, Switzerland.

Taraxacum officinale, Pissenlit, Dandelion, *Trifolium*, Trèfle, Clover, *Leucanthemum*, Marguerite, Daisy, *Ranunculus repens*, Bouton d'or, Buttercup

The hosts' advertised description of their retreat could explain Lowder's attraction to it:

Here simplicity takes on its true meaning, closely accompanied by sobriety... In this setting where nature alone reigns, guests revitalize themselves, take refuge from the frenzy of modern life. A place outside of time.

But if the allure of the place is traditional, Lowder's vision is radical as she composes startling spatial and formal visual juxtapositions with flattened telephoto views of Alpine buildings woven frame-by-frame into wide angle images of wildflowers.

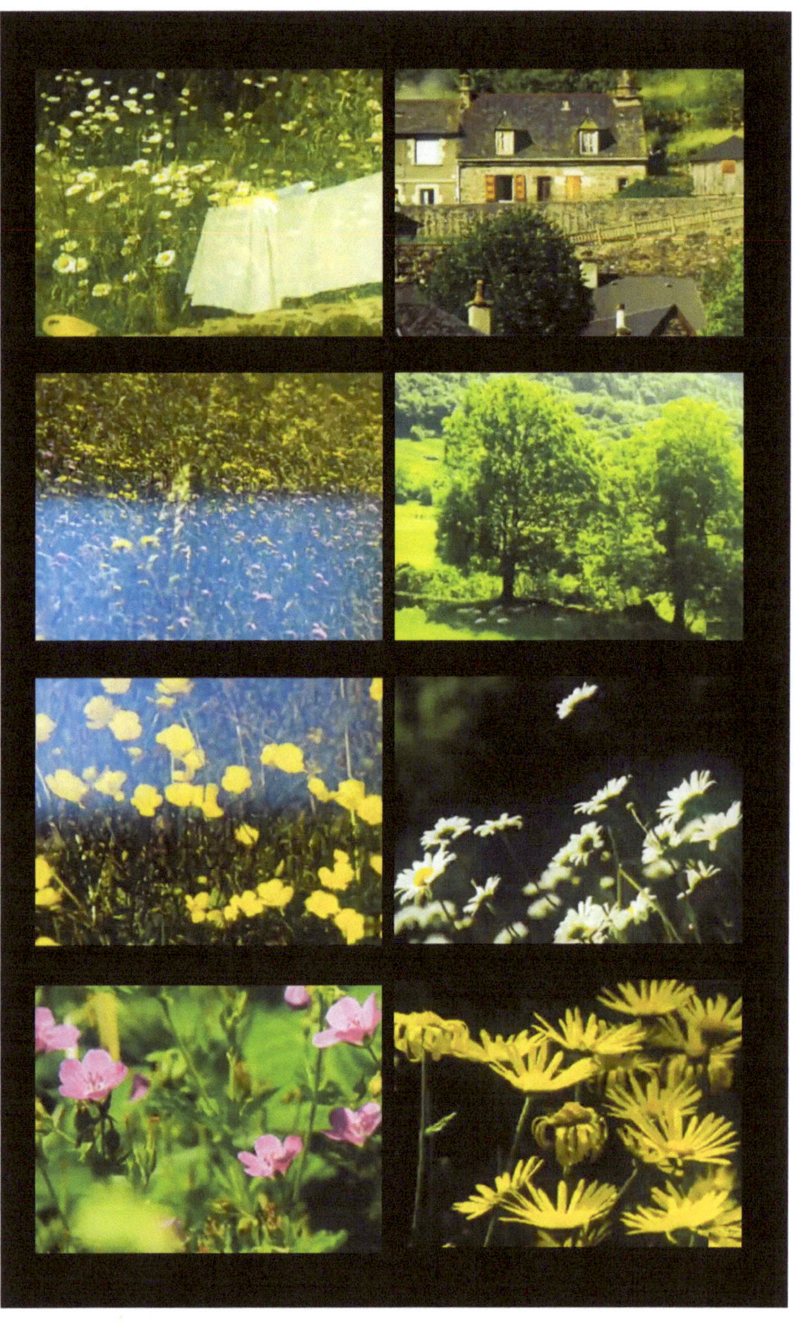

Bouquet 25 (2002)

BOUQUET 25 (2002)
LE TAHOUL, CANTAL

Bouquet 25 was shot in Cantal, around Le Tahoul, the Falgoux Valley and the Aulac Pass. This reel mingles the few flowers uneaten by the Salers cows with the village residents going about their affairs.

Leucanthemum, Marguerite, Daisy, *Viola,* Violette, Violet, *Myosotis arvensis,* Myosotis des champs, Field forget-me-not, *Taraxacum officinale,* Pissenlit, Dandelion, *Geranium robertianum,* Herbe à Robert, Herb Robert, *Lathraea Squamaria,* Lathrée écailleuse, Common toothwort, *Ranunculus repens,* Bouton d'or, Buttercup, *Genista,* Genêt, Broom, *Silene dioica,* Silène rose, Red campion

A grouping of houses in a village far from mass tourism and organized leisure activities, human actions seem integrated into the landscape. But although the subject is timeless, it is seen with a modern vision: the flicker of alternating film frames produces a kinetic energy that animates its subjects. The laundry drying in the sun shivers with an energy generated by a purely filmic optical phenomenon. In this context, the occasional, relatively rare, sequences of "natural" motion - such as the gestures of a woman retrieving laundry from a clothesline have a mysterious irreality.

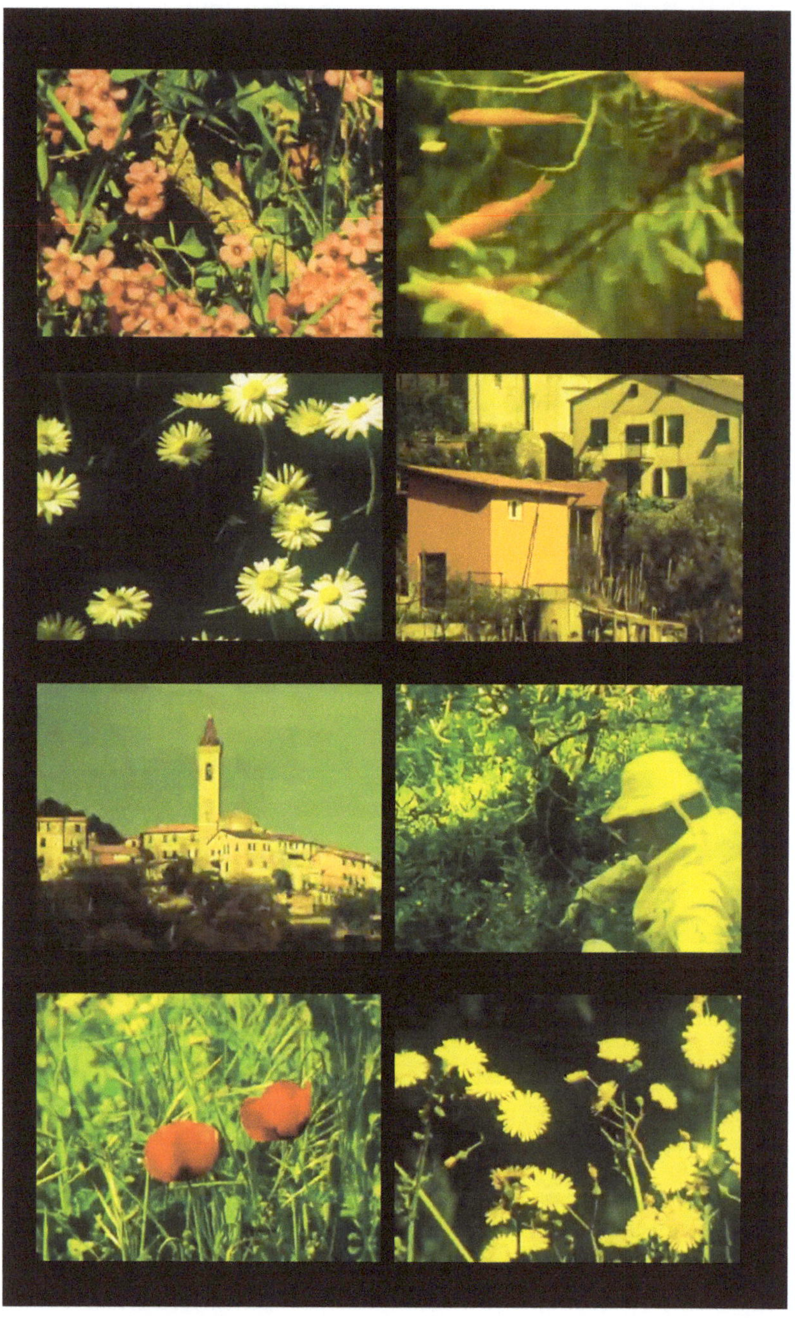

Bouquet 26 (2003)

BOUQUET 26 (2003)
LA TERRA DI MEZZO, LOCALITA CARMELO, CASTIGLIONE CHIAVARESE, LIGURIA, ITALY

Bouquet 26 was filmed in the middle of the animals of a small farm, La Terra di Mezzo, perched on hillside terraces of Liguria, Italy.

Sutera cordata, Bacopa, Ornemental bacopa, *Aquilegia*, Ancolie, Aquilegia or Columbine, *Ranunculus repens*, Bouton d'or, Buttercup, *Malva*, Mauve, Malva, *Calendula officinalis*, Souci, Pot marigold, *Senecio*, Séneçon, Ragwort, *Papaver*, Coquelicot, Poppy

A change of country - from France to Italy - is echoed by a shift in color palette to a dominant orange, crystalized in the goldfish in the dark water of a basin. Views of the steep terraces of the Ligurian coast also mark a departure from the flatter landscapes of rural France.

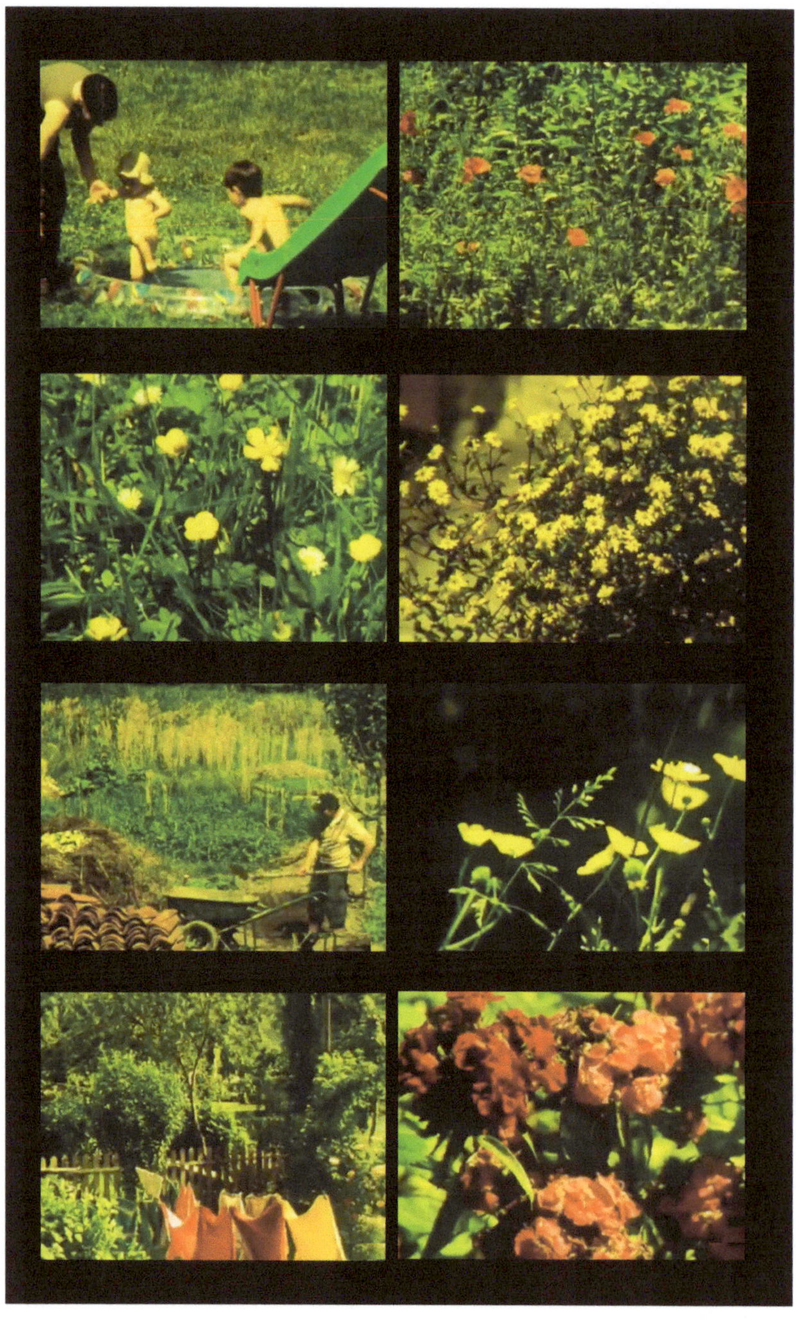

Bouquet 27 (2003)

BOUQUET 27 (2003)
CENTRE MACROBIOTIQUE ST. GAUDENS, HAUTE-GARONNE

Bouquet 27 moves around a macrobiotic centre in St. Gaudens, Haute-Garonne. Amongst glimpses of the surrounding countryside leading to the village of St. Béat, it shows its residents working on the land, repairing items or making rice biscuits.

Ranunculus repens, Bouton d'or, Buttercup, *Anthemis tinctoria,* Anthemis des teinturiers, Anthemis tonctoria, Golden chamomile, *Myosotis alpestris,* Myosotis des Alpes, Alpine forget-me-not, *Papaver,* Coqueli-cot, Poppy

The first shot of children on a water slide and falling water is a recurrent motif. In a sense, the viewer is also on a continuous water slide. A horizontal rectangle matte - perhaps created by filming through an opening in a farm building provides a rectangular echo of the format of widescreen motion picture film.

Here the people viewed are at work - repairing masonry, shoveling earth into a wheelbarrow - unlike the random tourist movement in earlier *Bouquets.*

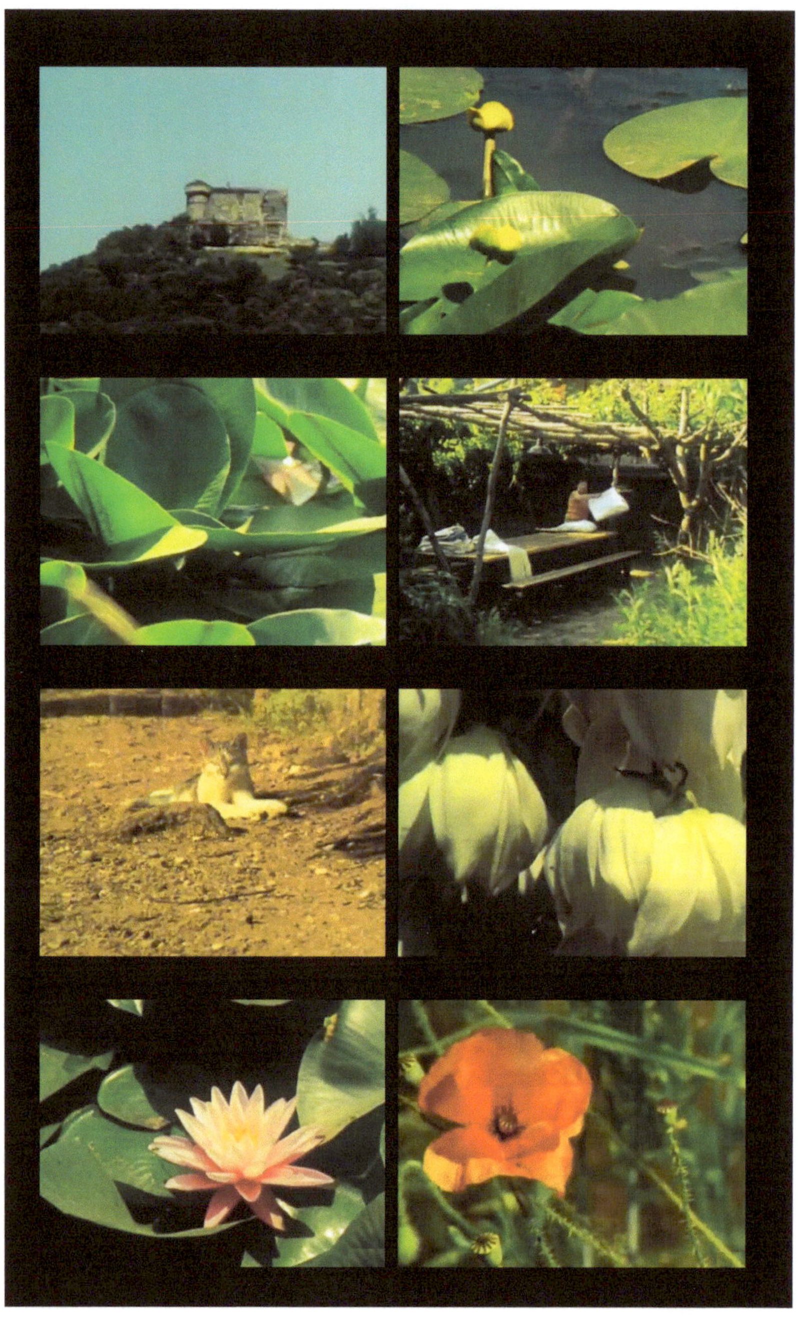

Bouquet 28 (2005)

BOUQUET 28 (2005)
LA BARAQUE, LIEU-DIT LES COUVRETTES, LOZÈRE

Bouquet 28 takes place on a farm, Mas de Cocagne, Aujac, Gard, which has developed from an abandoned coal-mining area into an agricultural-ecological site over twenty-five years. The topics include abundant floral vegetation, the Château d'Aujac on the hillside in the distance, work on the farm, builders erecting a roof, washing being hung up and, to end, a contented frog amongst the pink water lilies.

Cichorium intybus, Chicorée sauvage, Common chicory, *Senecio*, Séneçon, Ragwort, *Papaver*, Coquelicot, Poppy, *Ranunculus repens*, Bouton d'or, Buttercup, *Yucca filamentosa*, Yucca filamenteux, Common Yucca, Adam's needle and thread, *Leucanthemum*, Marguerite, Daisy, *Solanum rantonnetii*, Solanum, Solanum, *Nymphaea*, Nénuphar, Water lily

The close-up of a poppy moving in the wind is another example of the ambiguous boundary between natural wind-generated movement in time and the cinematic technique of time-lapse. The human figures move with a similar frenzy as they work on a roof, carry laundry, beat pillows, and hang up white sheets to dry in the wind.

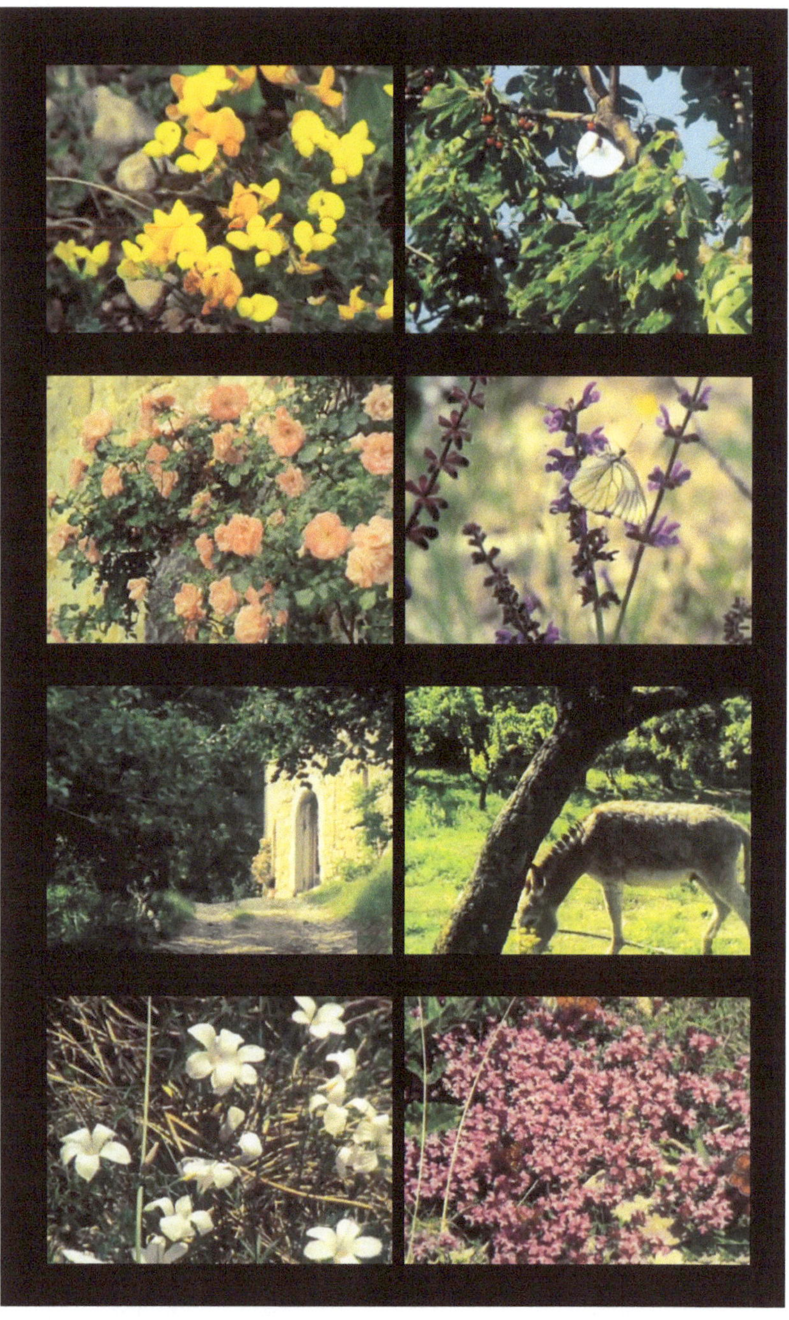

Bouquet 29 (2005)

BOUQUET 29 (2005)
FRA BOYER, FORÊT DOMANIALE DE L'OULE, MONTMORIN, HAUTES-ALPES

Bouquet 29 shows a very isolated 18th century farmhouse, Fra Boyer, on the borders of the Forêt Domaniale de l'Oule, near Montmorin, Hautes-Alpes. The floral vegetation attracts numerous butterflies and other flying insects, the family grows vegetables and collects the cherries while two donkeys help themselves.

Erinus alpinus, Érine des Alpes, Fairy foxglove, *Silene latifolia*, Silène, White campion, *Sinapis arvensis*, Moutarde sauvage, Wild mustard, *Vicia cracca*, Vesce cracca, Vetch, *Salva*, Sauge, Sage, *Rosa*, Rose, Rose, *Ranunculus repens*, Bouton d'or, Buttercup, *Trifolium*, Trèfle, Clover, *Calendula officinalis*, Souci, Pot marigold, *Geranium robertianum*, Herbe à Robert, Herb Robert, *Lotus corniculatus*, Lotier corniculé or Pied-de-poule, Bird's-foot trefoil

The timeless motions of donkeys grazing and gardening under cherry trees is confronted with the intrusion of modern consumer culture in the images of CDs strung in the trees. It takes a moment to realize that the role of the shiny disks is in fact a very ancient one - that of the scarecrow deterring birds from approaching to eat the fruit.

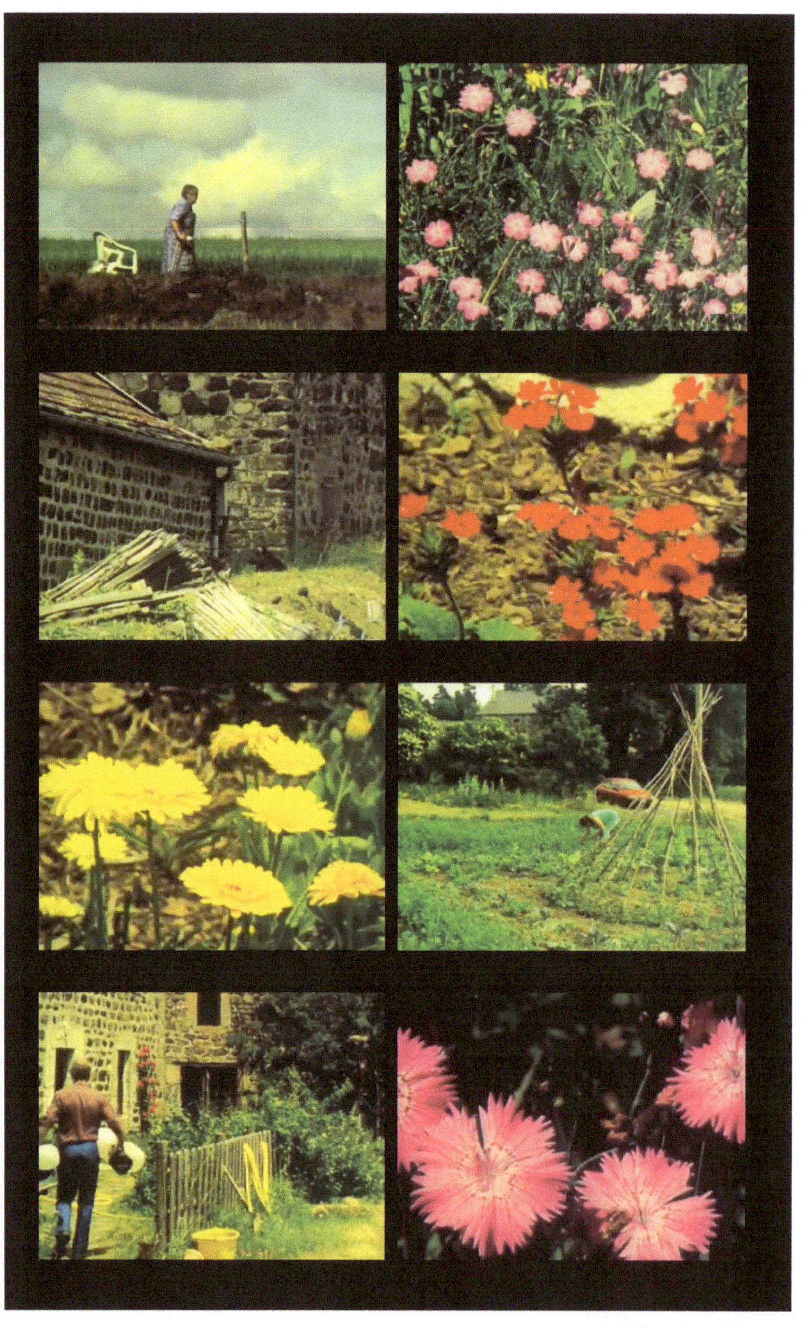

Bouquet 30 (2005)

BOUQUET 30 (2005)
LE LANTEÏROU, CHAMPAGNE

Bouquet 30 (2005) treats the farm of Le Lanteïrou, Champagne, near Les Vastres, Haute-Loire. One sees the cows, the farmer by the house, a member of the family in the bed he has built, complete with bedside lamp, under a nearby tree, and an elderly neighbor walking between the two white chairs set up at either end of her field amongst the vegetable patches.

Leucanthemum, Marguerite, Daisy, *Carduus*, Chardon, Thistle, *Avena fatua*, Avoine sauvage, Common wild oat, *Senecio*, Séneçon, Ragwort, *Trifolium*, Trèfle, Clover, *Dianthus*, Œillet, Dianthus or Pink, *Malva*, Mauve, Mallow, *Verbena*, Verveine, Verbena, *Salva*, Sauge, Sage, *Dianthus silvestris*, Œillet sauvage, Wood pink

Images such as a man sleeping outdoors in an indoor bed or an elderly woman with a plastic bag near a plastic lawn chair clash with the palette of botanical content. Lowder does not divert her gaze from the mundane modern details that intrude on the purity of a rural retreat - a man carrying plastic water jugs (clearly the lightest container for transporting water) or the labor-saving power of a large tractor.

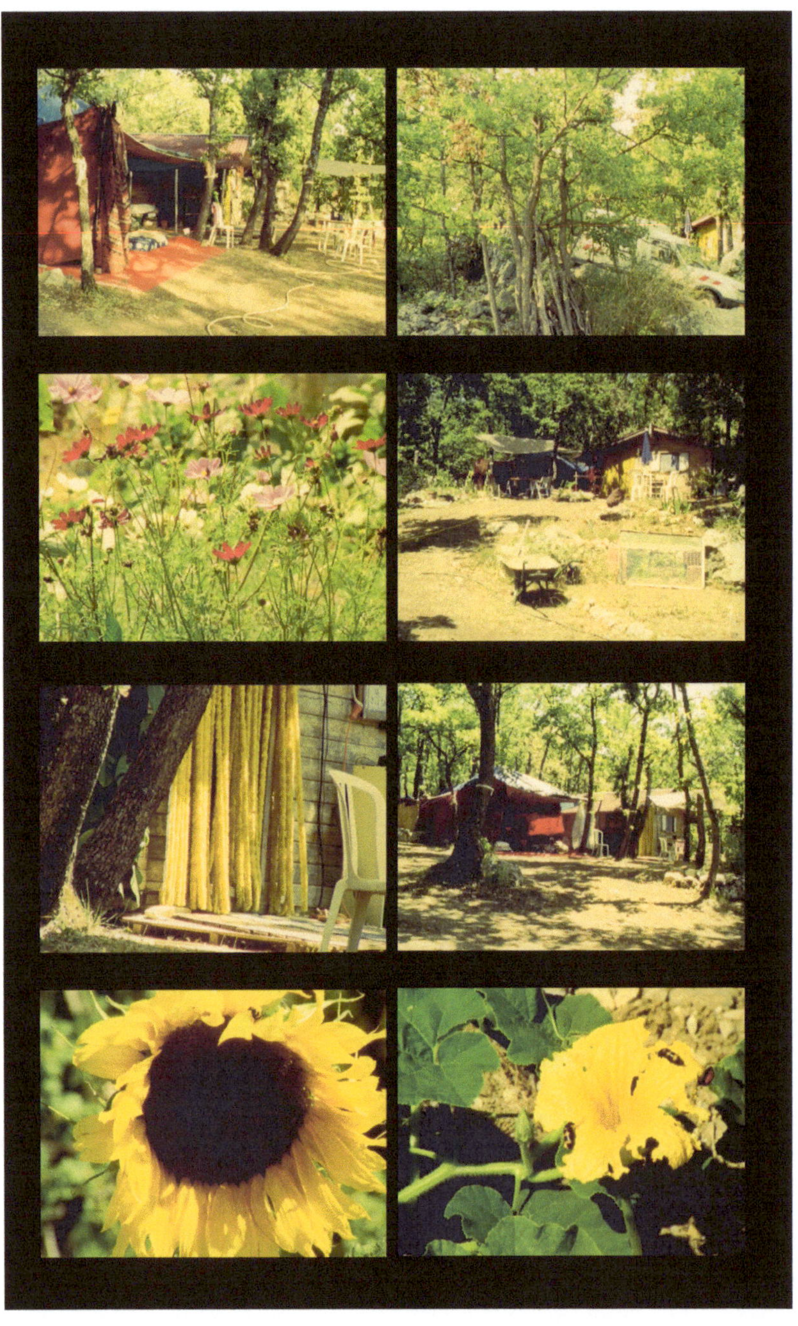

Bouquet 11 (2005)

BOUQUET 11 (2005)
OASIS DE LA ROCHE BLEUE, NEAR PLAISANS, DRÔME

Bouquet 11 takes place on an organic farm at an altitude of 650 meters, north of Mt. Ventoux (1912m), on four hectares of dry but fertile land abandoned some fifty years ago. After moving around, Ljiljiana and Luc wanted to find a spot to settle, to work in the ancestral tradition establishing a dialogue with nature. At the time I filmed they had grown, in a very short while, a magnificent amount of flowers, vegetables, fruits, and aromatic herbs and spices.

Coreopsis, Coréopsis, Coreopsis, *Helianthus*, Tournesol, Sunflower, *Cucurbita*, (Fleur de) potimarron, Red Kuri squash blossom, *Cosmos*, Cosmos, Cosmos, *Taraxacum officinale*, Pissenlit, Dandelion

The opening shot of a sprinkler watering a garden is a reminder of the centrality of moving water in Lowder's work. In this case, the time-lapse motion is used outside its usual context of flowers and combined with sequences of continuous motion to create another dimension of time. And again, there is no attempt to suggest that the natural retreat does not function without the support of fossil-burning conveniences as a vehicle departs from the isolated cabin. And synthetic materials such as plastic chairs surround a campsite with red and blue polyester tarpaulins.

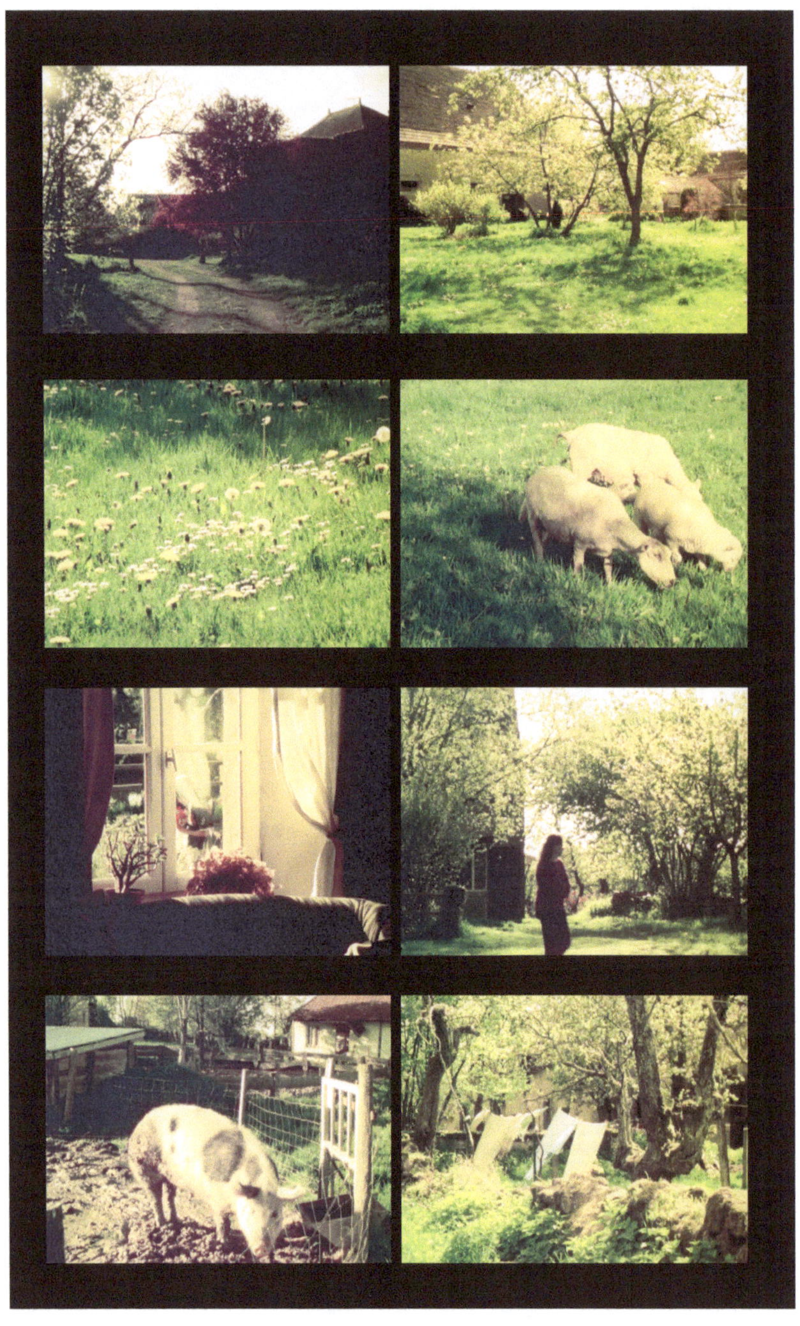

Bouquet 12 (2008)

BOUQUET 12 (2008)
FERME DE LA MHOTTE, SAINT-MENOUX, ALLIER

Bouquet 12 was filmed in an ecological domain consisting of magnificent old farm houses and an enormous barn situated in a sparsely inhabited area. Often, paying guests working on different projects came to stay there. The farm raised a few pigs and sheep and had a shop selling organic food. Some members of the family worked in the nearby Rudolf Steiner School and the barn was used for performing arts events. The cottage I stayed in had a very economical small Swedish rectangular log fire that both heated the room efficiently and cooked one's soup in no time.

Leucanthemum, Marguerite, Daisy, *Taraxacum officinale*, Pissenlit, Dandelion, *Myosotis sylvatica*, Myosotis des bois, Wood forget-me-not

The views of a pig in its sty seem far from the postcard tourist views of the first *Bouquets*, just as the Allier region is far from any popular vacation destination. Unlike the more idyllic settings of earlier *Bouquets*, the grazing sheep are shown reflected in stagnant water, insects are visible in the air, and the wildflowers are humble daisies and dandelions.

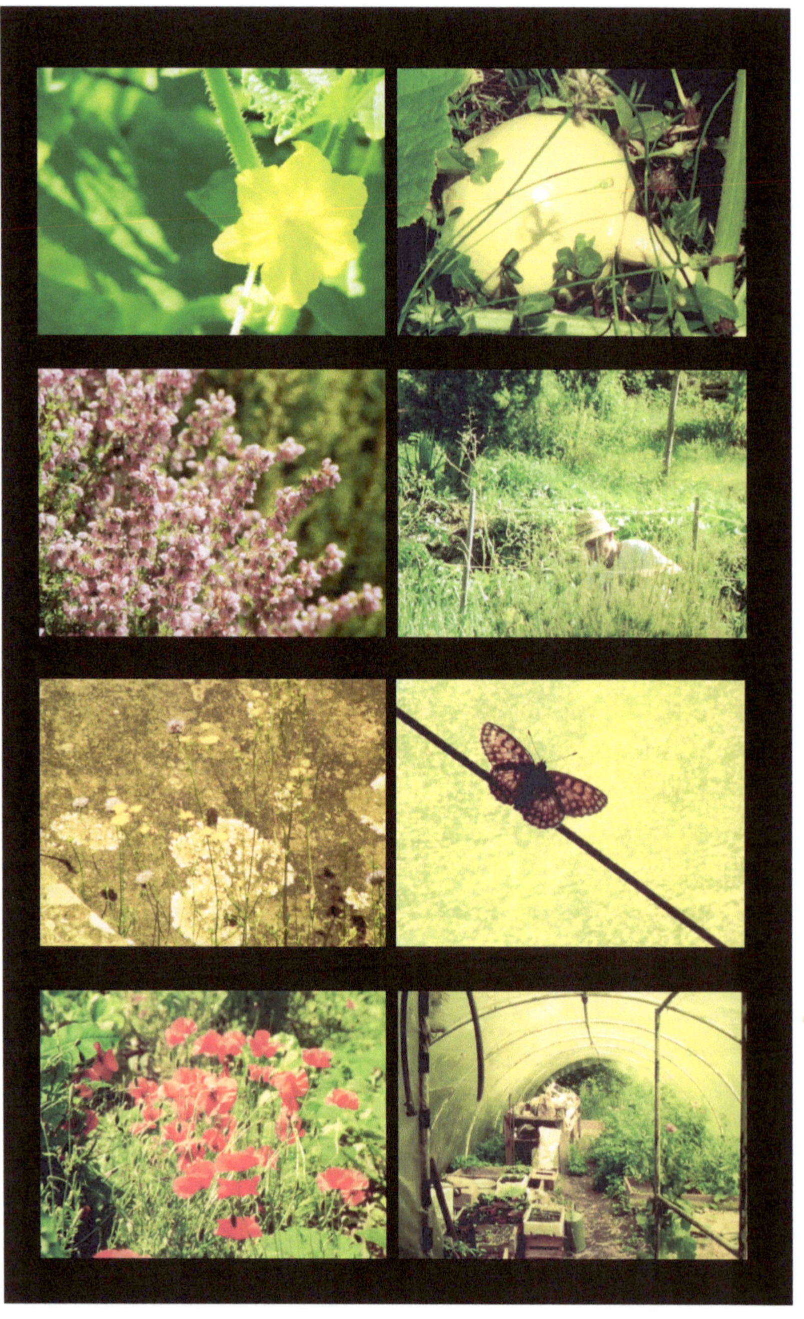

Bouquet 13 (2008)

BOUQUET 13 (2008)
LA FERME DU MAS DE COCAGNE, SITE AGROÉCOLOGIQUE DE LA BARAQUE, AUJAC, GARD

Pierre Buchberger and Martine Nivon, like many people during the late 1960s, left urban life to build their lives on an alternative basis. They acquired some fifty hectares of abandoned Cévennes coal mining land classified as industrial fallow land, terraced the land; grew vegetables; restored and built onto the farm houses; dug ponds to purify the water sources… Under their stewardship the location was restored to be a beautiful spot, augmented by the river below where one could swim.

Papaver, Coquelicot, Poppy, *Carduus*, Chardon, Thistle, *Matricaria chamomilla*, Camomille, Wild chamomile, *Sedum album*, Orpin blanc, White stonecrop, *Geranium robertianum*, Herbe à Robert, Herb Robert, *Daucus carota*, Carotte sauvage, Wild carrot or Queen Anne's lace, *Taraxacum officinale*, Pissenlit, Dandelion, *Cucurbita*, Courge, Squash, *Erica*, Bruyère, Heather, *Campsis radicans*, Bignone, Trumpet vine

Seemingly shot at the standard 16mm speed of 24 frames per second, the natural motion of the beating wings of a butterfly are a reminder of just how fluid is the demarcation of time in the *Bouquets*. Periods of hours can be compressed into a frenzy of seconds while in other sequences motion is barely visible at all.

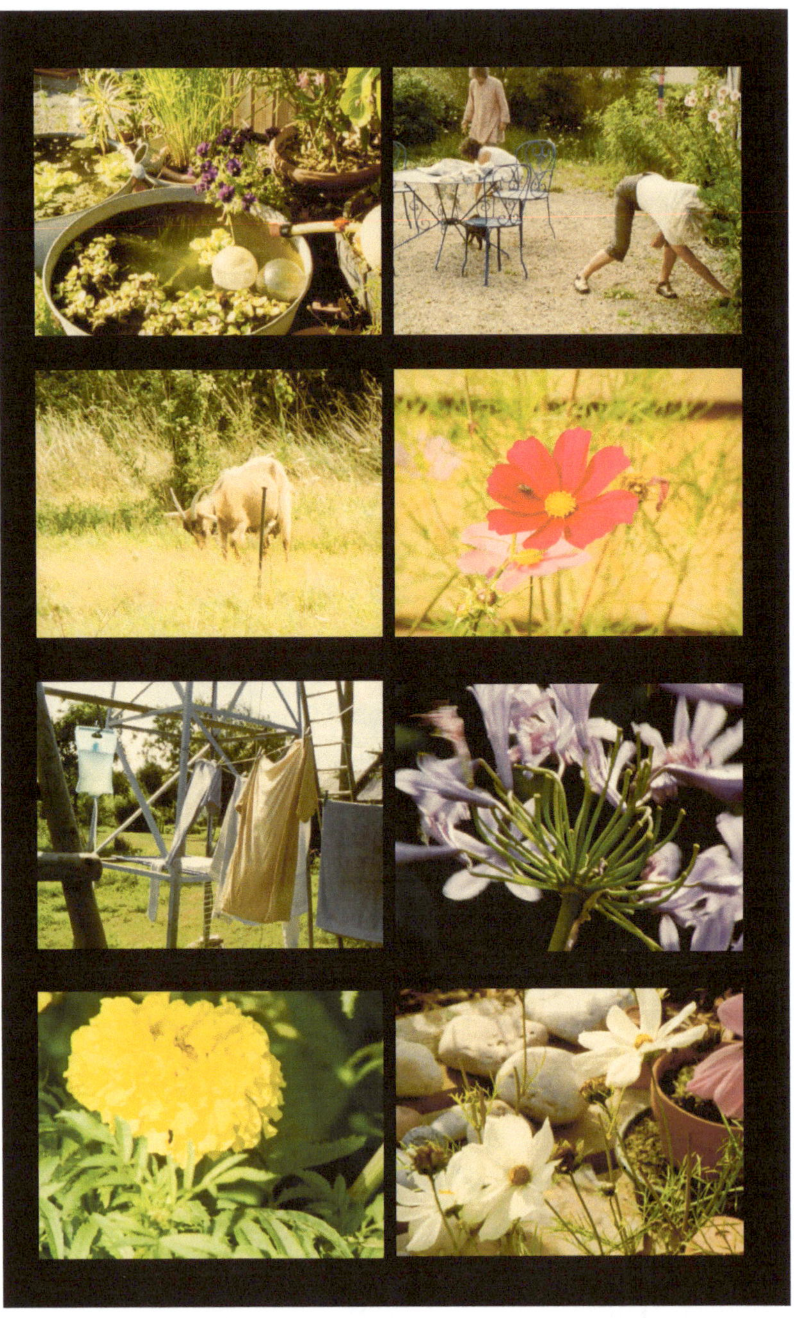

Bouquet 14 (2008)

BOUQUET 14 (2008)
ASSERAC, LOIRE-ATLANTIQUE

I stayed at Le Vieil Eclis while I was filming the gathering of sea salt for *Fleur de Sel* (2010). The farmers grew vegetables only for themselves, but Jacky Burgaud baked weekly large batches of very good organic bread for numerous people nearby... There were solar panels on the roof and a windmill for electricity, and a pond to purify the water. Over the years I had to go there quite a few times because it rains often in that area and sea salt will not crystallize without at least four consecutive days of sunshine.

Cosmos, Cosmos, Cosmos, *Tagetes patula*, Œillet d'Inde, French marigold, *Agapanthus*, Agapanthe, Lily of the Nile, *Nymphaea*, Nénuphar, Water lily, *Malva*, Mauve, Mallow, *Viola*, Pensée, Pansy, *Bougainvillea*, Bougainvillée, Bougainvillea

The *Bouquets* seem to celebrate how farm life forces the domestic and industrial worlds, the traditional and the modern, to cohabitate: a windmill next to a concrete pylon and a children's swing set, the recurrent image of laundry drying in the wind next to a parked car. Water bubbles on a lily pond and a plastic yellow duck water toy, showing discoloration of age, a domestic cat reclining on a vinyl table cover under a metal chair.

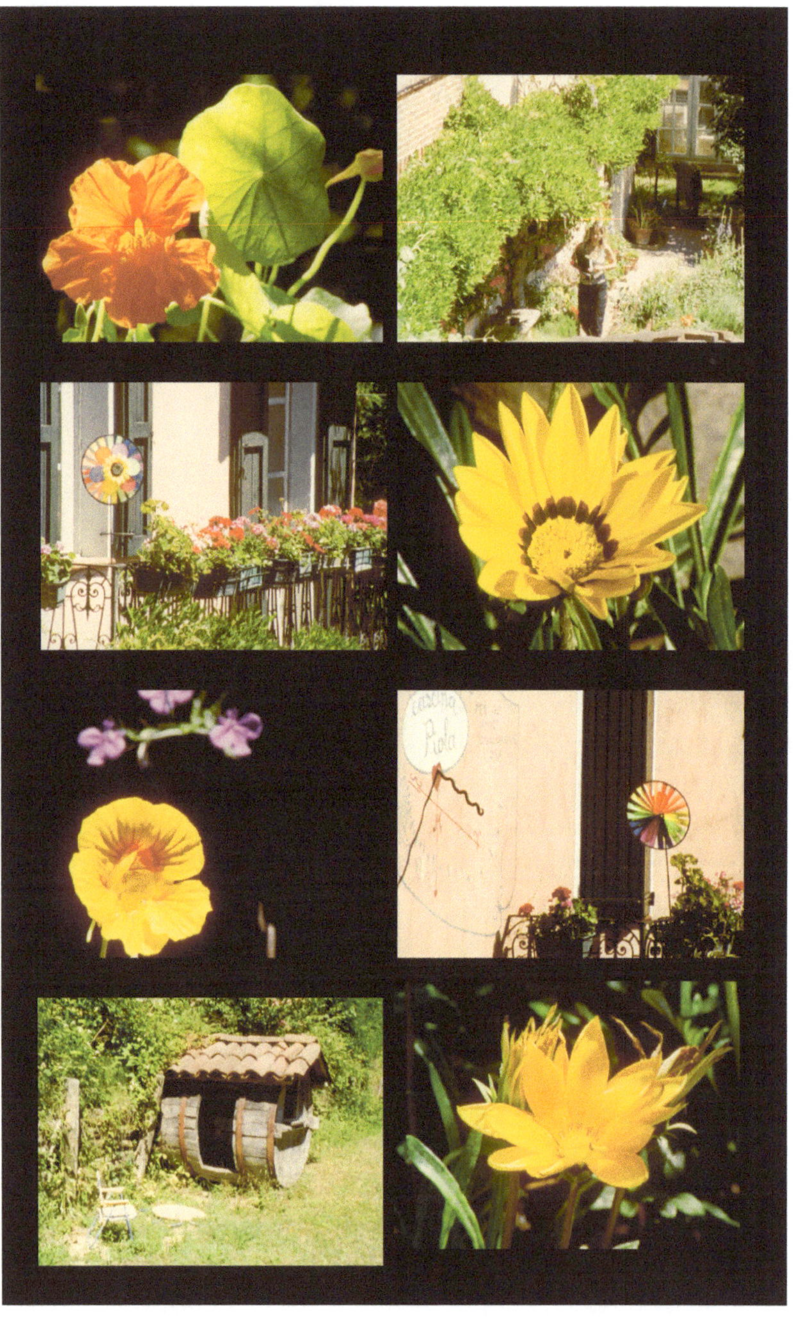

Bouquet 15 (2009)

BOUQUET 15 (2009)
AZIENDA AGRICOLA CASCINA PIOLA, SERRA CAPRIGLIO, ASTI

Over the years I often stayed at Cascina Piola... It had solar panels and its own water source. In a few nearby fields they produced an enormous amount of an ancient variety of red peppers - a regional specialty... The farm is in the heart of the region known for Italy's slow food movement, of which it is a part.

Tropaeolum, Capucine, Nasturtium, *Campanula*, Campanule, Bellflower, *Lilium lancifolium*, Lis tigré, Tiger lily, *Gazania rigens*, Gazania, Gazania or Treasure flower, *Pelargonium*, Géranium, Geranium, *Plumbago auriculata*, Plumbago du Cap, Cape leadwort, *Misopates orontium*, Muflier, Snapdragon, *Gerbera jamesonii,* Gerbera, Gerbera or Transvaal daisy, *Coreopsis*, Coréopsis, Coreopsis, *Begonia*, Bégonia, Begonia, *Geranium*, Géranium sauvage, Wild geranium, *Dianthus*, Œillet, Dianthus or Pink, *Rosa*, Rose, Rose

Again, details of modern technology cohabit with farm life unchanged for centuries. Solar panels are visible behind a traditional wooden farm trailer. And the primitive functionality of a multi-colored wind spinner recalls that of the aperture shutter - the basic mechanism of 20th century cinema.

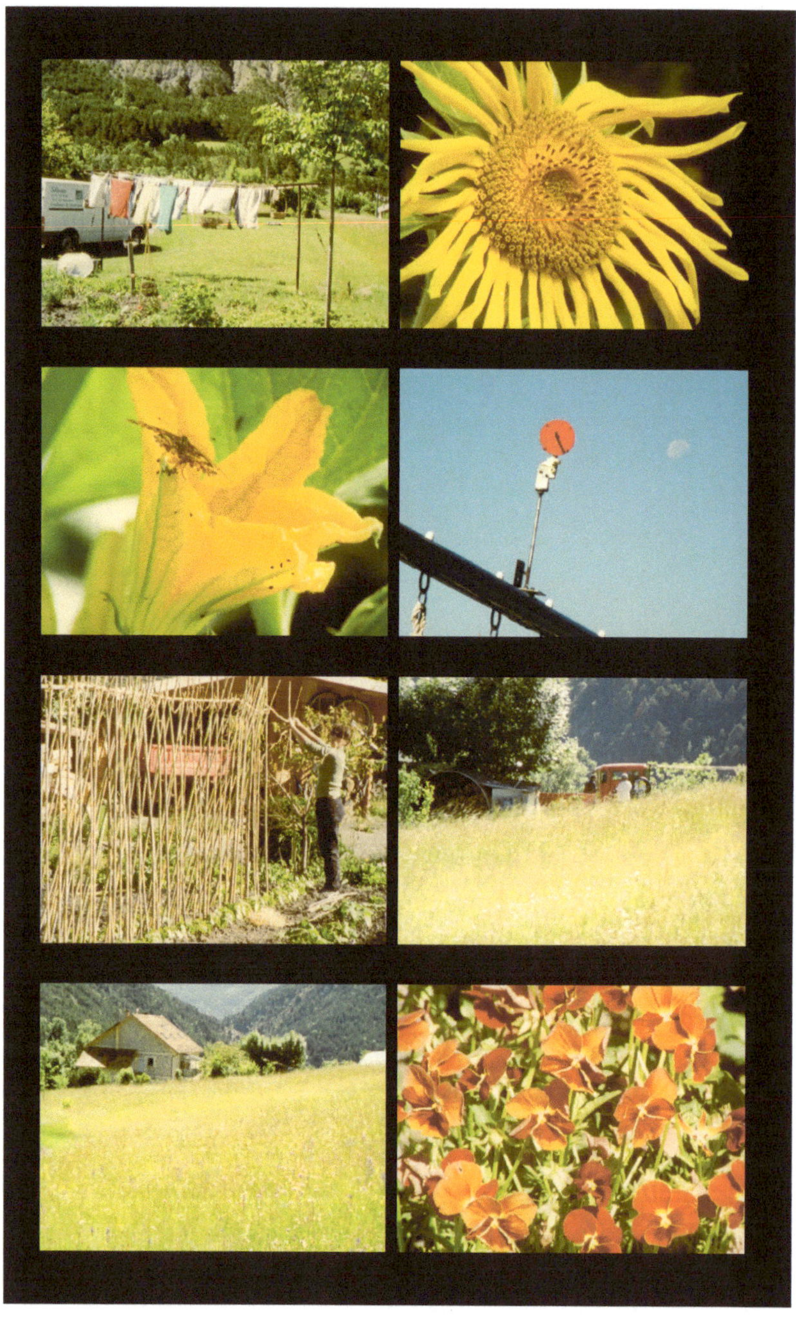

Bouquet 16 (2009)

BOUQUET 16 (2009)
PRADS-HAUTE-BLÉONE, BASSES-ALPES

The farm of Sylvie and Gérard Nicolino was known for the great variety of jams they sold in organic shops and fairs. It was an ideal place for trekkers, as higher up the road petered out with no one around except the odd bright green lizard.

Ranunculus repens, Bouton d'or, Buttercup, *Viola*, Pensée, Pansy, *Jasminum officinale*, Jasmin blanc, Jasmine, *Petunia*, Pétunia, Petunia, *Dianthus*, Œillet, Dianthus or Pink, *Trifolium*, Trèfle, Clover, *Avena fatua*, Avoine sauvage, Common wild oat, *Lotus corniculatus*, Lotier corniculé or Pied-de-poule, Bird's-foot trefoil, *Salvia*, Sauge, Sage, *Leucanthemum*, Marguerite, Daisy, *Gaillardia*, Gaillarde, Gaillardia or Blanket flower, *Silene latifolia*, Silène, White campion, *Cucurbita*, (Fleur de) courge, Squash blossom, *Helianthus*, Tournesol, Sunflower

The timeless natural world and the fleeting artificial one are often intermingled in the *Bouquets* in enigmatic ways: is the red disk against the sky a measurement device or a mobile sculpture? Seeds blow in the wind amid makeshift temporary buildings. A white delivery van and the colors of industrial machinery are in counterpoint with the greenery of the natural world.

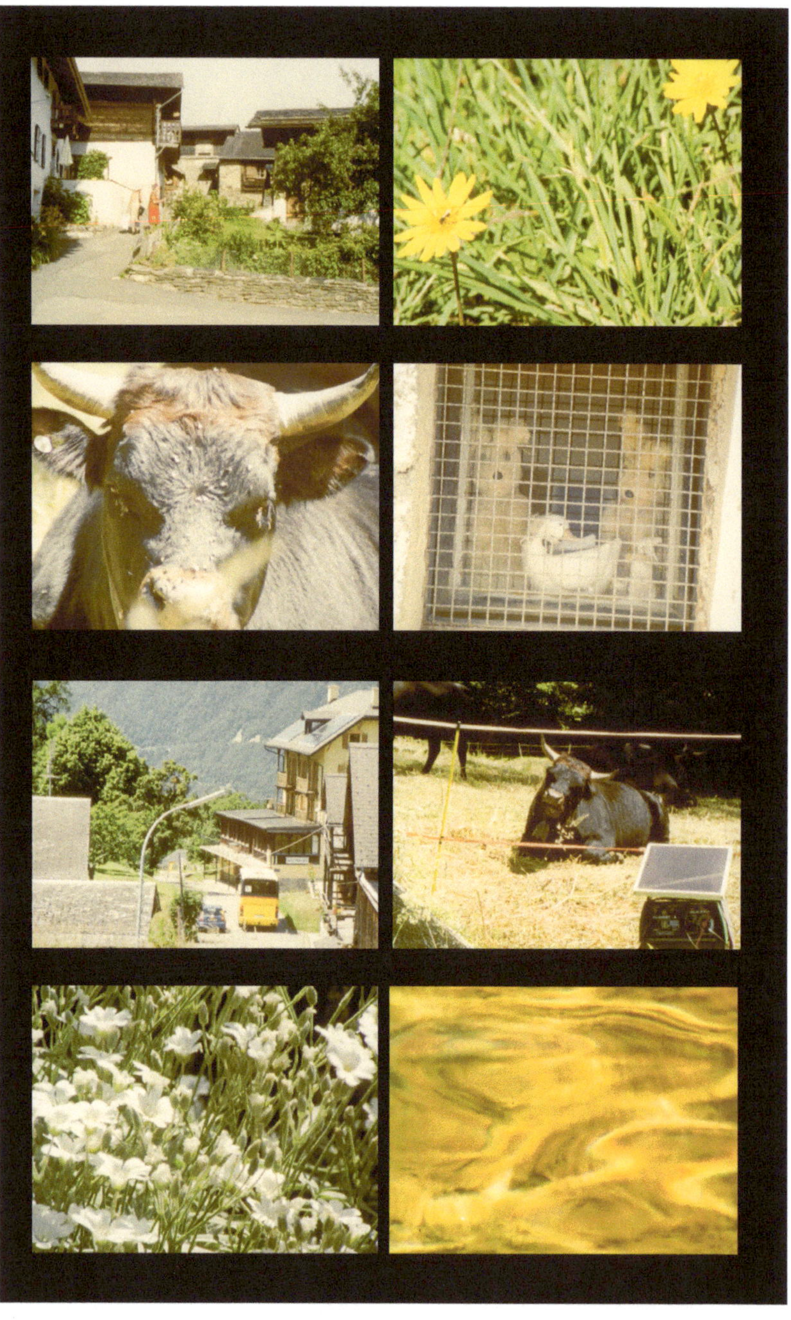

Bouquet 17 (2009)

BOUQUET 17 (2009)
HÔTEL BEAU-SITE, CHEMIN SUR MARTIGNY

I initially came to stay at Beau-Site to see an exhibition taking place nearby and, as it was too far to drive home the same day, I found a splendidly restored ecological hotel in an ancient hamlet just up the hill. I remember having supper one evening, overlooking the mountains as snow came down amidst lightning.

Arnica montana, Arnica, Mountain arnica, *Silene latifolia,* Silène, White campion, *Avena fatua,* Avoine sauvage, Common wild oat, *Trifolium,* Trèfle, Clover, *Daucus carota,* Carotte sauvage, Wild Carrot or Queen Anne's Lace, *Lilium martagon,* Lis Martagon, Martagon lily, *Senecio,* Séneçon, Ragwort, *Campanula,* Campanule, Bellflower, *Heuchera sanguinea,* Heuchère or Désespoir du peintre, Coral Bell

A yellow tourist bus drives in front of an imposing chalet (the same bus line that appeared eight years earlier in *Bouquet* 22) - the continuous sequence is unusual in its duration as the bus moves slowly downhill. Flies surround the head of a large black steer equipped with an ageless bell. The ancient breed of Alpine cattle (named after the Val d'Hérens region of Switzerland) are seen with a small solar panel unit in the foreground.

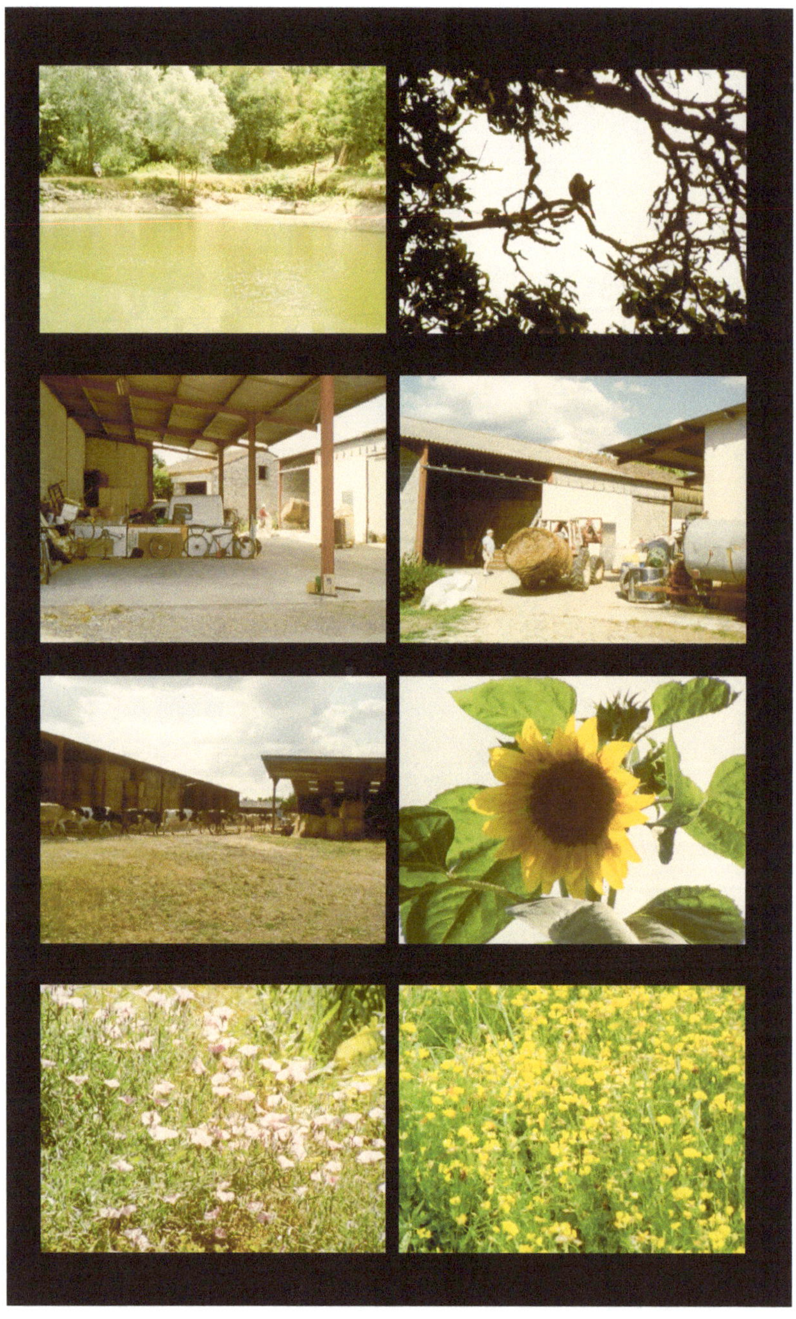

Bouquet 18 (2009)

BOUQUET 18 (2009)
FERME DE CROZEFOND, SAINT-AUBIN, LOT-ET-GARONNE

This farm, organic since 1961, is the only one in France to grow midnight primroses… I could not film the fields of flowers because they are well-named: as soon as there is light, they close. But I did discover an incredibly self-sustaining farm. The family made bread, cakes, cheese, honey, jams and all kinds of meat products.

Convolvulus arvensis, Liseron des champs, Field bindweed, *Lotus corniculatus*, Lotier corniculé or Pied-de-poule, Bird's-foot trefoil, *Salvia*, Sauge, Sage, *Zinnia*, Zinnia, Zinnia, *Helianthus*, Tournesol, Sunflower

From the first bursts of single frames whose subjects are barely discernible this *Bouquet* moves to the other extreme: an unusually long sequence - 25 seconds - of birds on a branch amounts to almost half of the one-minute duration of *Bouquet 18*.

Lowder's documentation of the random accumulation of farm life continues - bicycles to be repaired, furniture pieces to be discarded, parked vehicles, a corrugated roof. A large herd of dairy cows heads into barn. This is not idealized pristine nature but the accoutrements of a small business: farm equipment, a water tank trailer, a roll of hay on a tractor fork lift.

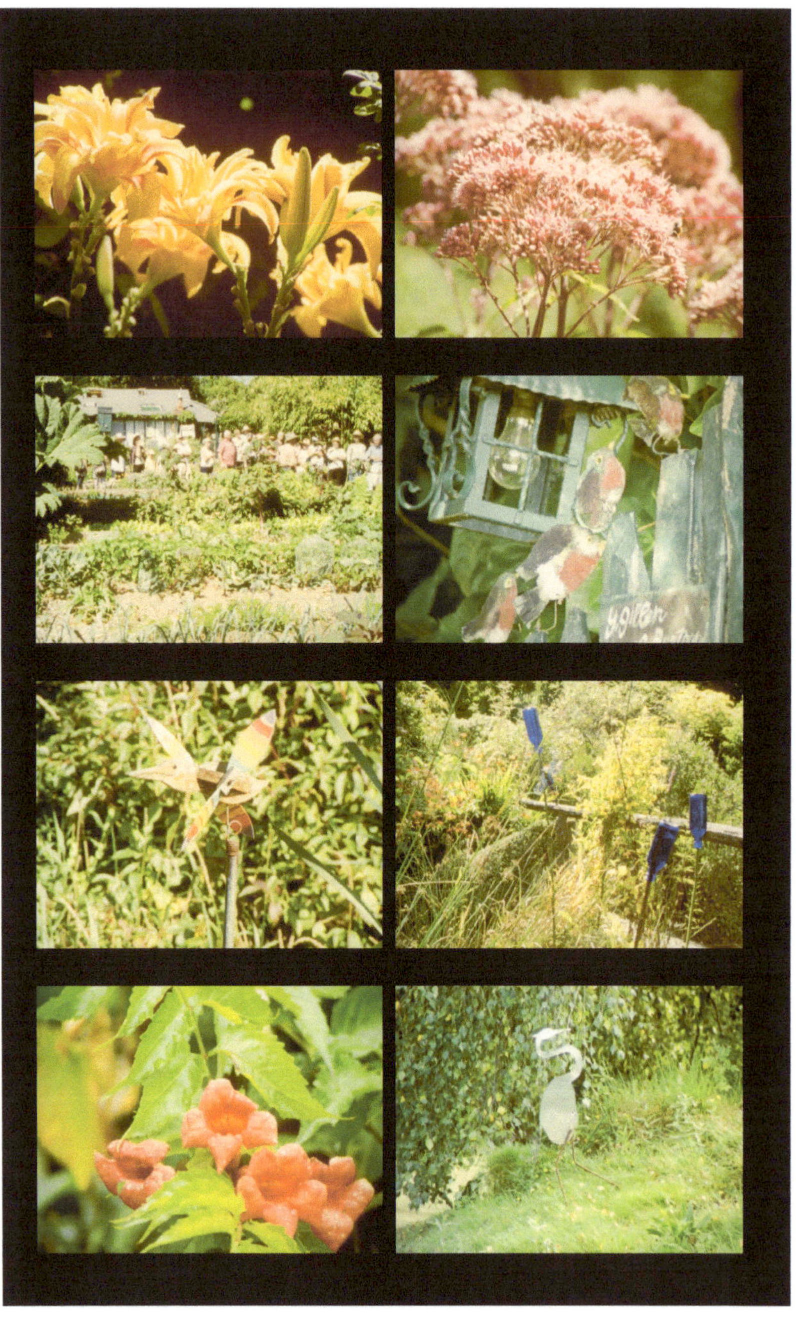

Bouquet 19 (2009)

BOUQUET 19 (2009)
PARC NATUREL RÉGIONAL DE BRIÈRE, HOSCAS, LOIRE-ATLANTIQUE

The Jardins du Marais was converted from marsh land into a vast botanical paradise. Annick Bertrand and Yves Gillen converted their caravan into a beautiful home complete with solar panels and a windmill for electricity. They grow their vegetables without any electrical machines, carefully planting the right plants next to each other to avoid incompatibilities and parasites.

Lilium lancifolium, Lis tigré, Tiger lily, *Lathyrus odoratus*, Pois de senteur, Sweetpea, *Sedum telephium*, Orpin reprise, Orpine, *Veronicastum virginicum*, Véronique de Virginie, Veronicastrum, *Hydrangea*, Hortensia, Hydrangea, *Borago officinalis*, Bourrache, Borage, *Calendula officinalis*, Souci, Pot marigold, *Rosa*, Rose, Rose, *Campsis radicans*, Bignone, Trumpet vine

The optical effects of the *Bouquets* - a succession of single16mm film frames - constantly blend with recordings of "natural" motion - the optical phenomenon of "persistence of vision" based on the inability of the human eye to distinguish minute alterations in a succession of still images. Among the latter are images of wind-driven devices - ranging from the low technology of a scarecrow to the high-technology of wind-turbines.

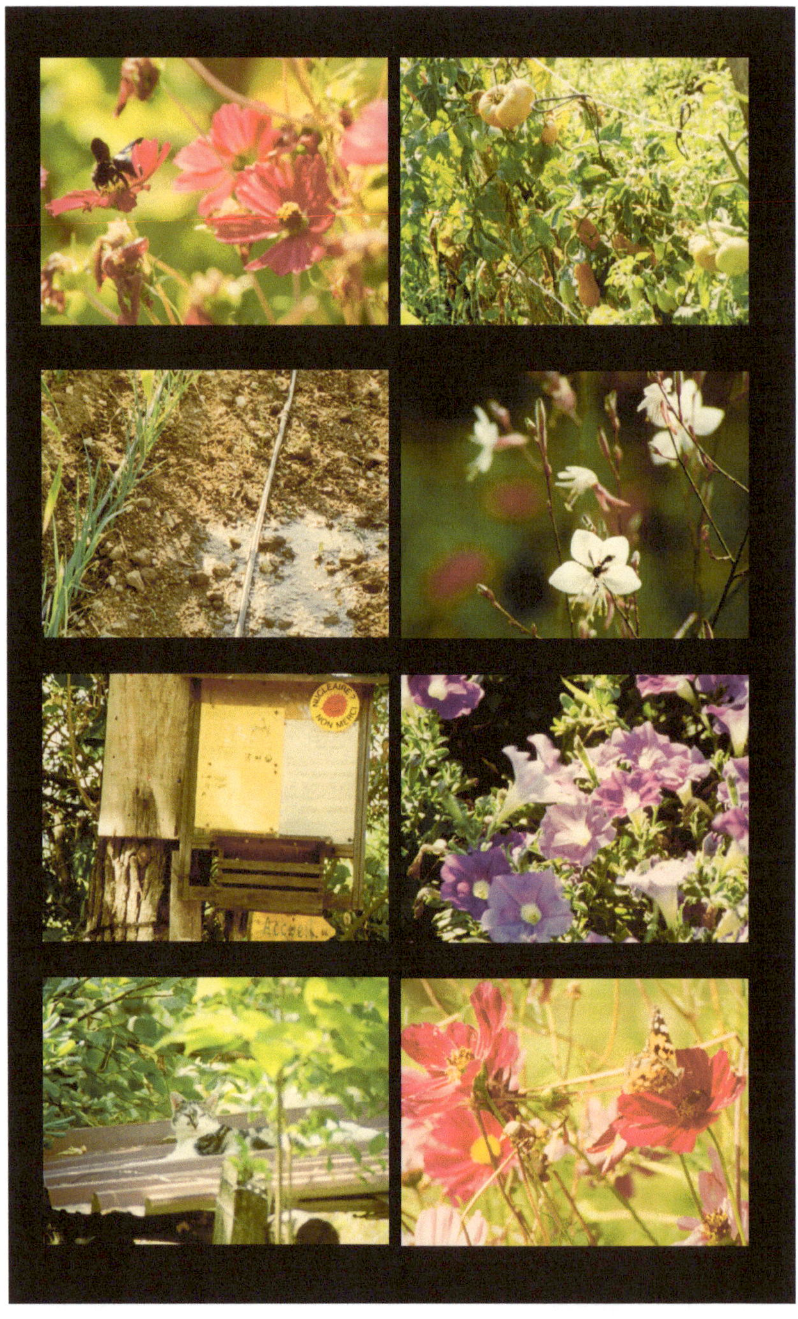

Bouquet 20 (2009)

BOUQUET 20 (2009)
LA FERME DU MAS DE COCAGNE, SITE AGROÉCOLOGIQUE DE LA BARAQUE, AUJAC, GARD

I returned to this farm one year after filming *Bouquet 13* there. The same place at a different time makes a different film.

Cosmos, Cosmos, Cosmos, *Calendula officinalis,* Souci, Pot marigold, *Gaura, Gaura,* Gaura, *Petunia,* Pétunia, Petunia

Realistic depictions of abrupt natural movements - such as those of insects - are often indistinguishable from the time-lapse technique used often in the *Bouquets* which is often syncopated into short bursts with other sorts of motion such as that of a mechanical water sprinkler.

And haphazard, eccentric aspects of human construction are frequently celebrated: an improvised message board with an anti-nuclear sticker, a cat using corrugated sheet metal roofing for its bed.

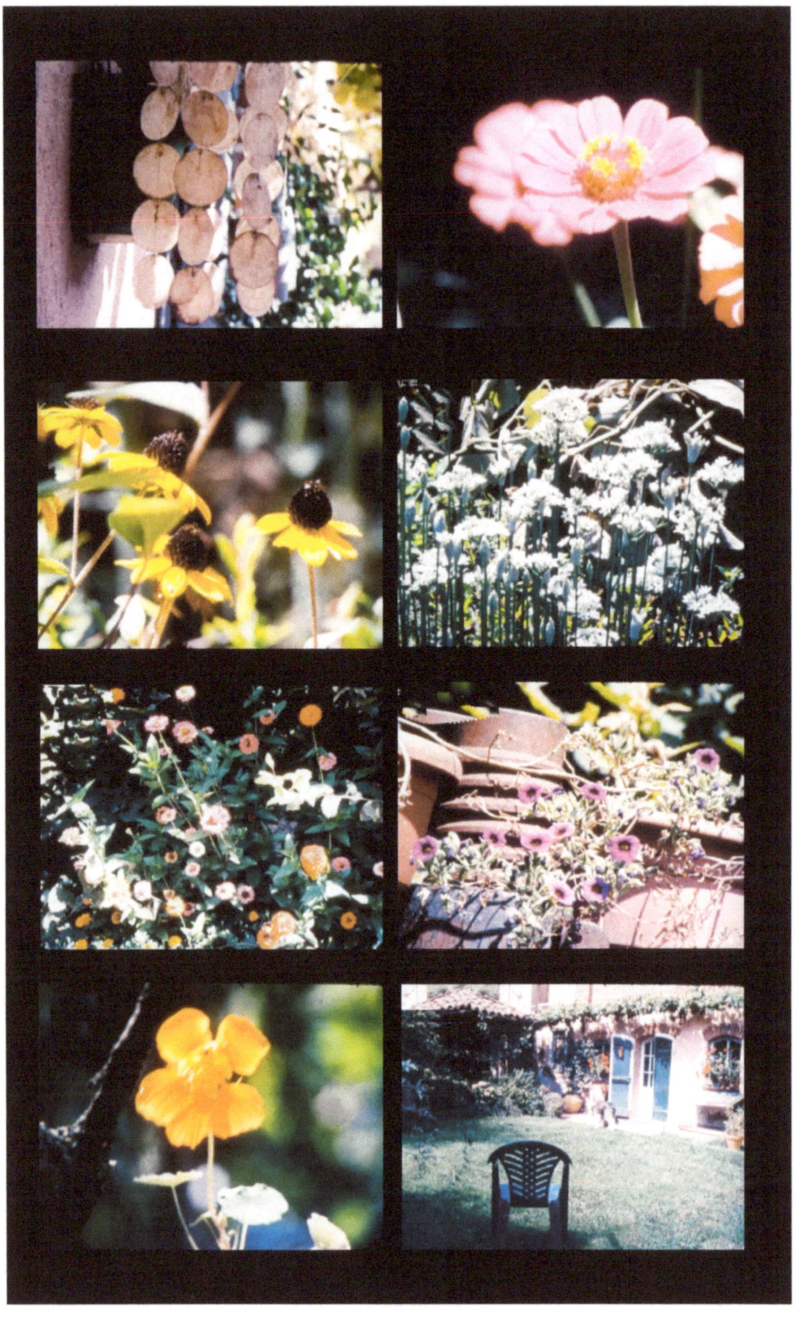

Bouquet 31 (2014)

BOUQUET 31 (2014)
CASCINA PIOLA, SERRA CAPRIGLIO, ASTI, PIEMONTE

Bouquet 31 picks out some of the items that contribute to the poetry of this small farm south of Turin.

Begonia, Bégonia, Begonia, *Aster*, Aster, Aster, *Rudbeckia*, Rudbeckia, Black-eyed Susan, *Pelargonium*, Géranium, Geranium, *Tropaeolum*, Capucine, Nasturtium, *Petunia*, Pétunia, Petunia, *Zinnia*, Zinnia, Zinnia, *Allium ursinum*, Aïl des ours, Wild garlic

As they were almost all shot in mid-summer, the *Bouquets* frequently convey a sense of languor - a dog lazily paces across a summer lawn, a cat rolls in the grass, humans slowly go about daily tasks. But the calm can be broken at any moment with bursts of frenetic energy - spinning wind chimes or a cluster of single-frame views of flowers. Anticipating these small kinetic explosions gives an underlying tension to even the most soporific summer scenes.

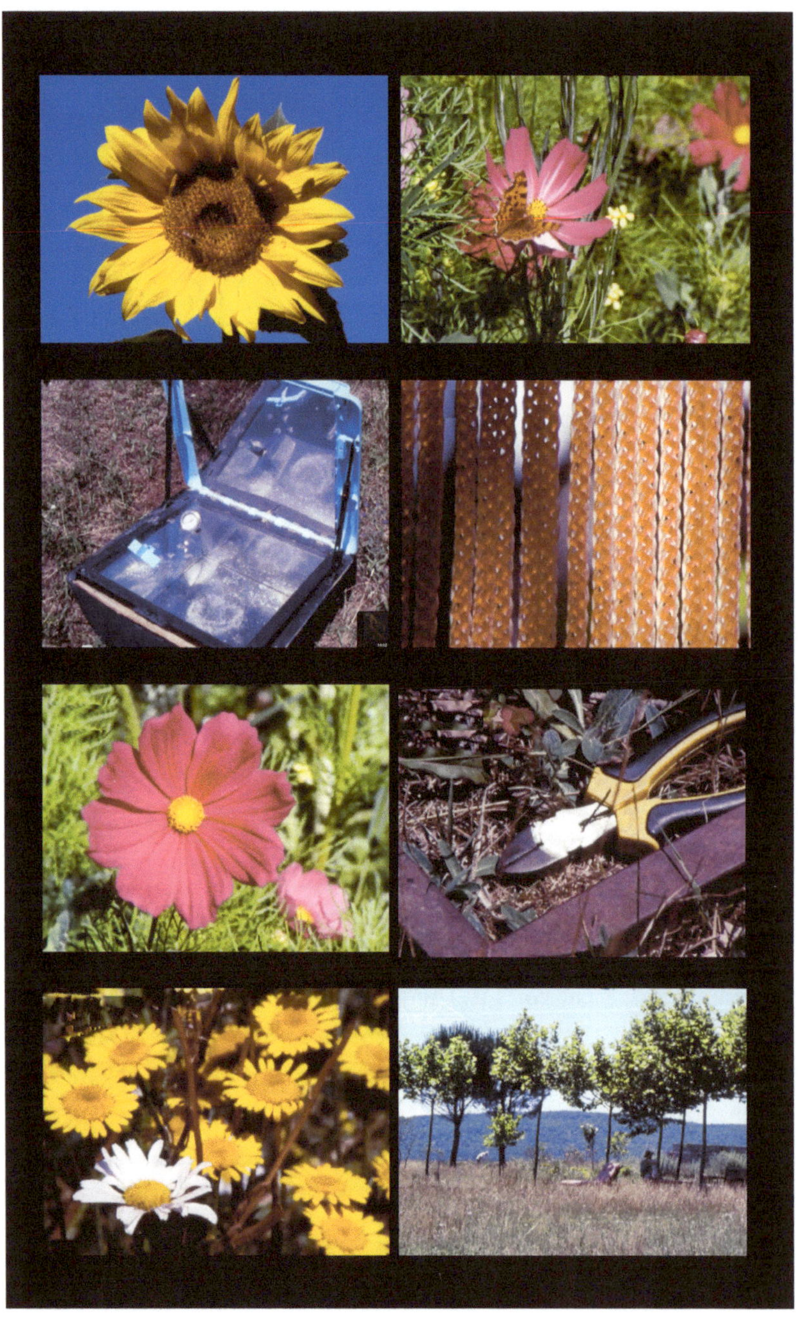

Bouquet 32 (2014)

BOUQUET 32 (2015)
ROUTE DE DAUPHIN, SAINT-MICHEL-L'OBSERVATOIRE, ALPES-DE-HAUTE-PROVENCE

Bouquet 32 presents a view of a farm that both produces some of the vegetables for the residents and grows a large variety of sunflowers.

Anthemis tinctoria, Anthémis des teinturiers, Yellow chamomile, *Leucanthemum*, Marguerite, Daisy, *Cosmos*, Cosmos, Cosmos, *Helianthus*, Tournesol, Sunflower, *Lilium lancifolium*, Lis tigré, Tiger lily, *Papaver*, Coquelicot, Poppy

The *Bouquets* are celebrations of deep summer. While the soft wind only slightly rustles the tree leaves, the lone figure seen in long shot sitting in the shade contemplates an expansive mountain vista, punctuated by a butterfly batting its wings, swallows finding their perch on a wire and bees pollinating trembling flowers.

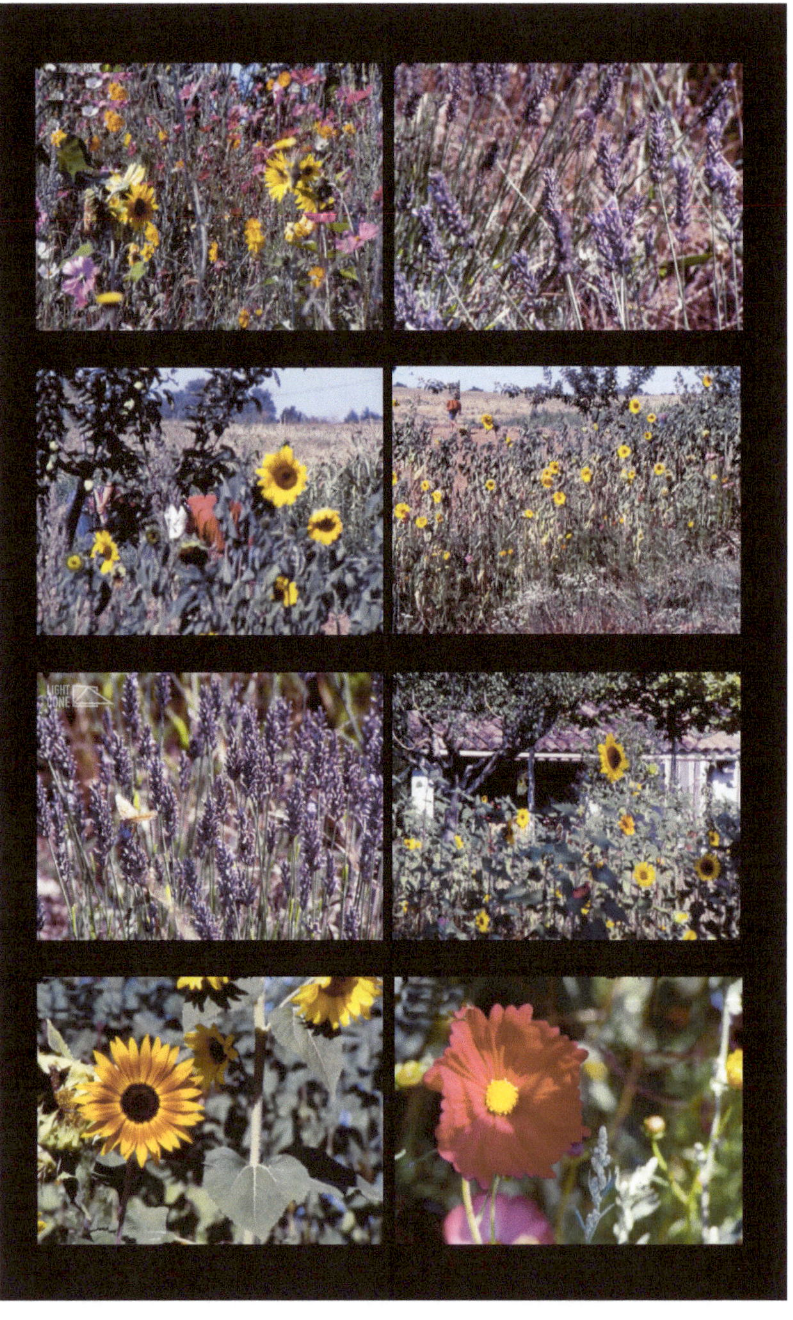

Bouquet 33 (2015)

BOUQUET 33 (2015)

ROUTE DE DAUPHIN, SAINT-MICHEL-L'OBSERVATOIRE, ALPES-DE-HAUTE-PROVENCE

Bouquet 33 gives another view of the same farm seen previously in *Bouquet 32*.

Cosmos, Cosmos, Cosmos, *Coreopsis*, Coréopsis, Coreopsis, *Helianthus*, Tournesol, Sunflower, *Lavandula*, Lavande, Lavender, *Daucus carota*, Carotte sauvage, Wild carrot or Queen Anne's lace

A palisade of sunflowers quiver in front of an open field. A water sprinkler nozzle embedded in wild flowers oscillates. The human activity in the shade of a corrugated out-building roof seems equally purposeful even if its purpose is unclear. The beating wings of a butterfly seem synchronized with the wind-animated flowers. Here again the *Bouquets* reveal unsuspected underlying rhythms in rural life.

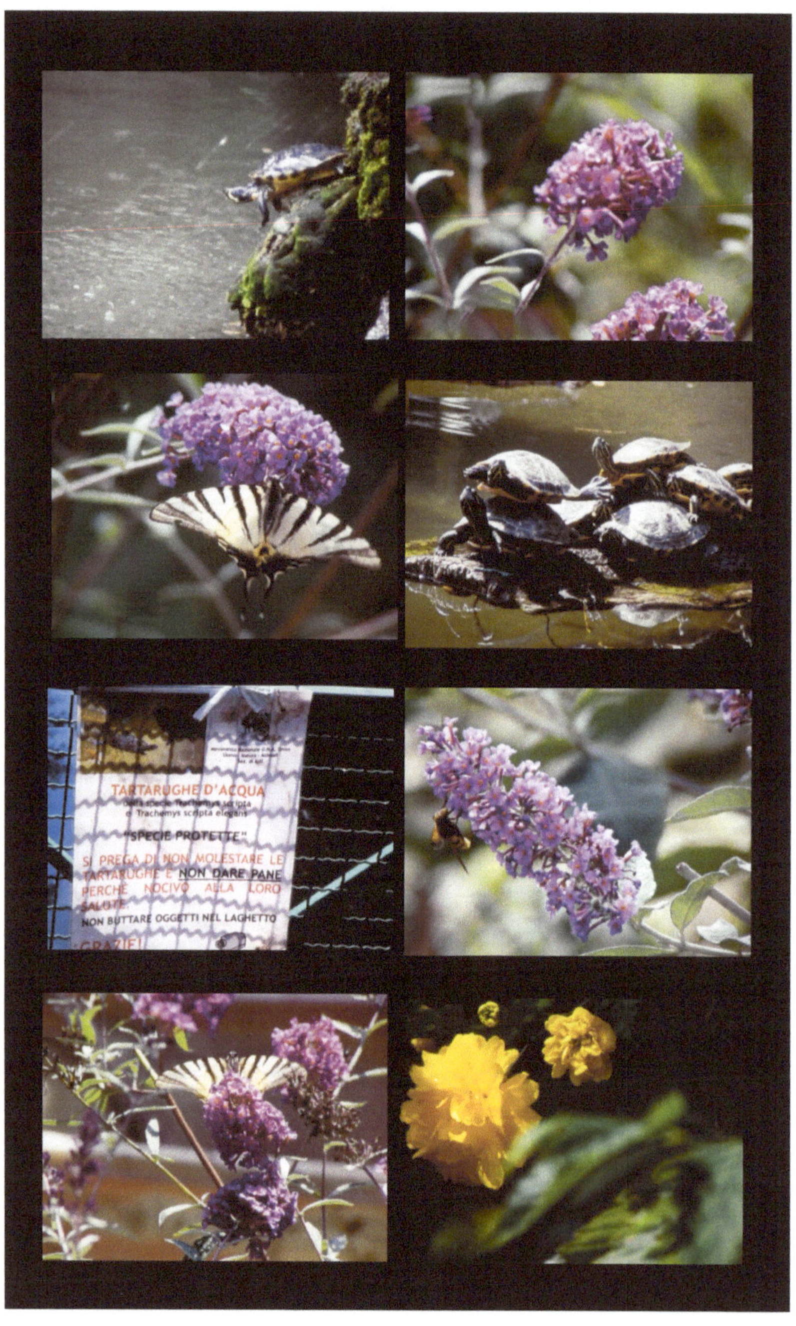

Bouquet 34 (2015)

BOUQUET 34 (2015)
CASCINA PIOLA, SERRA CAPRIGLIO, ASTI, PIEMONTE

Filmed a year after *Bouquet 33, Bouquet 34* gives another version of the farm Cascina Piola, previously seen in *Bouquets 15* and *31*. One has a glimpse of a variety of turtles kept in a pond in a nearby town, Asti.

Buddleia davidii, Buddléia or Arbre aux papillons, Buddleia or Butterfly bush, *Begonia*, Bégonia, Begonia, *Kerria Japonica*, Corête du Japon, Japanese kerria

In the work of a butterfly suspended from a flower, there is an inversion of gravitation that is symptomatic of a natural order whose rhythm is independent of human logic. A woman walks into a garden decisively but her objective is no more apparent than that of the basking turtle suddenly deciding to drop into the water. In the world of the *Bouquets* the actions of butterflies and bees often have more discernible purpose than any of the larger fauna, particularly humans.

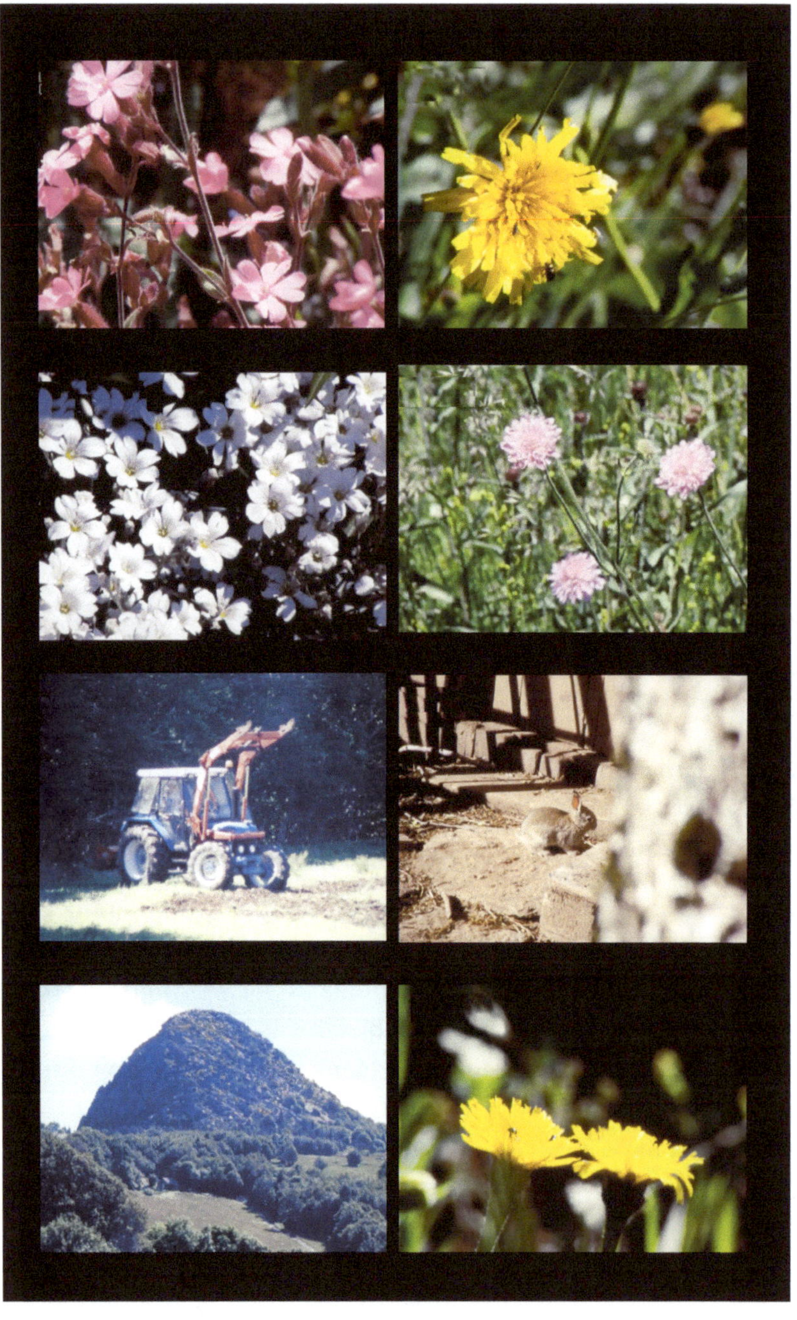

Bouquet 35 (2016)

BOUQUET 35 (2016)
AUBERGE DE BACHASSON, ROUTE DU GERBIER DE JONC, SAINTE-EULALIE, ARDÈCHE

Bouquet 35 films the Auberge de Bachasson, located near the Source de la Loire. The farm has a flock of sheep, takes in guests and has a large indoor and outdoor restaurant. The farm makes their own charcuterie, a great speciality of the region, which they serve in the restaurant.

Silene dioica, Silène rose, Red campion, *Silene latifolia*, Silène blanche, White campion, *Leucanthemum*, Marguerite, Daisy, *Helianthemum*, Hélianthème, Helianthemum or Sunrose, *Scabiosa*, Scabieuse, Scabiosa or Pincushion flower, *Viola*, Pensée, Pansy, *Taraxacum*, Pissenlit, Dandelion

A farmyard is visible in the distance as a tractor maneuvers in the foreground, a rabbit can be glimpsed in high grass, its nose twitching like the quivering flowers. The scene resembles those of many of the preceding *Bouquets*, but then, in an unprecedented reversal, it is Lowder's camera that shakes while the rabbit remains immobile.

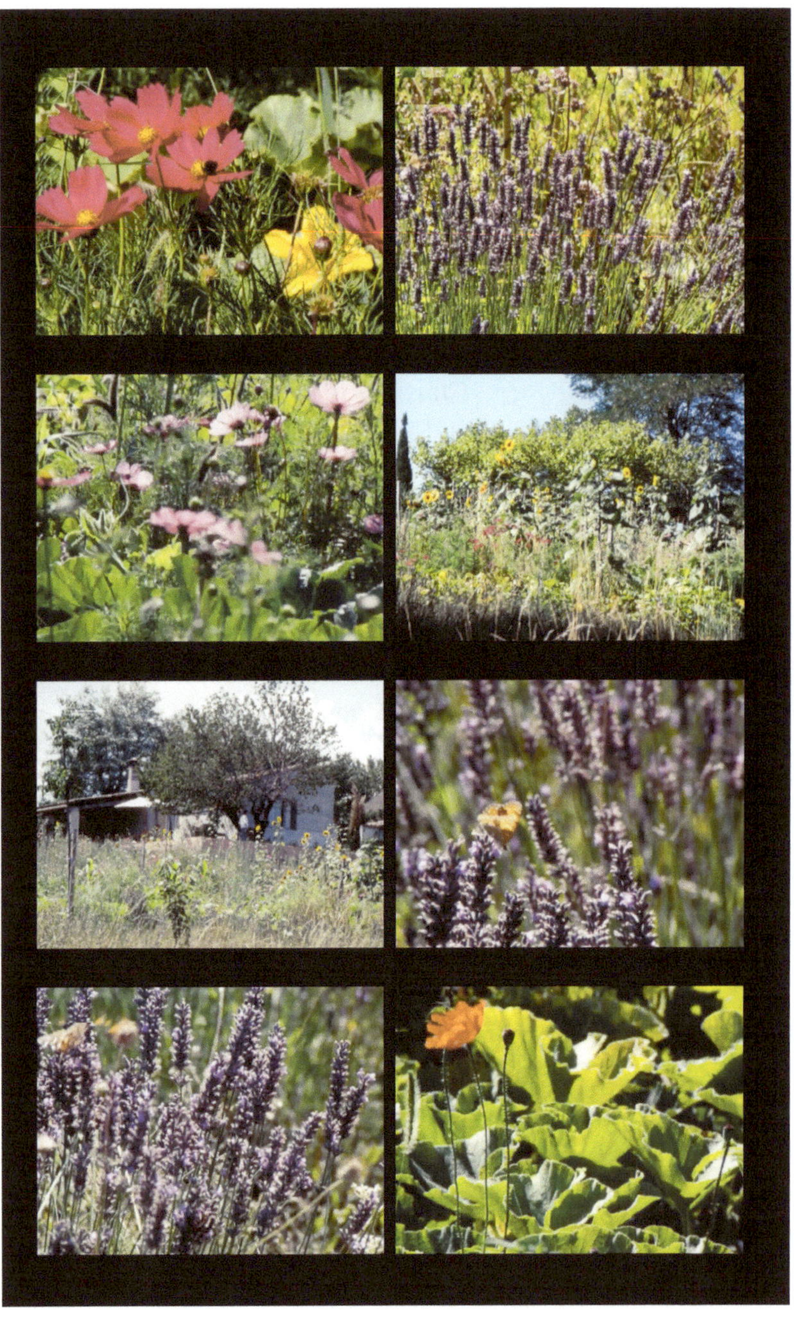

Bouquet 36 (2016)

BOUQUET 36 (2016)
ROUTE DE DAUPHIN, SAINT-MICHEL-L'OBSERVATOIRE, ALPES-DE-HAUTE-PROVENCE

Bouquet 36 returns a year later to La Fée d'Arlane, the farm seen previously in *Bouquets 32* and *33*. One sees the abundant variety of flowers and the people who happen to be there.

Lavandula, Lavande, Lavender, *Cosmos*, Cosmos, Cosmos, *Cucurbita*, (Fleur de) courge, Squash blossom, *Helianthus*, Tournesol, Sunflower, *Papaver*, Coquelicot, Poppy

The nature of motion in the *Bouquets* is sometimes explicable, sometimes not. Do the flowers quiver because of the wind or are they animated by Lowder's frame-by-frame filming technique? A child ambles up the path to a house, but then stops, uncertain of his goal. There is a fragmentary glimpse of other human figures whose motion can seem no less arbitrary than that of the sunflower in the foreground.

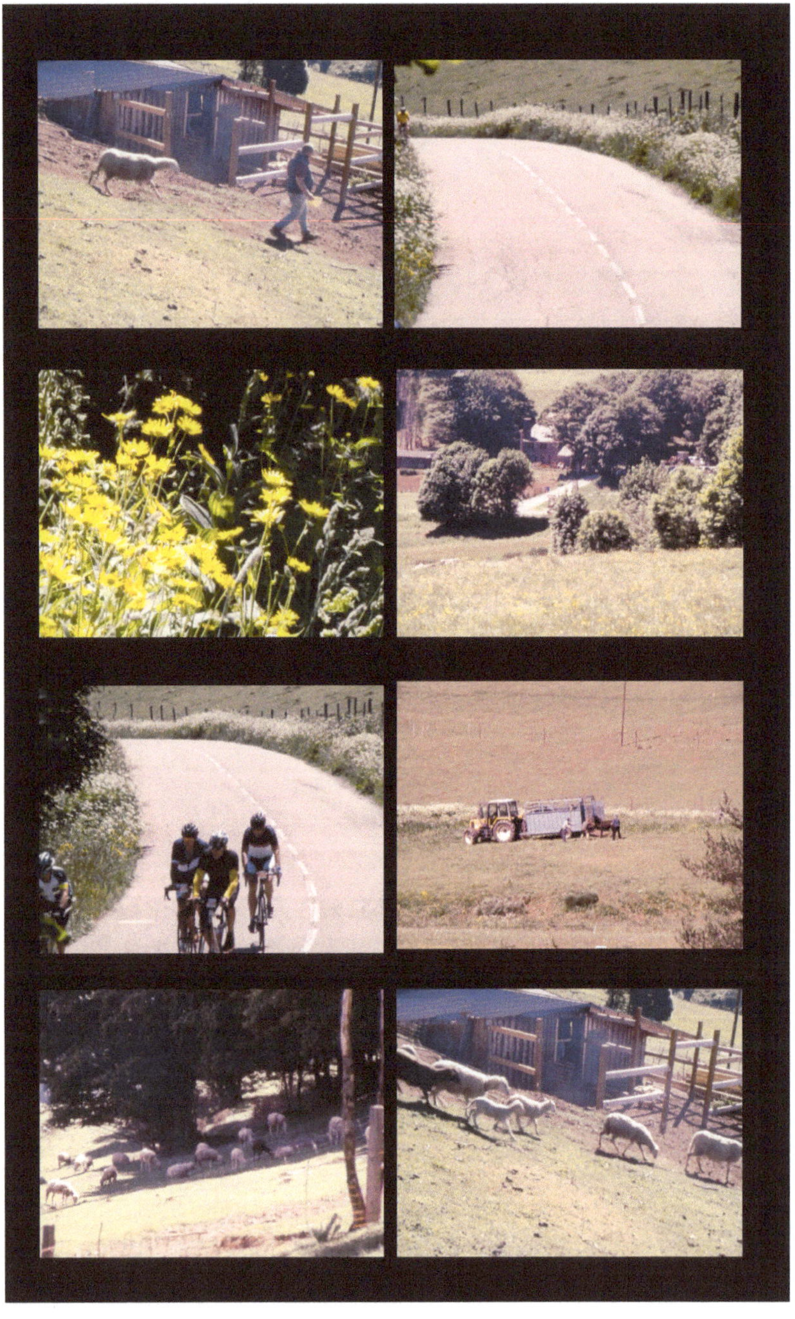

Bouquet 37 (2018)

BOUQUET 37 (2018)
AUBERGE DE BACHASSON, ROUTE DU GERBIER DE JONC, SAINTE-EULALIE, ARDÈCHE

Bouquet 37 returned a couple of years later to the Auberge de Bachasson. One sees a part of the huge bicycle event with 20,000 participants, climbing up the steep road near the farm which arrives at the base (1417m) of the Mont Gerbier-de-Jonc (1551m) from which the river Loire derives its source.

Helianthus, Soleil vivace, Perennial sunflower

The process of herding a recalcitrant donkey into a truck-drawn van is viewed from a distance. Seen from such a remove, human activity takes on the random solemnity of insect life. Cyclists slowly climbing a rural road seem to have less purpose than the sheep following their shepherd towards their paddock. The views of the laggardly cyclists recall those of the very first *Bouquet* - shot on Mont Ventoux almost a quarter century earlier, a reminder of the extraordinary coherence of Lowder's unique vision.

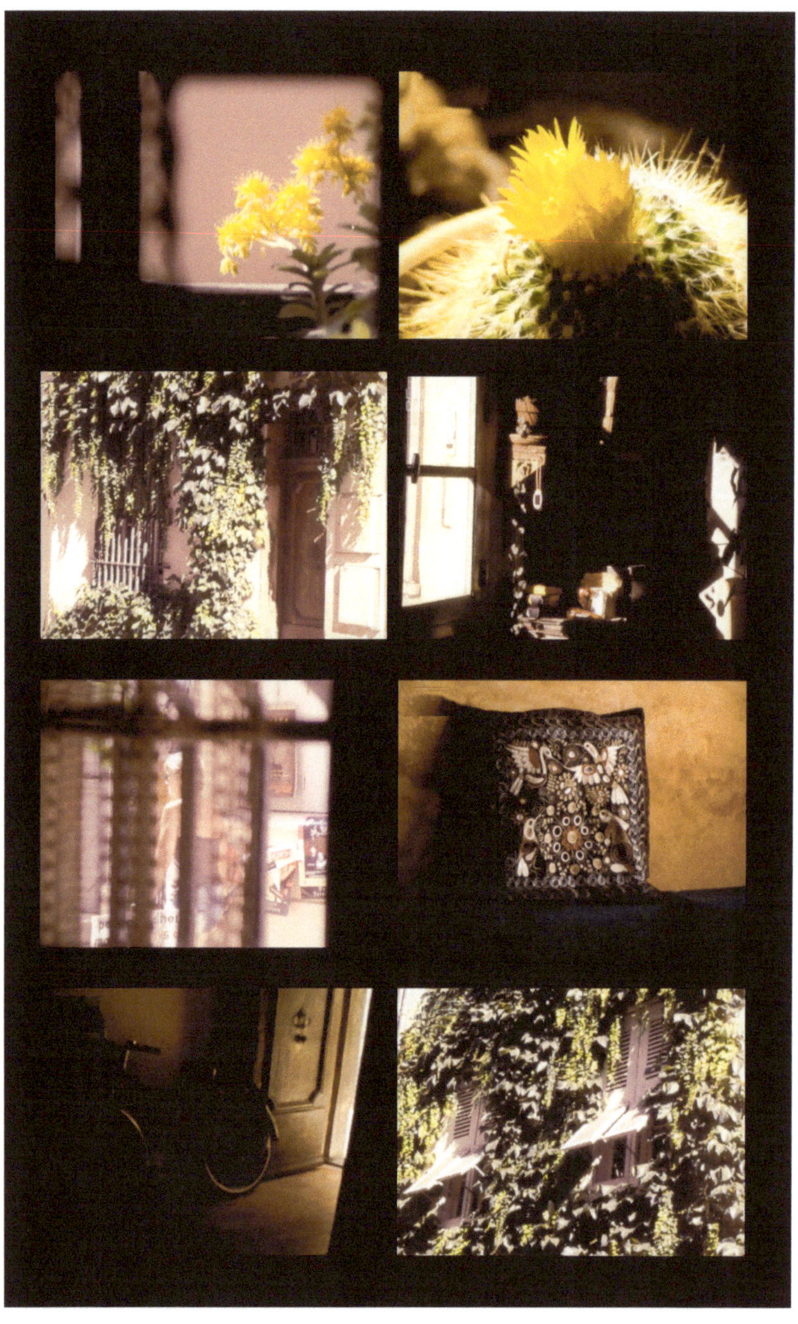

Bouquet 38 (2019)

BOUQUET 38 (2019)
72 RUE DES LICES, AVIGNON, VAUCLUSE

Bouquet 38 provides a glimpse of where we live. I chose to film things that I like, the yellow flowers of a cactus that blooms every spring, a Peruvian cushion embroidered with birds and rabbits, a present from my sister, my now 72-year-old bicycle which was given to Alain when he was 11 years old and the creeper covering our house.

Sedum palmeri, Sedum palmeri, Sedum palmeri, *Parthenocissus tricuspidata*, Vigne vierge, Japanese ivy, *Parodia chrysacanthion*, Cactus Parodia, Golden powder puff

Shadow-play in a domestic study, a bicycle leans against the wall just inside the door opened to bright sunlight, shutters cantilevered to provide shade from Provençal summer heat. Bees cluster in the vines which cover the facade, passersby can be glimpsed through the curtained window in the street which is festooned with posters - evidence of the theater festival which invades the usually quiet streets of Avignon every July. The shards of sunlight on an interior wall advance in time-lapse fits and starts. For once, the filmmaker is not a traveling guest but weaving a portrait of her own home.

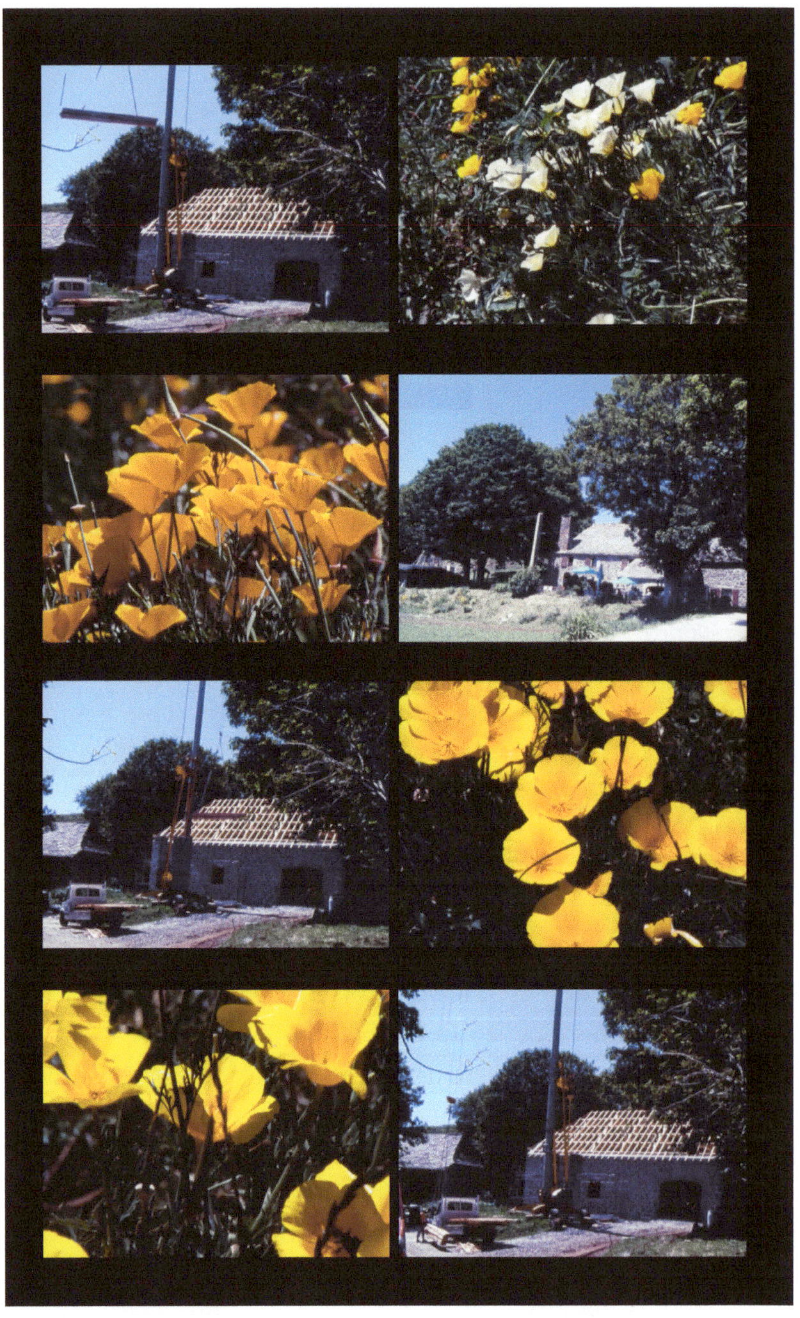

Bouquet 39 (2020)

BOUQUET 39 (2020)

AUBERGE DE BACHASSON, ROUTE DU GERBIER DE JONC, SAINTE-EULALIE, ARDÈCHE

Bouquet 39 was filmed two years after *Bouquet 37* at the Auberge de Bachasson, at a moment when a large building, constructed as ecologically as possible by a local group of builders, was being completed in order to provide a specific space for preparing the charcuterie delicatessen products as well as making available a large area for other activities.

Eschscholzia californica, Pavot de Californie, California poppy

Constructing a farm building in the hot summer sun, a crane slowly lifts lumber from the bed of a truck towards the unfinished roof. It is not only one of the rare activities depicted in the *Bouquets* whose purpose is completely straightforward but also constitutes the longest continuous sequence in the entire series.

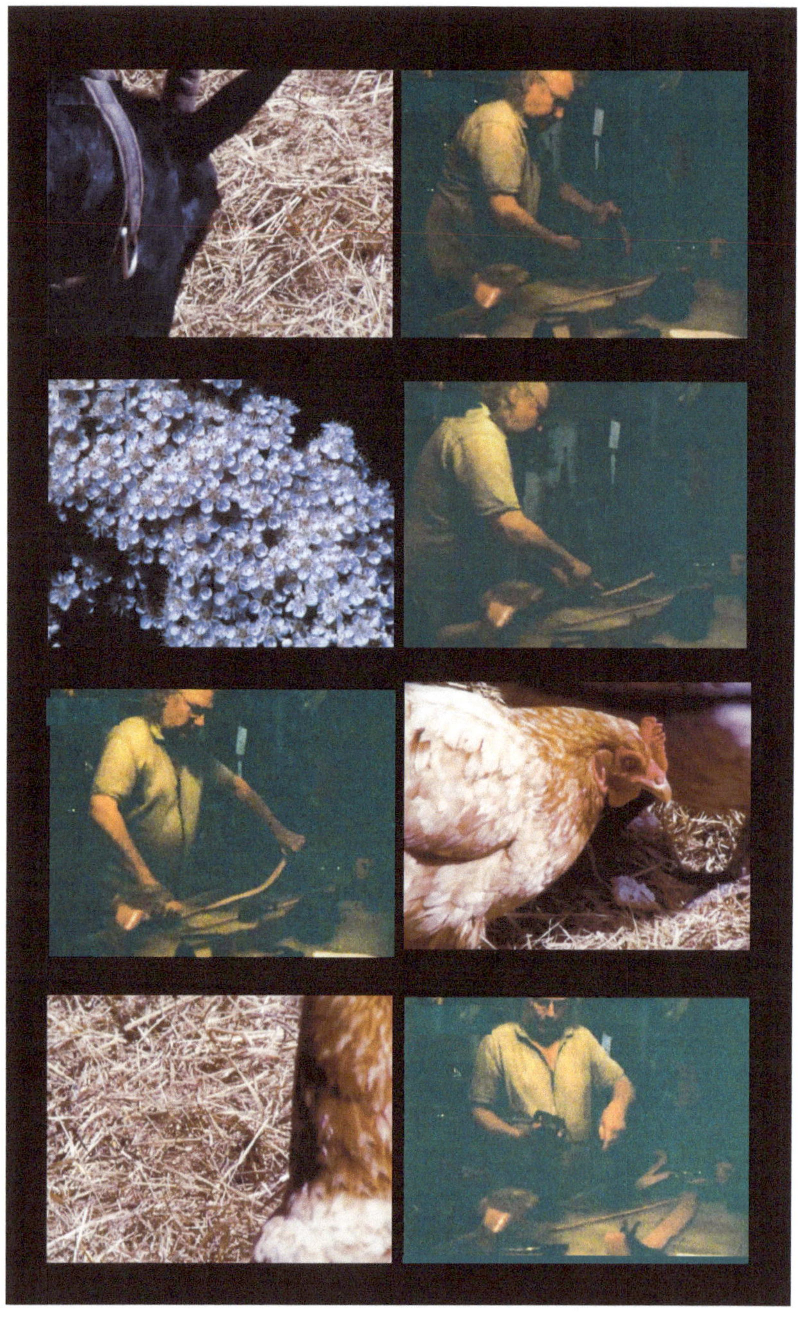

Bouquet 40 (2022)

BOUQUET 40 (2022)
LE MOUSCAILLOU, ESCOUSSENS, TARN

Bouquet 40 was filmed in a place located in the Parc naturel régional du Haut-Languedoc where we see Eric Alexandre in the process of cutting a strip of leather, the main piece for assembling one of his sandals. Sliding it back and forth allows him to adjust the sandal to the right size to fit a foot. For a moment one sees the chickens who were eaten soon afterwards by a fox.

Cratægus, Aubépine, Hawthorn

Just as *Bouquet 38* showed the artist's own home instead of accommodation for travelers and *Bouquet 39* depicted an unusually long single action, *Bouquet 40* is likewise totally uncharacteristic of its predecessors. Here there is only one continuous shot - of a sandal maker at work. And where almost all of the previous *Bouquets* were shot outside in high summer sunlight, producing intense and varied colors, everything here is inside in deep shadow and almost monochromatic. After almost three decades, *Bouquet 40* appears to be a coda.

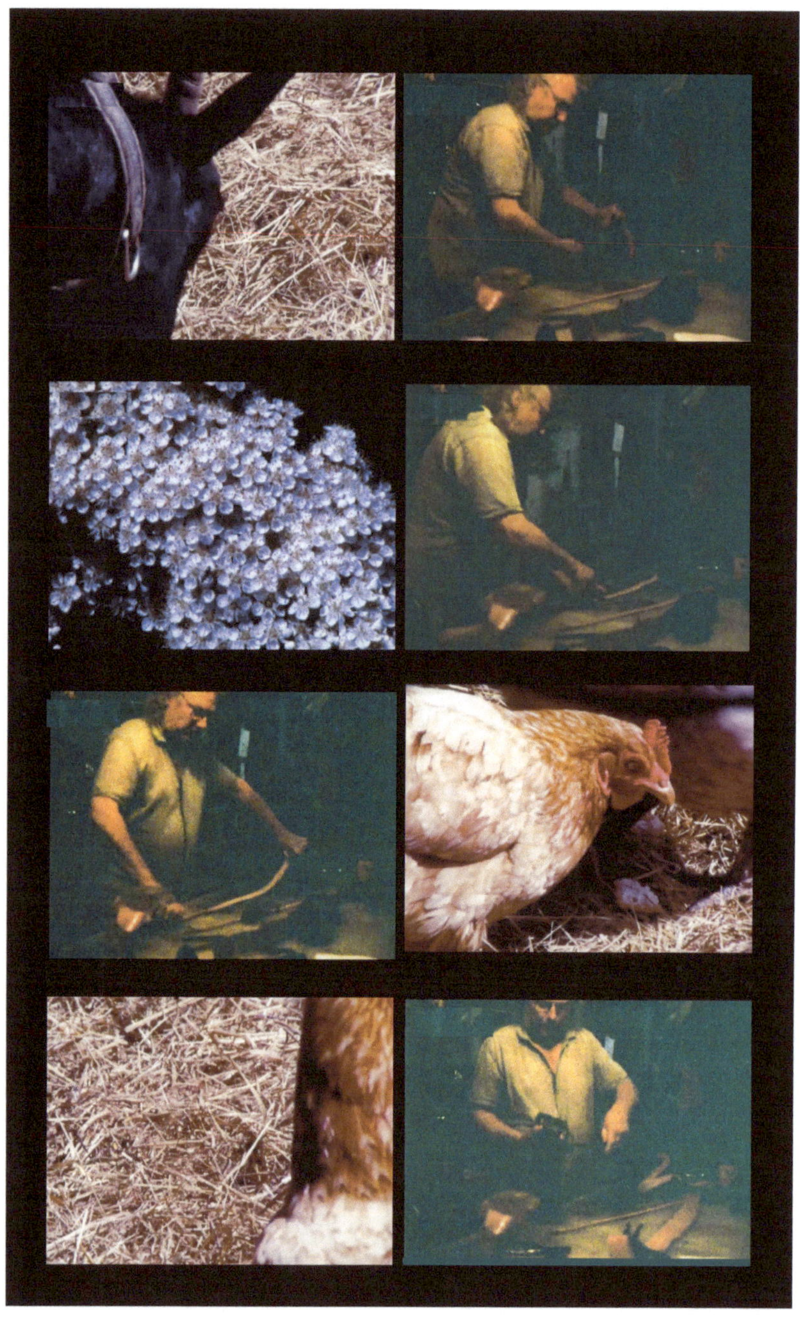

Bouquet 40 (2022)

PART 3 : WRITINGS

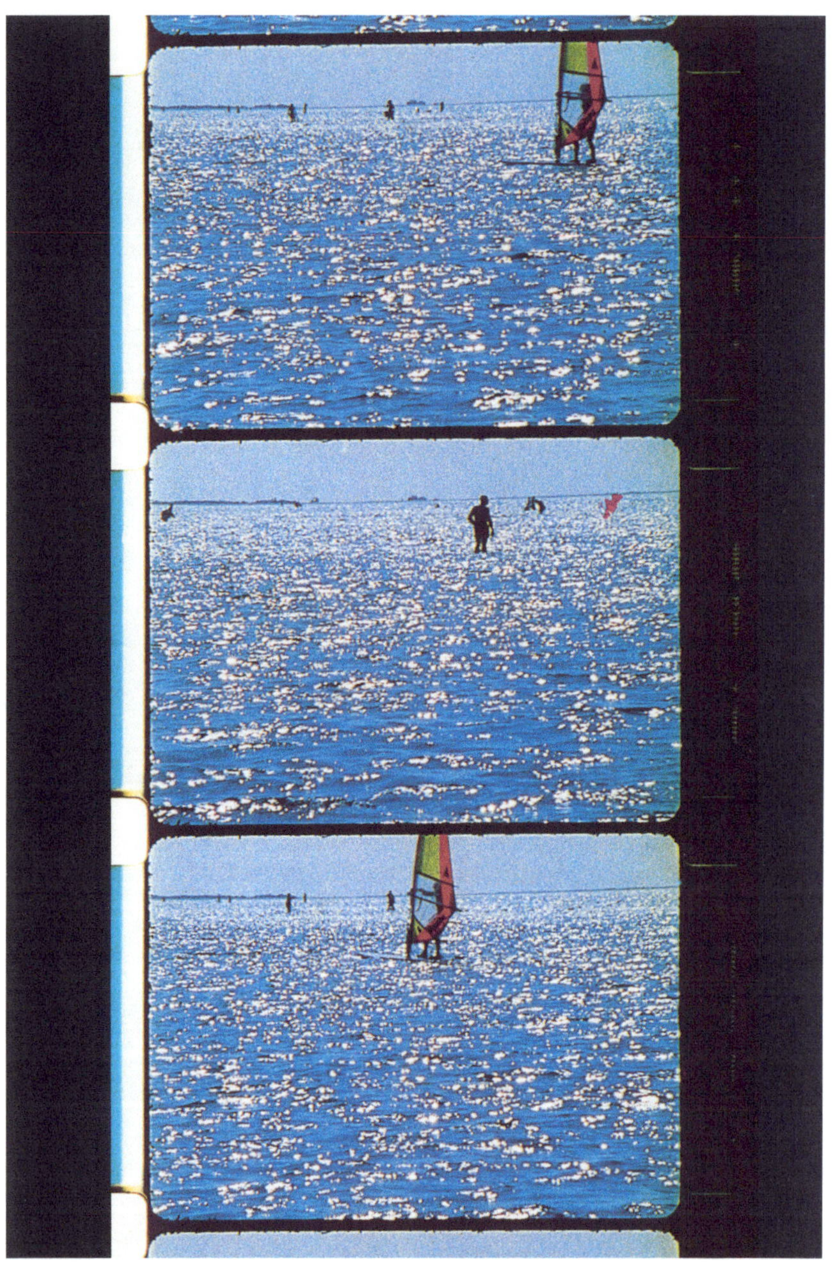

Bouquet 8 (1994)

REMARKS ON COLOR STEMMING FROM THE BOUQUETS

The *Bouquets* series (1994-1995) belongs to a series of visual explorations which touch on the spatial-temporal possibilities of the filmstrip. Explorations pursued for what will soon be twenty years, whose determinant sources perhaps deserve to be recalled.

Without assigning priority to any one of my interests over others, the first that comes to mind is a concern for the implications of devices powered by inventions that pre-date that of film; then comes a group of explorations starting in the 1960s and 70s devoted to perception; and, finally, the creation of procedures and actions today that are common in the practice of the contemporary visual arts.

Arising from varied geographical and historical origins, these interests have led me outside the cinematic paths of traditional filmmaking. Instead of seeking to establish a simulation of reality (a bird in a cage) - the creation of an illusion of motion by an apparent motion (a sequence of still images on a moving strip) - it consists of the creation of a cinematic motion which permits access to a perception of reality from a different perspective. While traditional cinematography consisted of two motions, that of the camera and that of the reality filmed, the actual mechanics of the camera reveal possibilities inherent in the arrangement of images arising from the movement of the filmstrip.

Another influence comes from the visual arts. Since around 1850, numerous artists have been attracted to the development of graphic and visual means of composing an image. Reaching an apogee during the great formalist period of the 1960s and 70s, these explorations contributed to the considerable enlargement of the gap between reality and its representation. The advantage of such a hiatus between what is represented and its representation is that by developing tools, both conceptual and material, film artists can introduce a broader and more complex spatial-temporal dimension into their work.

This aspect takes on a particular importance in the creation of a film which is based on the photographic image. Because, by retaining the preeminence of the physical qualities of the appearance of the image, such a device permits the viewer's attention to focus alternatively on the filmed scene or the filmed image of the filmstrip projected on the screen.

Structured in the camera during filming, the *Bouquets* series treats a variety of subjects, in order to compose a film bouquet by means of images gathered each time at the same site, at several different moments. By correlating the position and the preeminence of the photographic traits and qualities of a frame with a series of images of which it is a part, and no longer, in the manner of traditional film, by thinking of the composition of the image from shot to shot, it is possible to work on the details of a frame within the bouquet of selected images and, in doing so, intervene on the visual qualities that one wants to work on.

From this perspective, color (a film in black-and-white being also a film in color for a film artist) is an essential component of the film image. By taking into account the forms and lines, the variety, the nature of textures and contours of the elements of the scene to film present themselves to the film artist in the same way as to a painter when it comes to the possibility of modulating them at the moment of making them felt in the work.

On the other hand, when it comes to the mixing and juxtaposition of colors, there is usually a radical difference between the work of the painter and that of the filmmaker in regard to the means of making colors tangible: the application of pigment onto canvas for the former; the exposure of film to light by the latter. This difference carries a consequence. After having adjusted their recording device, usually filmmakers (unless they are using graphic special effects, such as mattes, or superimpositions, etc) record a single light over the entire surface of the frame. But in the *Bouquet* series, as in certain of my preceding films, this situation is partly evaded to the degree that the image perceived on the screen is a composite image created by the successive projection of a series of frames each representing an often very different image. No frame having been exposed more than once, what is perceived is not the perception of a physical image (what is seen on the screen is what is perceptible by examining the filmstrip), but an optical image, i.e. a film image whose different states perceived at the moment of the projection of the film are not apparent when studying the elements registered on the filmstrip.

Thus, for example, the scenes treated in *Bouquet 7,* filmed in the historic washhouse of Tonnerre. At one place in this film images of water and images of flowers can be perceived on the filmstrip, each one with a variety of different tones and tints but no mixture - neither of the distinct elements situated on the separate frames nor the inter-action of the colors caused by the optical overlapping, which seems to happen on the screen but which, in reality, is created by the treatment of forms and lines colored by the visual system. It is in this way that the tints of a series of wildflowers can be modified by interspersing them with those of another series of cultivated plants in a nearby park, or by the texture of the surrounding medieval houses, not to mention the local cat quite present on the filmstrip but only barely perceptible on the screen.

Depending on this process of intertwining very graphically different images, the colors, the forms, and the lines of a frame are perceived through the combination of their qualities with those of the preceding or successive contiguous frames. Compared to a physical superimposition, the advantage of such a way of working lies in the qualitative gap in the perception of colors and juxtaposed motifs which leads to a kind of spatial-temporal organization particular to this form of weaving images together. By the choice of color associations and configurations, tones can appear bolder and motion more dynamic than would be the case of superimposition of images on the same filmstrip.

This visual energy can be seen in the work of numerous experimental filmmakers who, by other means, bring similar cinematic processes into play. This is the case of the films of Cécile Fontaine who works by a manual insertion on the same filmstrip of forms and colors of images drawn from diverse sources. Among the advantages of this way of working is that it permits her effectively to mix on the screen portions of black-and-white images, printed on black and white film, with elements in color taken from color films. Similarly, in *Chronoma* (1977) by Jean-Michel Bouhours, numerous parts of a photograph of a high-tension metal pylon, to which bright colors have been added, move through different phases at the same time as there are changes of the tone, the rhythm of the autonomous alternations of colors and the rotations of this form around itself.

As in a certain kind of painting, it is the dynamism of the eye which captures and accentuates the colors juxtaposed with each other under specific cinematographic conditions, and this film process allows the development of a specific spatial-temporal dynamic which, by establishing relations between colored forms in motion, sustains for the ensemble of elements a certain autonomy and empowers its components.

- February, April, and July, 1995

Translated from "Propos sur la couleur en partant des Bouquets," *Poétique de la couleur. Anthologie* edited by N. Brenez and M. McKane. Paris: Auditorium du Louvre-Institut de l'image, 1995.

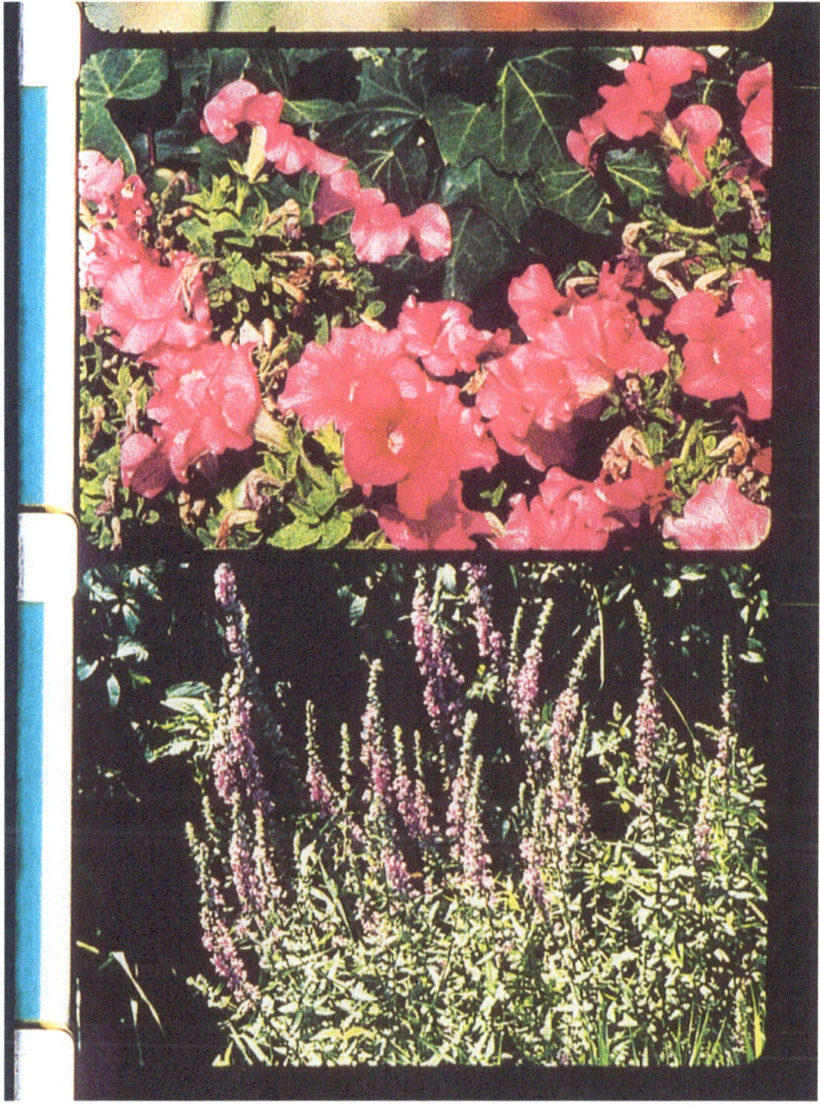

Bouquet 3, 1995

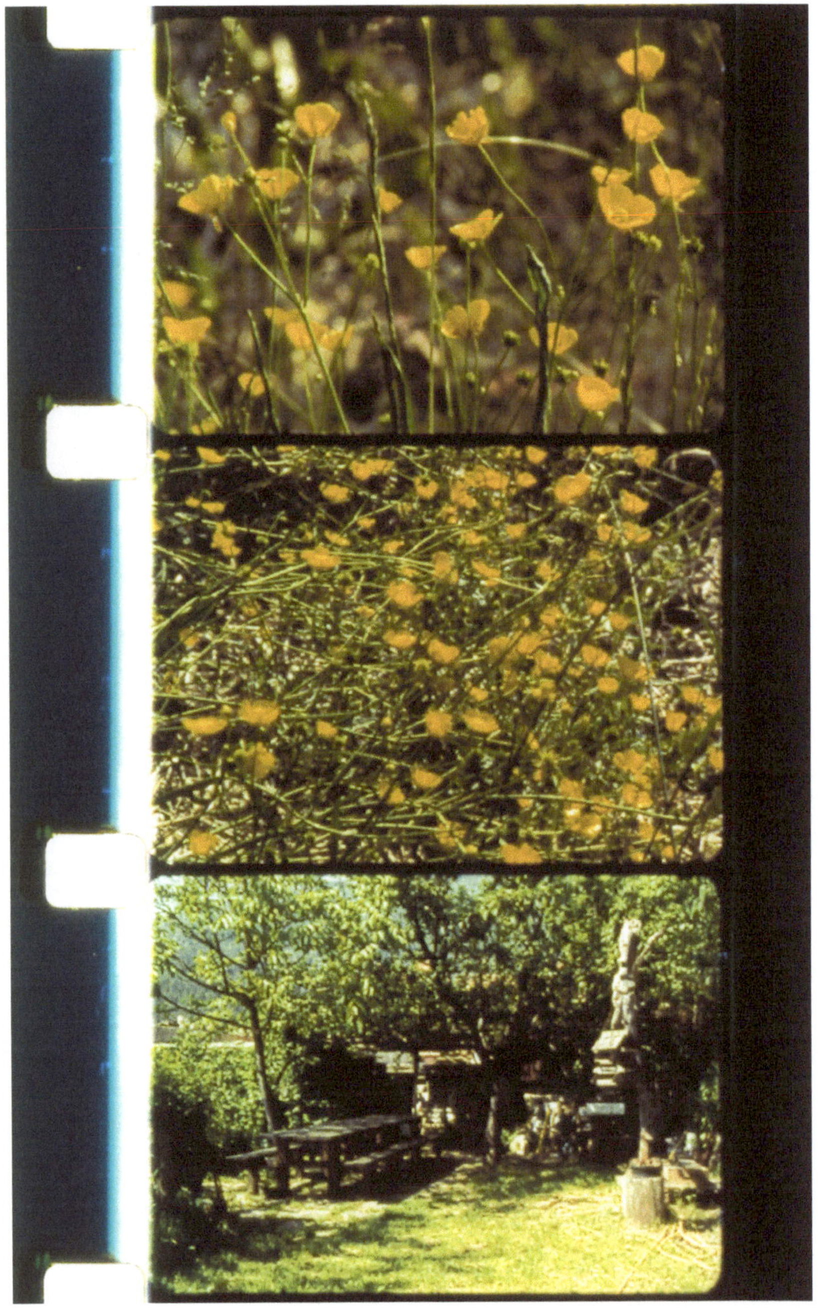

Bouquet 21 (2001)

LEAVING THE ARTIST'S STUDIO BEHIND
OR HOW TO MAKE BOUQUETS OUT OF FLOWERS AND FILM

Bouquets 1-10 (1994-1995), the first of ten of a series of one-minute films, is composed entirely in the camera during filming. The two three-second sections of black frames preceding and following each *Bouquet*, with a single frame of a flower for punctuation in between the end of one and the start of the next, are also created in the camera. Each *Bouquet* is designed to be exactly one minute (1440 frames) long, but since it is extremely difficult to correlate the numerous considerations involved in the filming procedure, occasionally errors occur and a few of the films are slightly longer or shorter than intended.

I have been working for a couple of decades on different ways to deal with the graphic and plastic features of the photographic image in relation to producing the filmstrip in the camera. I will try to indicate here some of the advantages and problems involved in the adopted procedure as it applies to this particular series of films.

The above could be taken to infer that everything is pre-calculated in order to facilitate the filming process. Unfortunately for the filmmaker nothing could be further from the truth. Over the years my films have become shorter and shorter, their preparation longer and longer and their execution more and more difficult. This is partly due to my increasing the number of considerations upon which the filming procedures are based in order to be able to treat a wider range of subject matter. All of which is intentional even if it makes progress very slow.

In my early produced-in-the-camera pieces, I filmed a scene from a single viewpoint adjusting the focus frame-by-frame successively according to scores destined to deal with spatio-temporal possibilities of the chosen site in various ways. The three minute film *Les Tournesols* (1982) is one example of this way of working. Due to the varying time-lengths our perceptual system needs to treat different types of visual stimulus, parts of images situated on separate frames are seen, under certain circumstances, depending on the graphic and plastic features of the successive frames, to appear simultaneously or as over-lapping each other on the screen.

In the *Bouquets* series, as in a previous film, *Impromptu* (1989), and for a part of *Quiproquo* (1992), instead of filming each frame successively so that the order of appearance of each image on the filmstrip corre-sponds to the order in which each frame is filmed, another recording procedure, allowing the projected sequence to no longer correspond to the order in which the images are filmed, was developed. This anachronic feature first appeared in the *Scènes de la vie française* series (1985-1986) but was not achieved in that case in the camera but by weaving two filmstrips together in the printing. The alternative printing of the two series of images was accomplished by a means both simple and complicated which the length of this article does not allow me to go into here. It is sufficient to say that the simplicity was due to using the usual lab printing techniques without an optical printer, while the complexity was provoked by asking the technicians to modify slightly their production line procedures.

· · ·

The important point is that in the *Scènes de la vie française* series the procedure required two filmstrips to be recorded from the same view-point at different times. In other words, one had, for example, in the film on Paris, a scene of the sailboat pond in the Luxembourg gardens from a set point of view shot in June 1983, November 1983 and November 1984 presented in three versions successively: first of all June 1983, with the palms and orange trees out in their boxes combined with a winterly November 1984, then the same June 1983 mingled with an autumnally November 1983 and finally November 1983 mixed with November 1984. Boats on the pond sail through palm tree trunks, people in winter coats casting no shadows walk past others in summer clothes in bright sunshine. Another sequence in the same film recorded on the same dates mixes three different boats on the Canal St. Martin, a small motor driven November 1984 vessel proceeding in the opposite direction to the big June 1983 barge or the November 1983 medium-sized flat bottomed boat.

The first film presenting an image of one space at two different times composed in the camera is *Impromptu*. This piece is based on a relatively simple structure compared to that of the *Bouquets*. First I filmed the odd frames (first, third, fifth, etc.), covering up the lens for the even ones (second, fourth, etc.) in between. Then I rewound the film back to the first frame and filmed the even frames in the same way so that all of the images on the filmstrip were exposed. This was done on a spring-driven camera which one has to wind up manually at regular intervals. The result is an image of a situation at two different times of day. The process takes a while so this could mean the even frames were filmed in the morning and the others in the afternoon. In *Impromptu*, for instance, one of the images is composed of the movement and light and shade of the leaves that a lime tree had between a given three or four hours and the arrangement of shapes and coloring of the same tree during the following three or four hours. Some items of the scene such as the position of the tree's trunk remain relatively stationary even if light and color change continuously.

After alternating these frames in the camera I also filmed a short piece of the tree at 24 frames per second, in order to compare this traditional set of frames with the frame-by-frame section. As I started to do this, the owners of the tree arrived in a blue van with their little white dog to plant some tomatoes. Although having to answer questions as to why I was trespassing while continuing to film made the latter even more difficult, in retrospect I was delighted at the unexpected appearance because it convinced me of what I suspected to be one of the interesting aspects of this way of working: one does not know how a scene will evolve and the procedure has to be able to accommodate unpredictable movements and transformations. This is an important point as it is one of the factors that makes it possible to establish a visual relationship between the filmed reality and the functioning of the film in cinematographic terms.

Near the end of *Impromptu,* for a series of images of small backlit trees on the edge of the village Brant, I forgot to adjust the exposure. In this case I had intended that the two intermingled series of images be as similar as possible on that score. This obliged me to rewind the film a third time to add a little more light on another run through in order to equalize that set of frames. In the end the exposure of the two appears nearly identical.

I have always had an aversion for following recipes and never had a light meter. I prefer to develop a sense of judgment regarding light and thus be freer to concentrate on other matters. My forgetfulness in this case, however, made me realize that I could put the film through the camera within reason as often as needed and film the images in any order as long as I could keep track of what was on the frames that had already been exposed.

The possibility to film anachronically in the camera was developed further in parts of *Quiproquo*. Although in this film most of the sequences are also filmed from a single viewpoint, in parts, such as the front title sequence and a field of flowers further on, I composed the image with three sets of frames recording very different parts of the filmed area. In other words, the spatial and temporal dimensions gained a certain freedom in relation to the order in which they appear on the filmstrip.

These developments form the basis for *Bouquets 1-10* as far as the practical, material organization of the images is concerned. Others will evolve as the series continues. Each film is composed of a 16mm one minute strip filmed frame-by-frame in an anachronic order adjusted to the related needs of the fabrication procedures and the site filmed. The limits of the blending of different spatio-temporal entities are reduced to what functions in cinematographic terms.

This still leaves open the problems of what to film and why and in what order, like in any other type of film. As every filmmaker knows from experience, it is not advisable to bring together an arbitrary choice of images. Mere pixilation just produces more or less decorative confusion.

What to film. In my case I tend to choose places I like to be in but here a balance has to be found between the paradoxical situation that these have to correspond not only to my comfort (such as, I like to be outdoors, with my feet on natural ground, preferably in the shade on a sunny day, far from polluted air, mass competition and the economic goals and interests of our society) but also to my curiosity, concern or involvement concerning the people and life that are a part of the filmed scene. In that sense, studying the visual characteristics of a particular location gradually renders evident features of the life there. The lime tree in *Impromptu* is a typical example. I spent ages exploring systematically nearly every pathway over an area of several hundred miles, sizing up all the trees as to their suitability for the project. The tree I eventually chose was by a very unused road; only two or three vehicles passed during the entire day I filmed there, but there were distinct signs that the place was inhabited, the fields and lime trees (a speciality of the area) were well kept, the little house just outside the frame and the well within it indicated someone's residence of not long ago had now become an agriculture outhouse. There were several No Trespassing signs on either side of the spot I stood on. In other words, a form of social life was there but in a visually sufficiently unobtrusive manner to allow the scene to present an incentive for me to work on it.

Hence the subtle reasons for filming a site are intermingled with practical and cinematographic concerns. One of these is how to keep track of what is already on the film strip, and the other is how to correlate the graphic and plastic features of the photographic images so that the frame-by-frame procedure does not produce just a variegated changing pattern or scene.

In order to have some bearings as to which frames have been filmed I make myself charts where I fill in, as I film, details of every one of the 1440 frames. I study the site and calculate more or less what I intend to do taking into account previous experience. While working, the filming process always highlights unsuspected incidents and characteristics of the situation.

· · ·

The second question of how to assemble evolving graphic and plastic features of the photographic image within a series of frames is very complex. Over the years and successive films from *Parcelle* (1979), *Rue des Teinturiers* (1979), *Champ Provençal* (1979), *Retour d'un repère composé* (1981) to *Les Tournesols* (1982), I have dealt with aspects of the problem when a single viewpoint is concerned. With the combination of several entirely different images the problem is similar in the sense that, with experience, one learns which features prevail over others and in what circumstances. An understanding of the mechanisms involved allows one to eliminate parts of an image and to reinforce the appearance of other characteristics.

In the case of spatial elements, the work is similar to that of a painter and a developed sensibility and trained eye in that field is a help. The colored forms can be manipulated in similar manner to the marks applied by an artist, they can be made to have soft edges, to be out of focus, accentuated or eliminated; the challenge consists in imagining their combination with what appears just before or after the frames under consideration while taking into account their continuously shifting graphic features.

On the temporal level, the work is similar to that of a musician. I fix my sheets securely to the tripod, or put stones or my foot on them if nothing else will do, and then play my instrument, the camera, as best I can. The reality filmed shares, with the grid-like charts to be filled-in, the function of a score. The difficulty of execution, of interpreting within the given constraints, demands the same concentration as the careful attention a musician gives to the beginnings and endings of first and last notes of a movement in a piece of music. In fact here the cinematographic score seems more devious than its musical counter-part as its rhythm changes continuously as the light modifies constantly the endlessly shifting forms and colors.

. . .

As a conclusion, but without going into the subject here, it should just be mentioned that this recapitulation of some of the main points concerning making bouquets out of flowers and film à la Rose Lowder leads out of the artist's studio. Traditional cinema practices recreated the artist's studio for practical reasons: it is far easier to work in a controlled area, protected from unpredictable elements such as wind and rain with all the necessary tools at hand. The characteristics of the workspace reflect on the work as cinematographers also adopt the traditional painter's composition of the image, inherited from the Renaissance, placing the filmed subject in the middle of the screen (or painting), its volume enhanced by light and shade simulating daylight (preferably a north light) and clearly situated in a representation of three-dimensional space on a two-dimensional surface according to the rules of perspective. Films such as the *Bouquets* relate to later periods of the history of art. There is the obvious relation to the *plein air* art movement in France but also to numerous contemporary art and music movements. This type of work requires one to explore quite a few pathways in a number of fields as the title of the series, *Bouquets*, refers not only to a choice of recorded flowers but also to a particular composition of film frames.

Rose Lowder, Avignon, May 1997

Published in *Cantrills Filmnotes* 85-86, June 1997: 55.

FILM AS VISUAL ART

In choosing film as a visual art as a subject for reflection, I have necessarily been obliged to distance myself from two traditional ways of looking at the medium: on the one hand, I am not concerned with the notion of the director as the "auteur" directing actors, and, on the other, I do not take an approach that contrasts film with works of visual art (painting, for example), either by recounting the influence of traditional graphic rules on the visual aspect of the cinematographic image, or by comparing the different ways that diverse means of expression use to modulate through elements of the image the meaning of the subjects under discussion.

The reason I have chosen to look at film as a visual artist's medium is that, if the relations between painting and film have been frequently studied, it seems to me that traditional fiction film has progressively dealt with these expressive processes from the point of view of pictorial rules dating from the Renaissance. In doing so, the traditional cinematic image almost never takes into account the evolution of other visual aspects specific to more recent practices in the visual arts. Moreover, the obstacle encountered when approaching film as a visual art is that a vast body of films must be confronted that have not been sufficiently shown to have been properly taken into account in the history, aesthetics, or theory of film. Then visual artists were faced with new technology that resulted in the introduction of multimedia practices into the field of contemporary art. They have had access to ever more powerful tools such as computers which radically transform the way their work is made and, consequently, the visual character of the image.[1]

So here I would like to concentrate exclusively on filmmakers who are visual artists (often working in several media), who aspire to a certain number of visual possibilities previously unexplored by the film industry. In this way I will focus on filmmakers who, while possessing a broad historical vision of film, remain outside conventional techniques, and, in doing so, conceive of other ways of working by developing what can be called a visual artist's aesthetic, as it favors, with artistic means that can be relatively rudimentary and outside the norms of traditional film, very different approaches from those generally used in current commercial film. It is even difficult to capture in words the works in question here because their essential characteristics are based on complex visual strategies which are ill-suited to the analytical and descriptive formulas used for the study of fiction films. Based on links not from shot to shot or even frame to frame, but rather between elements or parts of a single frame or a series of images or other elements situated elsewhere on the filmstrip, these relations can pass unnoticed by viewers unaccustomed to these practices, because they grow out of aspects that do not exist or are never displayed in popular film, such as, for example, the accentuation of the texture, the sharpness, or the color of the filmed surfaces, the images intentionally under or over-exposed, or the unusual motions between the camera filming and the subject filmed.

These processes can constitute the visual structure of the continuity of a film, to such a degree that the work becomes incomprehensible to those unaware of these techniques. Often there is an actual manual manipulation of the filmstrip as in *Particles in Space* (1979) by Len Lye, *The Garden of Earthly Delights* (1981) by Stan Brakhage, or *Overeating*

(1984) by Cécile Fontaine, hand-developing as in *L'arbre bleu* (2001) or *Big Band* (2001) by Marcelle Thirache, editing in the camera during filming for *Bouquets 21-24*, made by myself, among many others.

For these films, it is a case of films in which the physical characteristics of the material have meaning and the process of creating on a strip of images determines the qualities perceived by the viewer, as a specific spatial-temporal experience. In this process, the composition of the image departs from that required for the organization of narrative continuity; this is the case, for example, of *Particles in Space* by Len Lye, where, unlike the image in numerous fiction films where certain visual elements take precedence over other components of the image, the eye is led, as in an "all-over" painting, to explore the entire surface of the image, in order to understand the totality of the visual composition of the work.

Having made numerous kinetic sculptures, Len Lye devoted himself to the study of graphic forms that engendered a cinematic motion, in other words, that focussed on the movement and evolution of visual forms based on a dynamic rhythm specific to the mechanics of cinematography and the art of film. Interesting aspects of these experiments also reappear in the inventive production of a small number of "documentaries" using actors, conceived by the same filmmaker (*Kill or Be Killed*, 1942).

But, in general, not having any filmmaking equipment available to him at the beginning, Len Lye adopted the means of direct filmmaking, painting directly on the filmstrip or scratching the film emulsion. By controlling the physical characteristics of film in this way, a parallel can be seen with the manual work of an artist-painter. An example would be *Particles in Space* which was entirely made by scratching black emulsion with different sharpened tools to create a strange scene of a cloud of particles made up of minuscule white elements whose appearance and movement are continually changing. Judging, at the beginning, that the image could not be looked at for more than 15 seconds, the filmmaker searched for a long time for appropriate music, and, having found it - the film begins and ends with the sound of his kinetic sculptures *Storm King* and *Twister* - as well as Nigerian Yoruba tribal drum music - he realized the work could last longer.

For Len Lye, who considered that "film is technically the best way to isolate visual motion," any graphic trace of reality, "geometric nothings," could as long as they were "extracted from civilized vision," use the physical contents of a form to allow him to compose movement: "As an artist I compose motion," Len Lye wrote.[2]

Other films are close to Len Lye's preoccupations but in a very different way. In the case of *Contrathemis: Composition II* (1941), a film by the painter-filmmaker Dwinnell Grant, the work is also based on abstract graphic elements, but in this case the artist refrains from adding sound. Conceived in another era, the film is based on drawings, held in place, affixed to the right corner by two bits of wood, filmed image by image at the rhythm of one drawing per frame. This technical process is common in animated films but, according to the filmmaker, it was the first attempt to develop a counterpoint of abstract visual themes. Moreover, the cinematic movements of the work have a completely different appearance from a cartoon and create a temporal evolution of forms in the space of the screen that is far more lyrical than the presence of dynamic energy produced by *Particles in Space*.

In the case of *The Garden of Earthly Delights* by Stan Brakhage, the work is made, as was his film *Mothlight*, by glueing elements along the strip of transparent film, in this instance pieces of vegetation found in the mountains. As is often the case with this way of working, the leaves and stems of plants, without regard to the division of frames, create optical interactions during their fairly long vertical passage on the screen. As its title suggests, the filmmaker conceived of this work as a homage to Hieronymus Bosch, even while expressing some reservations.

La Couleur de la forme (1960) by Hy Hirsh is also a sort of collage, but this time structured by realistic or abstract filmed images that are then mixed with superimpositions by using an optical print. The work deserves mention here because of the quality of its manipulations of color and the relations created between various scenes of different proportions and rhythms, such as, for example, enormous cats making their way through tiny football players in action on the field.

Overeating by Cécile Fontaine operates on other terms than the preceding films. This filmmaker's paradox is that her aversion to "technique," or rather the operation of filmmaking equipment or devices, led her to develop a series of highly meticulous technical procedures in order to create links between shots filmed by other people, on a manually assembled strip of film, without any magnification on a light table or any other specific film editing equipment. She has stated that, unlike some film artists who recycle fiction films, she mostly works with unknown films drawing mostly from documentaries, advertising films, newsreels, and home movies. Except for some rare exceptions, her films mix strips of varied subjects, different formats (8mm, Super 8, 16mm, or 35mm); in color and black and white, strips of silent and sound film. She employs chemical and graphic manipulations, for example, by removing the emulsion layer from a strip of film to glue it on to another strip, by scratching or cutting up parts of a layer of an image or in shifting the three layers of emulsion in the same scene. In the film *Overeating*, there is a relation between the treatment of the emulsion and the subject. Soaking the film in different solutions produces a distension of the emulsion which comes unglued from the base, then folded when it is re-glued. By repeating in a loop the image of a man greedily devouring a chicken, with the same manipulation of the soundtrack, the graphic and pictorial characteristics of the damaged image emphasize, with another sort of attention than that of a documentary image, the excessiveness and vulgarity of a glutton's body language.

A very short (less than a minute) movie trailer, *Tradition ist die Weitergabe des Feuers und nicht die Anbetung der Asche* (1999) by Gustav Deutsch, made by the Austrian Film Archives, also recycles images. But this time it consists of a representation of the beginning of the history of film, creating effects of a more poetic nature, rendered rather beautifully and giving, for a moment, the impression of a texture of paint on a fence superimposed on a building. A longer film, made by other processes, *Made Manifest* (1980) by Stan Brakhage, reveals, by means of subtle adjustments during filming, images of the sea and landscapes, providing a context conducive to a visual meditation. The filmmaker brings the expressive medium of film closer to music, since both means of expression are continuous, based on rhythm and motion. Brakhage evokes visual music as his reason for attempting by making his films silent to avoid the risk of confusion between two musics (visual and aural) playing simultaneously.

Two short films by Marcelle Thirache, *L'arbre bleu* and *Big Band*, demonstrate another way to manually manipulate the filmstrip. Both begin with the image of a plane tree, filmed from the filmmaker's window, on a day of blue skies, with a filter in the case of the first film, and with camera movements in the second. The particular visual character of these two reels, which were developed by the filmmaker, then worked on with ink and brushes, consists of weaving on the screen relations between filmed elements and colored graphic elements specific to the manual treatment to which the filmstrip is subjected.

In contrast to these two films by Thirache, where visual poetry predominates, *Bodybuilding* (1965) by Ernst Schmidt Jr., films the performances *Rumpsti Pumsti* and *BodyBuilding* (1965) of the Viennese Actionist Otto Muehl. At the time the artist was conceiving artistic actions only to be photographed or filmed. Despite its apparently documentary intent, this film presents a study of color and poses the question of how to record performances while simultaneously working cinematographically on the filmstrip.

In conclusion, I cannot resist including a small film of my own, structured in the camera during filming, *Bouquets 21, 22, 23, and 24*. Part of a series of films of one minute each (1440 frames), a projection time a little longer in the case of the four *Bouquets* projected at 18 frames-per-second, these experiments were developed to compose a film bouquet of images gathered in each instance at the same place, often at different moments. On the screen, the result is a composite image created by the projection of the recorded frames in another order than their successive placement on the filmstrip. As long as the camera permits rewinding the film during filming and a method can be found to locate the position of each frame, this way of working permits the recording of images, without superimposition, at any place on the roll of film, in any order. In conceiving a way of shooting images specific to the site where they are filmed, the structure of the filmstrip is intimately connected to what is likely to work visually in cinematographic terms. The process is far from easy to execute. In addition to the practical difficulties in accessing hard-to-reach places, such as, for example, the steep slopes of a mountain, unpredictable weather, the correlation of the graphic and visual characteristics of photographic images in a way that avoids resulting in a simple decorative effect, is far from simple. All the more so since when one works from reality, the vagaries which determine the temporality of a scene make its visual evolution highly unpredictable. Light changes continually, modifying the visual aspect of colors and forms; people, animals, and machines neither follow their expected trajectory nor obey a preconceived rhythm, making the evolution of film movement extremely difficult to control.

Raymond Depardon, comparing the making of a fiction film to one whose objective was to record reality, stated that "capturing reality is extremely time-consuming and is not much appreciated,"[3] suggesting that it is more difficult to control a documentary film than one based on the narration of a story.

Bouquets 21-24 were filmed respectively between the Lozère and the Ardèche, in the Savoy, near Mens and not far from Martigny in Switzerland. Occasionally such bizarre incidents occurred during their filming that I was surprised to be able to record any images at all.

To conclude, it seems to me necessary to mention that there still exists an endemic problem concerning the ease of access to the kind of works this conference has focussed on. It is not because I have attempted to see the visual aspect displayed by filmmakers referred to as experimental that the work can in a general way take its place among the visual arts. The explorations in question are often too specialized to be recognized by the arbiters of contemporary art since their ambitions are too far from the objectives of classical "art" cinema. On the practical side, film projection is much more complicated to set up (a dedicated space, the expense of renting a projector and hiring a projectionist, fixed projection times) than video art and with no guarantee of any profitability. It follows that, despite the growing interest of many people and the number of screenings devoted in recent years to such films which explore the fundamental nature of film, the filmmakers working in this field still find themselves in a no-man's land between the domains of contemporary art and that of film.

Translated from "Le cinéma comme art plastique", pp.190-197, *Le Septième art, le cinéma parmi les arts, Conférences du Collège d'Histoire de l'Art Cinématographique 2001-2002*, sous la direction de Jacques Aumont, Editions Léo Scheer, 2003.

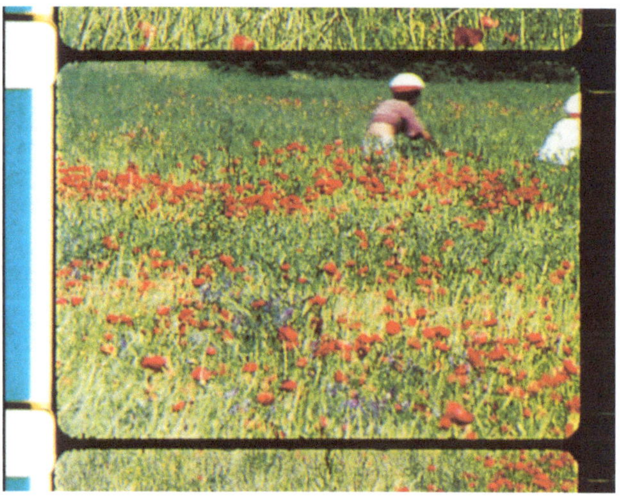

Bouquet 2 (1995)

FROM THE PICTORIAL TO THE FILMIC

THE UNPLANNED, THE UNEXPECTED, THE UNKNOWN

"The unplanned, the unexpected, the unknown," this subtitle reflects what was often my feeling in regards to the reaction, in cultural circles (including those of traditional cinema) to works of film which dared to depart from the norms of normal film production. And even if today we can be glad about the number of programs in the last years devoted to so-called "experimental" films by museums, cultural centers, and festivals of all sizes, I'm afraid that this has arrived too late, the context having imposed such difficult working conditions on film-makers that a great number of them have been discouraged by such a lack of social, artistic, and economic recognition, and have conse-quently progressively committed themselves to other forms of expres-sion or other activities altogether. Despite this negative aspect, this book calls on a positive point of view because, if I persist in working in this field of expression, it is precisely because it is able, by provoking a special spatial-temporal experience, to present an unex-pected opportunity for artistic practice, although always of course with the risk that such an ambition will remain inaccessible.

Looking back on what led me to this choice, I realize that I came to filmmaking a bit by accident. Having been around different artistic scenes since childhood, having worked in the studios of several visual artists in my birthplace, Lima, then in a number of art schools in Peru and then in London, I never planned to become a filmmaker. It was only at the beginning of the 1960s, when I was working in painting and sculpture while working in the film industry in London that the screenings organized by the poet Bob Cobbing in the back room of his bookstore, *Better Books,* made me aware of a great variety of films that were not visible in traditional movie theaters. Even if, at the time, I had no intention of making films myself, I realized that, unlike conventional films based on teams of highly specialized professionals, these works were most often conceived and created by a single person: the filmmaker, and, from this perspective, the practice of filmmaking could be incorporated into that of a visual artist. Consequently, while still editing films in a way that conformed to traditional processes, following the orders of producers or directors, I began to keep in mind the spatial-temporal possibilities of the filmstrip.

If the first works of Robert Breer, Stan Brakhage, or Jean Genet's film *Un chant d'amour,* censored for decades in the U.S. and France - the works shown at the time at *Better Books* - were unknown, they have, for the most part, since become classics in the history of experimental film. A small number of them have even been timidly accepted into the traditional history of film. So non-profit screening initiatives can serve as a breeding ground, a stimulus to many filmmakers in a dozen countries. And without this kind of activity, today, forty years later, a large number of works would have remained invisible.

When seeing them, even if my job in the film industry during this period left me no time to devote to substantial artistic explorations, I immediately understood that time marked by the successive passage of images printed onto a filmstrip, could vary according to the lines, forms and colors imprinted onto these frames, regardless of whether the motifs were abstract or figurative, photographic, graphic or the result of other processes. Their effect depended on the relationships established between the visual elements of the different images and their order of appearance on the screen. In other words, depending on how the visual elements that are taken into account in a pictorial work or a cinematic one, the modalities that form the dimension of time differ considerably. In the case of a painting, the organization of specific visual characteristics control, up to a point, the particular nature of the temporal perception of the work.

In the case of a film, if the particularity of the visual elements also constructs the work, their arrangement in relation to the progress of the projection becomes a primordial consideration. And so-called experimental filmmakers can be thanked for having deepened in a special way this aspect of the art of film by taking into account the specificity of its duration. In any case, it becomes obvious that by increasing the variety of procedures for making a film image, it is possible to broaden the way of conceiving the link between filmed (or not filmed) reality and the image created, and by developing more complex aesthetic processes, another kind of perception can be provoked, establishing a less direct visual relationship between what is considered to be the conventional appearance of reality, filmed or unfilmed, and the images in the work of art.

If, in my own film work, for around fifteen years, I did not complete anything, I nevertheless remained attentive to everything that was published or projected in the field in several countries. It was only when I was able to get away from the film industry that I was able to start to study how the mechanics of filmmaking related to perception. At that moment, in the middle of the 1970s, I had seen a large number of films whose visual structure was based in different ways on the optical relationships established by the arrangement of very small units of film frames, works in which either the series of images or the individual frame took the place normally assigned to the shot in the making of a traditional film.

Even though these works might open many new paths for filmmaking practice, they lead me to sense that there existed other possibilities, perhaps not possible by a simple arrangement of the visual relations of one frame to the next, but by mastering - something far from easy to do - the organization of a long series of images. In general at this period, the works that had succeeded in opening up new perspectives were based on the realization of a working process that was preconceived in order to treat in a precise way most especially certain deliberate aspects of the visual material.

From the middle of the 1960s, throughout the 1970s and for a large part of the 1980s, the structure of many films was based on this way of arranging the images. The optical effects highlighted by these works were often astonishing even if it became progressively obvious that it was difficult to get around the limits of this way of working, because it tended to create a relatively rigid repetitive motif which, if one is not careful, risks transforming the process into a steam roller that flattens out all the graphic or photographic subtlety of the image.

It is by taking into account this way of making a film that, before even having the use of a camera, I began to explore the apparatus of filmmaking by a somewhat primitive approach consisting of the projection of loops of filmstrips, made by using transparent 16mm leader, a hole puncher, and a felt tip marker. These practical studies, even when carried out in a methodic and relatively meticulous way, brought many surprises and optical subtleties that were difficult to control. Accompanying these observations from theoretical reading on the functioning of perception, I was able to notice different degrees of separation between what is seen on the screen and what is perceptible on the filmstrip, and that the variety of visual effects bringing out a selective group of characteristics of the frame relied primarily on the arrangement of images on the film.

Based on these studies, my discoveries supplied me with the basis for a certain number of my first films, *Parcelle* (1979), *Rue des Teinturiers* (1979), *Champ Provençal* (1979), *Retour d'un repère* (1979), *Retour d'un repère composé* (1981) and *Les Tournesols* (1982), composed image-by-image in the camera during filming, in which for practical reasons, being inexperienced, I filmed scenes of reality from a single point of view while adjusting the focus of each frame in a way that manipulated certain visual qualities, and this, in order to bring out in different ways the visual malleability and certain spatial-temporal characteristics of the place used. By taking into account a principle of the functioning of perception that holds that different categories of optical stimulation are processed at different speeds, it is possible to conceive a series of images which integrate the overlapping of different perceived visual elements to provoke a composite film image. Notwithstanding, one of the problems frequently encountered when working image-by-image or with small bunches of frames is that the result tends to produce an unwanted, somewhat decorative, flickering that is most frequently devoid of any graphic interest or meaning.

The question of how to arrange the lines, the particularities, the characteristics of photographic images composing a series of frames in order to avoid such pitfalls can be complicated. Whether the film image is composed of frames shot from a single point of view or images shot in several places does not much change the ways of finding a solution, except that denser visual content sometimes requires more time to overcome the difficulties encountered. With experience, I have learned to recognize the traits and the characteristics of an image which can dominate the others. A whole group of experiments on this question has made it possible, for example, to erase or reduce certain parts of the frame in order to highlight others as the film progresses. The advantage of the work of filmmakers operating in this field is that they can look for other ways of linking the different elements making up the film frame. By proceeding in this way, these filmmakers compose a distinctly cinematic image, its optical dynamism often based uniquely on the arrangement of spatial-temporal relationships.

The manipulation of the content of the images, if it is done correctly, gives a meaning to the work, but it is no longer based on the same criteria as those commonly used by narrative films. This fact is the source of much misunderstanding for those who attempt to apply the same rules to the study of experimental films as those used to examine popular commercial films.

As regards my own films, I have progressively increased the number of considerations concerning filming procedures in order to be able to deal with a greater diversity of subjects. First I filmed relatively stable scenes from a single angle while changing the focus, the street in *Rue des Teinturiers*, a peach orchard in *Champ Provençal*, the garden of Rocher des Doms in *Retour d'un repère* and *Retour d'un repère composé*, several fields of sunflowers for *Les Tournesols*.

For most of these films, each 3 minute roll was filmed in one day, I just introduced a temporal dimension in another way in *Champ Provençal* by filming three rolls at different periods, flowering, coming into leaf, fruiting. This treatment of the seasons continued in the series *Scènes de la vie française* (1985-1986) where the images filmed from the same angle at different moments were woven by printing in a way that mixed the appearance of the same scene at different seasons, like, for example, the Luxembourg Gardens during the summer of 1983, showing the palm trees and orange trees brought outside in the sun mixed with the same place during the winter of 1984, showing passersby in winter coats on a cloudy day. This manipulation of the dimension of time led me to work on the image composed in the camera during filming by shooting a series of frames image-by-image or in small groups of images at different moments for *Impromptu* (1989) and *Quiproquo* (1992).

Up to this point, the appearance of images on the filmstrip corresponded to the order in which they were filmed, but, an exposure error in a roll of *Impromptu*, having caused me to film a series of frames of the same scene in superimposition in order to get the right exposure, led me to another way of working. In making this correction I realized that, since my camera could go both forwards and backwards, by rewinding the roll of film I could position images at any place in the roll, regardless of when it was shot, as long as I could devise a system to identify the exact place in the roll where frames had already been exposed and where they had not. The series of films of one minute each, *Bouquets 1-10* (1994-1995), and those that followed, develop this way of working, by weaving different scenes of reality shot alternately at different moments over at least three passes of the film through the camera. The fishing boats at the port of Sète bathing in the poppy fields in *Les Coquelicots* (2002), or sailboats leaving the harbor of Marseille to wander through meadows in *Voiliers et Coqueli-cots* (2001), continue to explore this direction.

After I had found this way of working, with the help of homemade mattes and scores filled with notes taken during filming in order to be able to remember the images recorded, the question arose of the value of following such a meticulous process. In fact, in a general way, it was a question of bringing the pictorial together with the cinematic onto a common ground in respect to the arrangement of the visual qualities of a work. In looking at the painting *Petit intérieur bleu* by Matisse, it can be noticed there is a very limited choice of objects represented; certain have obviously been excluded, the arrangement of forms in the space is very specific, the ensemble provoking relationships between the way different components of the material have been treated, manipulated, placed. The whole forms a visual composition which establishes flexible relations between the work and our experience of reality at the same time that it engenders an experience of a nature different from what we could have imagined.

This way of responding to passing from the pictorial to the cinematic involves, as we have seen above, an arrangement of frames along the filmstrip that enables a mastery of the predominance of the temporal dimension. It is by working with this essential aspect of the mechanics of cinematography that I have been able to observe that filming in a particular place, selecting the elements which attract me in order to make them appear during the projection of a series of images, was a series of actions that lead to the pictorial. It developed into a spatial-temporal experience which brought out the characteristic trait of filmed reality while at the same time creating a work possessing a specific character.

Translated from "Du pictural au filmique. L'imprévu, l'inattendu, l'inconnu", pp.71-76, *L'image en mouvement*, Editions des Archives du Film Expérimental d'Avignon, Avignon, 2002.

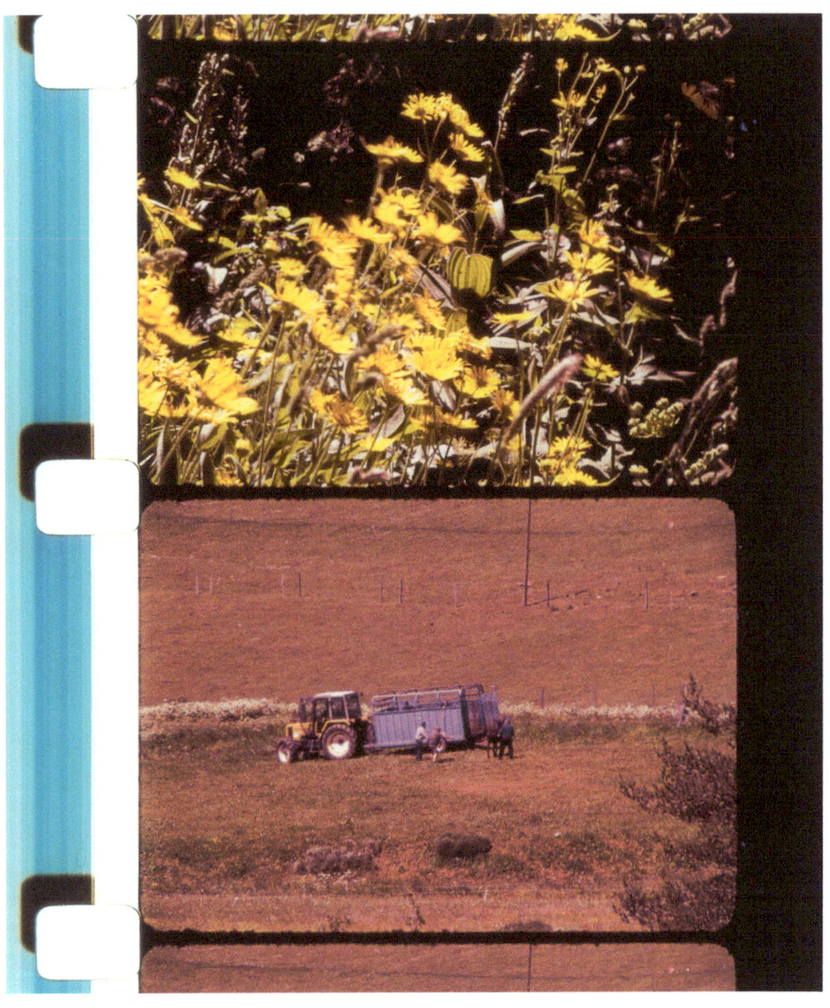

Bouquet 37 (2018)

FILMING FRAME-BY-FRAME AS A MEANS OF IMAGE COMPOSITION

By examining step-by-step my approach to filmmaking I am going to try to summarize the evolution of my process of composing images in the camera during the filming of scenes of daily life.

Having for a long time practiced a number of other visual media before starting to make films, I began to film in a way that borrowed from these different modes of expression different ways to modulate the visual characteristics of an image. Departing from the generally accepted norms of traditional cinema, it is possible, in relation to the flat, two-dimensional surface of the screen, to vary the focus from completely blurred to absolutely sharp and, by this means, to associate images of different tones of grey or a variety of nuances of colors with other more precisely defined and representational images. To the definition of forms, lines, and textures, can be added the possibility of using films with different sensitivity to light to bring out the film grain more or less explicitly in order to let it play a visual, graphic, or photographic role in the work's intent. It is in this way that by associating figurative and non-figurative images, the art of film has been able to become part of the evolution that has characterized the visual arts in the 20th century.

But in considering the way in which the dimension of time effects a work, one discovers a whole range of possibilities of modulating visual content which vary depending on whether it is a perception of a static object, such as a painting, or one evolving over time such as a film. Time plays a role in both cases but not in the same way. For a static work of art, it is a question of presenting forms, lines, textures and colors of the elements of the subject in two or three dimensions requiring the viewers' gaze, and often also their physical movements around a room in order to perceive the details of a work in relation to its whole from different distances. The duration of this activity depends as much on the motivation and the mood of the observers of the work as it does either on the circumstances in which they find themselves or the nature of the work on exhibit.

But when it is a question of a motion-based work of art which develops through a visual transformation over time, as is the case with the films considered here, and specifically if it is based on the nature of the visual elements of which it consists, it is the arrangement of the latter in relation to the filmstrip which becomes the primary parameter. Indeed, taking into account the temporality of projection in the composition of a film leads to the observation that the complexity of the film image is determined as much, if not more, by the combinations of the interactions of the components of the frames between themselves as it is by the nature of their visual appearance when viewed individually, one at a time.

It is from this perspective that I filmed the three films, grouped onto a single reel, *Roulement, rouerie, aubage,* two waterwheels on the Canal de la Sorgue in Avignon. The choice of this subject stemmed in part from the nature and the function of the mechanisms of these objects presenting several parameters, the evolution of which could, by the malleability of photographic process, be modulated during the filming. The successive movement of the paddles, more or less regular according to the length and width of their boards, permitted, by the adjustment of the focus in relation to the framing, to isolate certain characteristics of the wheels turning around their axis to compose a series of spatial-temporal experiments. At the beginning of *Roulement*, remembering a decade in the film industry when I was obliged to search for overexposed frames, I filmed one of the waterwheels just at the moment of the year when the sun was positioned so that the wet wooden paddles caught the rays of sunlight on each turn and overexposed several frames of film by its reflections. Having the rotation of the subject be a part of the filming process was a way to allowed the wheel to participate in the way it was presented.

It was also a way to continuously sustain the image on the screen on a line of demarcation situated between the realm of graphics, photography and representation in order to constantly slide between one or the other of these ways of perceiving things. This way of working by manipulating in the camera the appearance of the image while shooting according to the shifting characteristics of the subject in order to use the variations inherent to photographic realism, became a principle that I was then to pursue, to establish connections between certain aspects of the recorded reality and the nature of the image perceived when projected on film.

It was with this orientation that, for *Roulement, rouerie, aubage*, the series of focus points in relation to the framing in order to modulate the image in the camera without any editing was a way to specify the degree to which one could actually modify the traces of reality recorded on film. The framed image, focussed in several ways, permitted the movement of the water wheels to close off the point of view for variable durations, like opening windows of details and establishing filmic rhythms of the subject barely visible to the observer of this scene. The use of black and white film of differing sensibilities accentuated the graphic aspects of reality such as the edges of objects, the intersections, and sharpness of the texture of the wood or to bring out the poetic aspect of the subject filmed, permitting, for example, each paddle appearing out-of-focus on the upper part of the frame to be transformed into a powerful granular undulating wave, almost overflowing, before again becoming tranquilly clear as it progressively descended towards the lens. Filmed in a similar way in color, the same sequence had a tendency to present a more volumetric character, allowing the establishment of other relationships between the pictorial and the filmic space.

In an analogous way, in *Couleurs mécaniques*, I continued these experiments involving focussing in relation to framing by recording brightly colored parts of a fairground merry-go-round, a subject also characterized by a rotating motion. But this time the arrangement of the bits of reality was conceived in a way to make the nuances of color stand out as much as possible. Placing the camera in specific places allowed me to work with different degrees of definition and focus in order to emphasize the movement of people and parts of the merry-go-round's structure in relation to the background, while at the same time juxtaposing the bright emerald green of a strip of wood with the bright red of the floorboards, and, in this way, capturing the wheels turning at different speeds so that they seemed to be turning in reverse, then to introduce an upward movement of lights while, in reality, they were moving downwards, leaving the latter to open up as they floated up, or to suddenly disappear.

By modulating in this manner the perceptible qualities of a trace of recorded reality, one enters a domain where, by erasing in different ways the "realistic" character of the image, one departs from a simulation of reality in order to attempt to compose a series of frames capable of dealing with a cinematic idea. In this situation we place ourselves on the frontier where we can move from a so-called "representational" image to another of a more graphical character based on the malleability of the film image, which brings us into the domain of spatial-temporal experience where description and abstraction rarely occur. It is here that we encounter several problems.

In fact, one of the pitfalls of this filmic choice lies in the difficulty of conceiving a relation between the aspects of filmed reality and the reality transmitted by the film, while at the same time not allowing aestheticism to predominate. Actually this choice which consists of navigating between realism, naturalism and expressionism turns out to be as fascinating as it is difficult to confront.

At the same time as I made these films composed in the camera using focussing in relation to framing, I was also working on the possibilities of composing the image by shooting frame-by-frame. Starting in the 1960s and 1970s, numerous films from different sources were based on images composed of small numbers of single frames, revealing in a dazzling way, with astounding optical effects, new perspectives for the spatial-temporal arrangement of the elements of the filmic image.

A large number of these films were based on executing a pre-conceived idea of using certain already determined aspects of visual content in a specific way. From the visual capacity of this process of working with a succession of frames, I retained the importance of the choice of the process for structuring the work's form. After having systematically explored a variety of optical effects with a series of loops, I composed the images of *Parcelle* frame-by-frame, in the camera without any editing. As much in order to simplify my work as to test a certain number of specific ideas, this film was composed by recording a small number of graphic elements, interspersing them on the film strip frame-by-frame. Tiny red, yellow or blue squares or circles on a black background whose frequency and number continually increased or decreased, were juxtaposed with each other in different ways, sometimes interspersed with white, black, red, yellow or blue mono-chrome frames. The functioning of perception when faced with these projection-generated successions of images provokes the appearance of an overlapping of visual forms, making the forms and parts of forms, recorded as successive frames on the filmstrip, appear simulta-neous on the screen.

These two ways of structuring a work - focussing in relation to framing and frame-by-frame recording - provided the basis for a form of filmic composition which, by adapting them to the evolution of the perceptual qualities of reality understood cinematographically, allowed me to structure the image in the camera. I shot several films around Avignon according to these principles. *Rue des Teinturiers*, filmed between March and July from a balcony overlooking this street along the Canal de la Sorgue, *Champ Provençal*, filmed from April to June in an orchard of peach trees, and *Retour d'un repère composé*, shot under a tree in the garden of the Rocher des Doms. In all these cases, depending on the expressive possibilities of the location, the films were based on the selection of specific elements through the use of focussing, frame-by-frame shooting, concentrating on a limited number of elements present at the scene, the way in which their graphic or photographic qualities could be separated, isolated and recorded as distinct single frames on the filmstrip to establish the relationship necessary to function visually as an integral composition. Thus relatively complex actions were conceived especially for each film according to the evolution of the appearance of the filmed reality. By adopting a visual transposition of a poetic construct of Malaysian origin, the pantoum, *Retour d'un repère* employs the most meticulous structure in this series of films where the focus points interacted frame-by-frame in relation to the filmed space and the visual forms, graphic or photographic, recorded on the filmstrip in a way to make them appear intertwined with each other.

Nevertheless, one of the disadvantages of this way of working frame-by-frame is that often the procedure tends to produce an unwanted flickering that is somewhat decorative but devoid of any visual interest or meaning. By fixing the focus frame-by-frame in a slightly more controlled way with images of flowers in several fields at various focal distances, I was able, in the film *Les Tournesols*, to resolve to a certain degree this problem of instability in the image.

For all these films, the tendency was to gather the images in a single place at a single time, while filming from the same point of view but at different periods of blossoming, foliage, and fruiting, for *Champ Provençal*, then mix different seasons and years in the printing of the film for the series *Scènes de la vie française*. Subsequently I went on to broaden the temporal aspect in *Impromptu* and *Quiproquo*, with series of frames spread over time. Up to this point, the appearance of images on the filmstrip (and on the screen) corresponded rigorously to the order in which they were shot, but an exposure error in a reel of *Impromptu* led me to re-film in superimposition a part of the same scene in order to get the right result. In making this correction, I realized that I could, since my camera permitted rewinding the film during shooting, control the exposure of images on any section of the roll, without superimposition, in any order - a kind of image "weaving."

This way of filming in alternation was carried out in *Bouquets*, a series of films, each one minute long, dealing with a variety of subjects. The image of each *Bouquet* was composed through several passes through the camera, frame-by-frame, woven in an alternating order in the same place at different moments. Mixing plants found at a given location with whatever activities happened to take place at the time, each bouquet of flowers became, by this way of gathering frames, a bouquet of images.

From the moment one adopts this way of composing the filmic image, one finds oneself on common ground with other visual arts for certain aspects of the way of doing things. As in the process which consists of creating a painting, filming frame-by-frame permits one to explore one's cinematic propositions. In the case of one or two *Bouquets*, not having the time to continue filming, I was obliged to shoot fewer images than planned. Depending on the characteristics of the images already recorded on the film, the act of leaving, in an intermittent way, a certain number of black images can sometimes intensify certain aspects of the reality portrayed in the exposed images.

It could be that it is possible, by this way of shooting, to work in a way that, on the screen, a part of the frame disappears or is attenuated, allowing other elements of the image to appear more clearly, it is difficult to master the numerous optical subtleties provoked by the overlapping of characteristics during the projection of the film. The difficulty encountered in controlling this aspect of my practice, both of an aesthetic and technical nature, is also revealed when I compose the filmed image in the camera at different moments in different places. For *Les Coquelicots* and *Voiliers et Coquelicots,* near Arles, Bédarrides, and the grotto of Thouzon, I filmed frames, woven image by image in different alternating orders, in fields of poppies, shot in close-up, at a distance, backlit, and from every angle, in order to then film on the parts of the film not yet exposed the fishing boats of Sète, for *Les Coquelicots,* and sailboats leaving the port of Marseille for *Voiliers et Coquelicots.* The assemblage of the two series of images in the camera during filming in these different places permitted the fishing boats and sailboats to navigate on their own power through the flowers on the screen. But this combination of frames creates optical interactions during their slow irregular movement across the screen to orchestrate a sort of visual music based on the evolving rhythms which provoke a variety of surprises for the viewer during the projection.

In fact, not much is needed to make everything appear differently. The date, the time of day, the weather, the geography of the place, awareness at the moment of filming, many things can intervene when one adopts filming frame-by-frame as a means of image composition. And because my process is evolving, it is more difficult for me to draw a conclusion than to just, for the time being, end my account here.

Translated from "De l'enregistrement comme moyen de composition de l'image," *Pratiques 14 : Expéri-mentations cinématographiques : une vision de l'art élargie,* Marsaud Perrodin, Roselyne (ed), Automne 2003 : 44-54. Presses universitaires de Rennes, 2003.

IMPROVISED COMPOSITION OF THE FILM IMAGE IN THE CAMERA

I shall start with a truism by saying that the final result of a work of art is directly related to the way it is made.

Over the years, while composing the cinematographic image in the camera during filming, I found it necessary to develop a variety of drawn diagrams, scores or charts in order to keep track of what was being inscribed on the filmstrip as well as where what was being filmed was situated on the roll. As the camera I use allows me to wind the unexposed film back and forth, I can therefore film frames anywhere, in any order, anytime on the negative roll.

These scores became a crucial tool for a major part of my work as it was their gradual elaboration that helped develop more complex ways to interweave film frames in the camera which led to producing a greater amount of visual combinations and interactions.

One has to remember that creating a way to record what was being filmed and how it was being filmed, as I was working, in some perma-nent legible form by written or graphic means, was done purely for my own use. I needed both to know what I was doing as I was filming as well as to be able to check later on what had been done given the results.

I found it very difficult to represent visually what was done technically while at the same time documenting what took place in the scene. When filming out-of-doors without artificial lighting devices, the visual characteristics of the means of expression rest on very diverse evolving features. The change of light due to the movement of sun or clouds, the modification of filmed items and their shadows due to natural elements, wind, rain, sun or clouds, the unpredictable movement of birds, animals, people, machines, are all interacting reciprocally on each other.

The need to devise some written or diagrammatic method to take into account such sets of connected material or immaterial things (trees moved by the wind are visible whereas the wind itself can only be felt or known due to its effect on the trees) only became evident very gradually. A subject filmed in the usual technical way, i.e. continuously for a certain amount of time such as in the case of *Roulement, rouerie, aubage* (1978) or *Couleurs mécaniques* (1979), even though in those films a few modulations such as focussing and framing were involved, just requires a simple logbook to note down, amongst other things, the number of the roll, date, light indications, film stock and its speed, lens, filters, et cetera. It was only when frames were filmed individually and eventually woven together in the camera during filming that more meticulous diagrams were necessary.

One of my first films filmed frame-by-frame was *Parcelle* (1979). Using an art gallery invitation with a tiny white square in the middle of a black card as a guide to place alternatively three equally tiny yellow, blue and red squares or circles, I tested systematically to what extent items presented on frames following in succession can appear simultaneously on the screen. A whole series of rotations concerning one, two or three frames of the same image were varied to give more or less importance to the squares or circles on their black, white, or by the means of filters, blue, yellow, red, backgrounds.

. . .

As could be expected, all sorts of successive features appear simultaneously on the screen. A circle of one color inscribes itself within the boundaries of a square of another color on a diversity of colored backgrounds. Consisting of a sort of geometric still life using a card and little bits of paper in order to move them around easily, *Parcelle* was entirely suitable to analyse how the cinematographic procedure allows different elements following in succession on the film strip to appear to overlap when projected on the screen.

After *Parcelle* I worked in a similar way on scenes of reality, a street viewed from home, *Rue des Teinturiers* (1979), a nearby orchard, *Champ Provençal* (1979). In both cases I had to invent a different sort of document to write down what was done.

The two films are based on a fixed framing for each of their rolls and a series of focus points ranging from one nearby item to another in the distance. There is one rotation between the focus points, back and forth so as to avoid a traditional smooth advance or retreat within the filmed space. Another rotation concerned the number of frames filmed at each focus point, for instance, in alternation, 1, 2, 3, 2, 1. Taken as a whole, this meant that each time a focus point was filmed, the number of frames was different from the previous time it was registered. The idea was to render selected items in the scene autonomous so that they could intermingle with each other when projected in succession on the screen.

So, besides a few technical details, the diagrams for the two films show progression through each roll, the order of the focus points, the number of frames filmed for each focus point and a few indications about the weather, date and time of day, et cetera. There are also small black and white drawings of the scenes with the numbered focus points marked on them.

The problem was that although these films showed how one could make separate items on successive frames blend with each other on the screen, this was not without a certain amount of flickering or vibration inherent to the filming procedure. It took some time to work around this difficulty.

For *Retour d'un repère* I filmed a branch of a fine cedar tree in the local park. This film was also based on the rotation of a number of focal points in correlation with a rotation of the number of frames they were filmed, except here I consulted our literary rhetorical dictionary which led me to discover, and to adapt, a Malaysian poetic measure, the pantoum. This rhetorical figure consists of gradually including a new element while dropping one of the previous ones as the poem continues.

The filming of *Retour d'un repère* follows a similar pattern to that of a pantoum. The procedure is based on seven different points in space, from the nearest point one to the furthest point seven. As was the case with the earlier films filmed frame-by-frame, several focus points converge continuously on the screen to form a mobile visual composition.

In addition to the two rotations, the order of the filmed focal points and the number of frames filmed, the sun also rotates, lighting up the branch at one moment while visitors' brightly colored clothes passing by reflect in the pond below the branch. As the result renders a more complex visual structure, difficult to perceive in three minutes, the final film is made up of eight identical prints. One tends to see something different each time the roll is repeated.

I still wanted to have a more stable image on the screen. I think this is the case with *Les Tournesols* (1982). The reasons are that although in this film I am filming frame-by-frame in a similar way to the previous films, the subject of several fields of sunflowers provided an allover pattern and the heliotropic movement of the flowers following the rotation of the sun predominated over the flickering caused by recording the successive focal points strewn over the area. Those two features, pictorially similar flowers covering the whole image and the slight continuous movement of their form made the image on the screen seem relatively steady.

All these films were composed during filming in the camera meaning each roll remains in the final print as it was exposed.

Up to this point all the films' frames were registered in the order that they are projected on the screen.

My next stage was to interweave frames filmed in alternation at two different times from a single viewpoint. This was the case with the four different scenes in *Impromptu* (1989). At one point, for example, a selected number of frames were first filmed in front of a farm lime tree at 1p.m., then, after winding the roll back in the camera, the unexposed frames were filmed a couple of hours later. The result is that the tree trunk remains stationary on the screen while the tree's leaves vary their position, color, light and shade much more than is usual as what is seen on the screen is the blending of the two periods when the scene was filmed.

A 1p.m - 3p.m. lime tree! Then, as I continued, for punctuation, to film the tree traditionally, the couple of farmers turned up in their blue van with their little white dog to plant their tomatoes.

This way of working inadvertently opened new pathways, helped by an important mistake that I made in the last roll of the film. While filming alternatively the second series of images in front of trees in a meadow, I had set the aperture at f/8 instead of f/5.6. After quick reflection I rewound the roll and then refilmed those frames at f/22 in order for the images filmed at two different periods to correspond to each other in terms of lighting.

This error was very significant as it made me realize that I could film anywhere on the roll, at any time, no matter where. No need to keep to a single fixed viewpoint nor to film from the beginning of a piece of negative to the end of the roll in that order.

This started a second stage which consisted of exposing frames on a roll in non chronological order. First attempted in *Quiproquo* (1992), then partly adopted in the first *Bouquets 1- 10* (1994-1995), this way of working was developed more fully in *Bouquets 21-30* (2001-2005) and *Bouquets 11-20* (2005-2010). It is particularly evident in *Les Coquelicots* (2000) and *Voiliers et Coquelicots* (2001).

Until now the filming process was sufficiently simple for written notes and a few diagrams to be adequate for the purpose, but given the more complex recording procedure of the *Bouquets*, I had to find a way not only to note down for future reference what was being done as it was being done but also to invent and create a clean chart or score for me to fill in as I was working both to allow me to film anywhere on the film strip without superimposing images and to imagine or deduce how the different frames would correspond in significant visual terms.

It took me ages to develop on paper a suitable system. There was a definite correlation between devising a method to write down the necessary information and developing the filming procedure. One has to trace through the films and the corresponding notebooks to see how the two developed.

At the beginning the diagrams were functional for the films concerned. The hand-drawn *Parcelle* diagram indicates clearly how the three rotating elements composing the film, the shapes in the images, black or white backgrounds, the different colors of the circles, squares or backgrounds appear on the filmstrip. That diagram, however, was made to measure and only suitable for that particular film.

The small black ink drawings for *Rue des Teinturiers* and *Champ Provençal* only take into account the framing and changing focus points of the filmed scenes. For *Impromptu* and *Quiproquo* some of the information is noted down in various ways regarding the filming of alternative frames at two different periods as well as the total number of images recorded for the different sequences. But for a description of what was filmed, and in what circumstances, light, et cetera, I had to resort to fairly laborious written observations.

Since this way of noting down bits of information did not take into account the essential aspects of what was being done nor how it was being done, during the filming of the *Bouquets* series, I had to find a way to make a chart that was both economical in size, something that could be easily transported and fixed to the tripod while filming, and functional, making it possible to record the essential features of what was done as I worked.

After several unsuccessful attempts of writing descriptions by hand, the first graphic chart depicting clearly every filmed frame, second by second, appeared for working out the titles for *Bouquets 1* and *2*. But this type of score was not adopted immediately since for *Bouquet 4* there is still a primitive version in black ink recapitulating what was done, indicating the number of frames and seconds as the roll is filmed, with written descriptions of what was filmed during each second and a few comments such as where the battery was flat, where I forgot to adjust the light, et cetera, as well as indications of the meters or feet filmed for each second in the roll. For anyone else, this page, lacking drawings, would have been almost impossible to interpret and I even took a while to do so myself.

I continued this sort of logbook method for a while and *Bouquets 5, 7, 10, 1* and *3* (1995) all adopt similar written descriptions. I made all sorts of attempts to devise a graphic system which would be easy to handle, to fill in, to interpret while at the same time giving more precise information.

There was a question of how to place the diagrams on the page, vertically or horizontally. Horizontal provided the information but was difficult to read when transferred into the notebook as it meant I had to turn the page around. However, that stage was a start as the figures of the two frame counters on the camera at the end of each of the ten seconds were indicated.

For *Voiliers et Coquelicots* the diagram was made to measure, vertical, full color, every second was noted down with elaborate, if concise, indications of what was on every frame of the film including an expanded version of the end titles similar to the scores I developed later on. Besides technical information, I also indicated in great detail, the dates and hours of filming, where the fields were situated and that the boats were sailing out of the Vieux-Port of Marseille.

For *Voiliers et Coquelicots* this score was sufficient as it was easy to depict in succession two frames of vermillion poppies, even if being filmed in different parts of the field required a change of tone or little drawings within the squares indicating the frames to distinguish them, to be followed by a Prussian blue frame for the boats. But this was not the case once the subject filmed lent itself less to such pictorial devices, as was the case with *Bouquet 21* (2001). This type of chart needed to be accompanied by a laborious effort both to note down and to read, written descriptions. This took so much time that with all my other occupations, I have still not transferred *Bouquets 22, 23* and *24* (2001) into a notebook.

Bouquet 25 (2002) inaugurates the first charts that deal graphically, frame-by-frame, second by second, with what was done during filming. The drawn diagram neither transposes what was filmed nor how as clearly as the later ones do, (see some of the pages for *Bouquets 15, 16, 17, 18* and *19*), but it does indicate how, in rewinding the roll, the images composing the scenes were taken at three different times for an exact number of frames, half a second, a whole second, or a number of seconds. There are also little drawings of various filmed items such as the washing on the line or the village cows in the field, et cetera, and graphic features to indicate how a scene filmed in one way for a second continued to be filmed in the same way for several seconds more while other scenes were being interwoven with it, each for a different number of seconds at two other periods of time.

For the first time, in *Bouquet 26* (2003) a diagonal line appeared to indicate when a scene was filmed normally and not interwoven with another item. *Bouquets 27* (2003), *28, 29, 30* (2005) continued to develop the same type of chart, where some filmed items were drawn schematically, accompanied by graphic signs indicating more explicitly where one of the woven or not woven images started and finished. Every frame was noted down. Many more recent films, *Bouquets 11-20* (2005-2010), *Jardin du Soleil* (2010), *Jardins du Marais* (2010), *Rien d'extraordinaire* (2010), *Sources* (2012) and *foryannfromrose* (2014) use this form of chart.

Once the filming of a roll is finished, the penciled information on the chart was copied into a notebook in black ink and colored to make the pages easier to consult. Afterwards, as these charts take time to make, the pencil notes were rubbed out in order to be able to reuse the charts.

For some films, such as *Habitat* (2006), I did not need a chart. There is no way that I could count the number of frames a frog takes to jump into the pond. Even if I could have had this information, given that, when projected on a screen, a second is 24 frames, and that you can see on the filmstrip that a frog's jump appears for only 2 frames, it is difficult to see how that could have been put on a chart in a useful way.

Nevertheless, the charts played a major role in allowing me to develop ways to blend intricately, frame-by-frame, a variety of images taken at different times and/or in different places.

Here we return to the title of this article. I chose improvised composition because although there is a basic filming procedure created to compose the image in the camera during filming, nothing else is planned before arriving at the place the filming is to be done. Although I select the location for environmental reasons, I chose the images to be filmed on the spot as it depended entirely on what cinematographic possibilities the subject offered at that precise moment.

Originally published as "Improvised composition of the film image in the camera," pp. 46-52, in *On Film*, OEI #69-70, Stockholm, 2015.

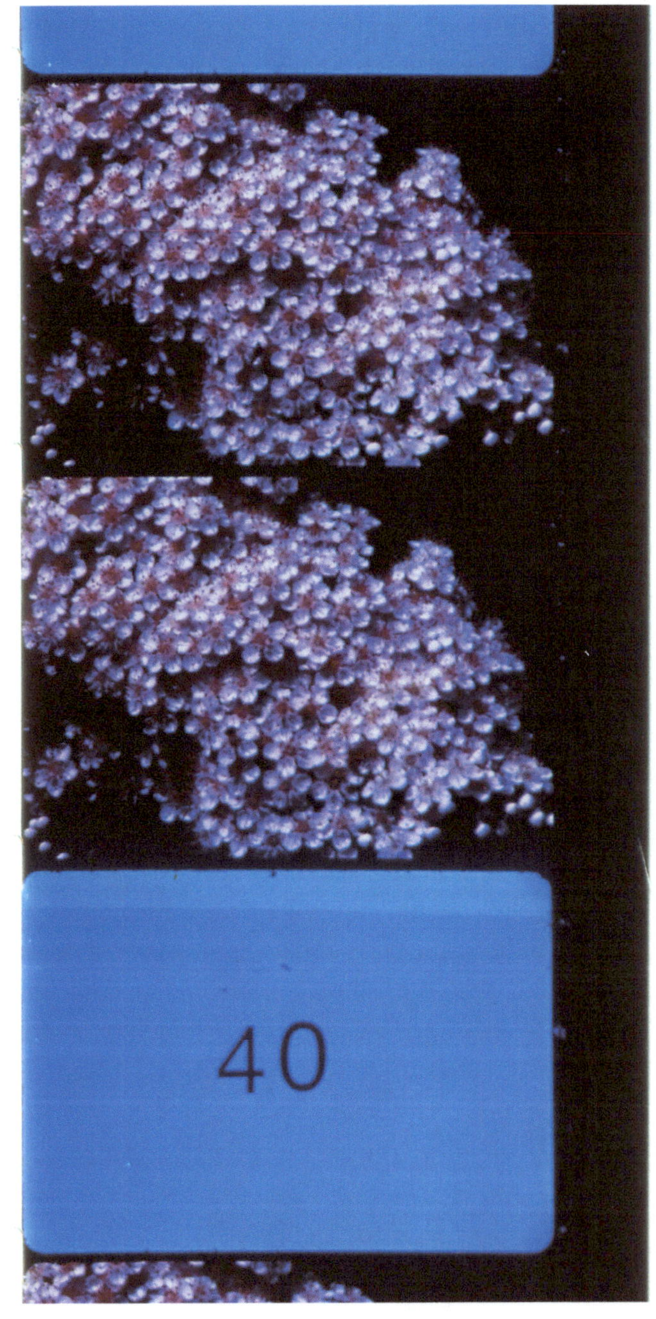

Bouquet 40 (2022)

NOTES ON CONTRIBUTORS

Enrico Camporesi oversees the research activities of the Centre Pompidou film department. His book *Futurs de l'obsolescence* (Éditions Mimésis, 2018) is about restoring artists' films.

Sarah Cooper is Professor of Film Studies at King's College London. In addition to her work on Rose Lowder, she has written on plants and film in articles on Jessica Hausner, F. Percy Smith, and Bo Wang and Pan Lu. Most recently she has served as Guest Editor of a Special Issue of *Philosophies*, "Thinking Cinema - with Plants," forthcoming in 2023.

Elena Duque is an artist, writer and teacher who makes her own experimental animated films and curates programs for (S8) Mostra de Cinema Periférico and the Seville European Film Festival. She edited *Val del Omar. Más allá de la órbita terrestre for* BAFICI in 2015, *8 super 8 for* (S8) Mostra de Cinema Periférico, and the zine *La mecánica de la luz.*

· · ·

Scott MacDonald is the author of 20 books including *A Critical Cinema: Interviews with Independent Filmmakers* (5 volumes), and most recently *Avant-Doc: Intersections of Documentary* and *Avant-Garde Cinema, The Sublimity of Document: Cinema as Diorama,* and (with Jacqueline Stewart) *William Greaves: Filmmaking as Mission.* He has curated films for Anthology Film Archives, the Harvard Film Archive, SFMoMA and other venues. Currently, he teaches at Hamilton College in New York State, where he curates the F.I.L.M. series.

Tara Merenda Nelson is a curator, programmer, filmmaker and lecturer in Rochester, New York. She is the Curator and Director of Public Programs at Visual Studies Workshop, whose archive preserves over 10,000 16mm film and early video titles. She programs the VSW Salon series, and, as an Associate Editor for the VSW FAB (Film Artist Books), an imprint of the VSW Press, edited and published *Bouquets 11-20: The Notebooks of Rose Lowder* in 2018.

Michael Sicinski is a critic and scholar specializing in avant-garde and experimental cinema who has also published more broadly on contemporary world cinema. He is on the faculty of the University of Houston, and writes regularly for various film magazines.

NOTES

EDITOR'S NOTE

1. From "The Pictorial to the Filmic: the unplanned, the unexpected, the unknown" (included in this volume).
2. Ibid.

TOWARD AN ECOLOGICAL CINEMA

1. Peter Kubelka's well-known essay "The Theory of Metrical Film" is included in P. Adams Sitney, *The Avant-Garde Film*, 139-59. Kubelka uses his early films as examples of "metrical structure" based on the assumption that the essential "articulation of cinema" takes place "not between shots but between frames." Lowder's research became her Ph.D. dissertation at the Université Paris-Nanterre: *Le film expérimental en tant qu'instrument de recherche visuelle: Contribution des cinéastes expérimentaux à une démarche exploratoire* (1987).
2. Lowder in Scott MacDonald, *A Critical Cinema 3: Interviews with Independent Filmmakers* (Berkeley: University of California Press, 1998), 219.
3. Lowder has lived in France since 1973, though she was born to British parents in Lima, Peru (in 1941), and worked for some years in London (at the BBC). She has an extensive knowledge of independent cinema from many parts of the world, in part because of her work as an archivist and programmer at the Archives du film expérimental d'Avignon, which she (and her partner, Alain-Alcide Sudre) established in 1982.
4. In the case of *Retour d'un repère*, this expansion was itself extended, first, in *Rapprochements* (1979), a two-projector film in which two prints of *Retour d'un repère* are projected one on top of the other (Lowder: "to see if I could make a brighter film," in MacDonald, *A Critical Cinema 3*, 234), and in 1981, in *Retour d'un repère composé*, a fifty-nine-minute reworking of the same material.
5. Lowder, in MacDonald, *A Critical Cinema 3*, 236.
6. The title of *Impromptu* refers to the fact that Lowder had been asked to screen the film before she considered it finished, and also to a series of accidents that occurred during and after the shooting. See MacDonald, *A Critical Cinema 3*, 237.
7. MacDonald and Lowder, in MacDonald, *A Critical Cinema 3*, 238-39.
8. The flowers are those that "happened to be on our balcony when I decided to introduce a pause of black in between each *Bouquet* with a single flower as punctuation" (Lowder, letter to the author, September 8, 1998): a red pourpier (portulaca or purslane); a white snapdragon; a small sunflower; a magenta portulaca, a yellow-orange marigold, a white arum lily (of the Araceae family); a black-centered, yellow-petaled rudbeckia, a yellow-orange portulaca; a white arum lily.

A FILMIC EXPLORATION BY MEANS OF BOTANICAL IMAGERY: NOTES ON ROSE LOWDER

1. On this topic, in an interview with William English, Lowder recalls attending a screening of Robert Breer's *Recreation* (1956) while she was living in London around 1964 (held at *Better Books*). In the filmmaker's words: "I found that very interesting. To me it was quite evident, right from the beginning, that the individual frames or pictures were not at all equal. They seemed to have a different time according to what was in the picture." English 1989, p. 106.
2. "While traditional cinematography consisted of two motions, that of the camera and that of the reality filmed, the actual mechanics of the camera reveal possibilities inherent in the arrangement of images arising from the movement of the filmstrip." Translated from Lowder, 1995, p. 147.
3. It is worth noting that Lowder has always combined theoretical writing together with her artistic practice. This is most evident in her Ph.D dissertation, under the direction of Jean Rouch. See Lowder, 1987.
4. The reference is to the article by P. Adams Sitney (Sitney, 1969).
5. Kubelka, 1978, p. 141.
6. MacDonald, 1998, p. 219.
7. Looking closely at the film strip one can see that the focus changes according to various "scores" such as: 1/2/3/2/1 or 1/2/2/3/2/2/1 (in which each number indicates how many frames share the same focus). The musical paradigm can be useful if one thinks of such strategy in terms of "variations" - according to light, weather, minor accidents. On this note, Lowder would also use what happened in the streets as a palette of color (as for instance choosing to shoot a red car in a shot that lacks warm colors, and so on).
8. MacDonald 1998, p. 231.
9. *Retour d'un repère* (1979) functions in a rather similar way. Later, in 1981, Lowder reworked the film's source material into another film, whose length is extended to nearly an hour. For an in-depth discussion of *Retour d'un repère composé* (1981) see Cartwright & Gidal 1986-87.
10. MacDonald 1998, p. 226.
11. Hamlyn 2003, p. 63.
12. For a discussion of the "flicker film" see Michaud 2006, pp. 121-134.
13. It is worth remembering that in the same year Lowder made another three-minute film from the same negative entitled *Les Tournesols colorés*. The two films can be screened together side by side, creating a new dynamic between the two different images.
14. On the relationship between filmic material and temporality Peter Gidal writes: "[d]uration can be theorized in relation to discontinuity, the piece of filmstrip-time which is cut at begin and end by the splice." Gidal 1989, p. 100.
15. MacDonald 2001, p. 84.
16. MacDonald 2005, p. 219.
17. For instance, *Bouquet 10* was shot on the lake Serre-Ponçon, and *Bouquet 7* in Tonnerre.

18. Lowder 1997.
19. Michaud, 2011, p. 40.
20. Quoted in Lévi-Strauss 1962, p. 6.

PERCEPTUAL-IMAGINATIVE SPACE AND THE BEAUTIFUL ECOLOGIES OF ROSE LOWDER'S BOUQUETS

1. Rose Lowder, *Rose by Rose Lowder* (Paris: Light Cone Editions, 2015), 86.
2. After completing *1-10*, Lowder began *11-20* but was not satisfied with them so made *21-30*, which she ended up completing first, hence their non-chronological order (*Rose by Rose Lowder*, 83). In a Master Class at Lux, London in September 2018 she said that she is still making *Bouquets*.
3. See her DVD Interview (2002) on "Cinéxpérimentaux 5: Rose Lowder" (Re:Voir, 2014).
4. William English, "Three Aspects of French Experiment: Interviews with yann beauvais and Rose Lowder and Alain-Alcide Sudre", Millennium Film Journal 23/24 (Winter 1990-1), 106-15.
5. Rose Lowder, "Le film expérimental en tant qu'instrument de recherche visuelle : contribution des cinéastes expérimentaux à une démarche exploratoire", 622, Light Cone archive, Paris.
6. Rose Lowder, "The Filming and the Film: A Brief Introduction to the Work, " March 1985, *Cantrills Filmnotes* 47/48 (August 1985), 56-60 (59).
7. P. Adams Sitney, *Visionary Film: The American Avant-Garde*, 1943-2000, 3rd edition (Oxford: Oxford University Press, 2002 [1974]), 347-70.
8. Rose Lowder, "Leaving the Artist's Studio Behind or How to Make Bouquets Out of Flowers and Film", Cantrills Filmnotes 85/86 (June 1997), 54-8 (55).
9. Lowder, "Le film expérimental," 205.
10. The volume *Perception: Mechanisms and Models* (San Francisco: W. H. Freeman and Company, 1972), edited by Richard Held and Whitman Richards, is a recurrent reference point.
11. Jean-Paul Sartre, *The Imaginary: A Phenomenological Psychology of the Imagination*, translated by Jonathan Webber (London: Routledge, 2010 [1940]), 235-39 and Maurice Merleau-Ponty, *Phenomenology of Perception*, translated by Colin Smith (London: Routledge, 2002 [1945]), 306-8.
12. Sartre, *The Imaginary*, 8.
13. Merleau-Ponty, *Phenomenology of Perception*, 236.
14. My exploration of imagination here differs therefore from the focus of my earlier *Film and the Imagined Image* (Edinburgh: Edinburgh University Press, 2019), which was devoted to how spectators conjure vivid mental images while watching film.
15. Maurice Merleau-Ponty, "Eye and Mind" in *The Merleau-Ponty Aesthetics Reader: Philosophy and Painting*, edited by Galen A. Johnson (Evanston: Northwestern University Press, 1993 [1960]), 121-49 (146). Initially close to Sartre in *Phenomenology of Perception* when writing about perception and imagination, Merleau-Ponty distances himself in his later work on imagination from his fellow phenomenologist. For more on this in relation to film, see Sarah Cooper, "Merleau-Ponty and Film: Docu-

menting the Imagination" in *Understanding Merleau-Ponty, Understanding Modernism*, edited by Ariane Mildenberg (New York: Bloomsbury, 2019), 157-69.

16. Joseph Addison, *Essays on the Pleasures of the Imagination*, Antwerp: Duverger & Co., 1828, 7. His essays appeared originally in The Spectator in 1712.

17. Addison, *Pleasures*, 3.

18. Immanuel Kant, *Observations on the Feeling of the Beautiful and Sublime and Other Writings*, edited and translated by Patrick Frierson and Paul Guyer, Cambridge: Cambridge University Press, 2011 [1764]), 14.

19. Immanuel Kant, *Critique of Judgment*, translated by Werner S. Pluhar, Indianapolis: Hackett Publishing Company, 1987 [1790]), 114.

20. Kant, *Critique of Judgment*, 112-13.

21. Kant, *Critique of Judgment*, 115.

22. Kant, *Critique of Judgment*, 115.

23. Elaine Scarry, *On Beauty and Being Just* (Princeton: Princeton University Press, 1999), 84.

24. When Scarry addresses imaginability elsewhere, the size of the object to be imagined is important. Flowers are exemplary objects for her: their size, shape and localization, as well as the rarity of their petals, lend themselves to vivid imagining. See her *Dreaming by the Book*, Princeton: Princeton University Press, 2001 [1999]), 40-71.

25. Guinevere Narraway, "Strange Seeing: Re-viewing Nature in the Films of Rose Lowder" in *Screening Nature: Cinema Beyond the Human*, edited by Anat Pick and Guinevere Narraway, Oxford: Berghahn, 2013, 213-24 (221).

26. Scarry, "On Beauty and Being Just," 51. For a critique of the denigration of the pretty specific to film, see Rosalind Galt, *Pretty: Film and the Decorative Image*, New York: Columbia University Press, 2011.

27. Scarry, "On Beauty and Being Just," 94.

28. Scarry, "On Beauty and Being Just," 3-6.

29. Enrico Camporesi, "A Filmic Exploration by Means of Botanical Imagery: Notes on Rose Lowder" (reprinted in this volume.)

30. Lowder, DVD Interview (2002).

31. Scarry, "On Beauty and Being Just," 88.

32. Scarry, "On Beauty and Being Just," 61.

33. Scott MacDonald, "Toward an Eco-Cinema," ISLE 11:2, July 2004, 107-32, (109); Narraway, "Strange Seeing," 221.

34. Luce Irigaray and Michael Marder, *Through Vegetal Being: Two Philosophical Perspectives*, New York: Columbia University Press, 2016, 48.

35. Iris Murdoch, "The Sovereignty of Good over Other Concepts" in *The Sovereignty of Good*, London: Routledge, 2014 [1970]), 75-100 (88).

36. Murdoch, "The Sovereignty," 88. *Perceptual-Imaginative Space*, 329.

37. Murdoch, "The Sovereignty," 82.

38. Murdoch, "The Sovereignty," 82.

39. Murdoch, "The Sovereignty," 83.

40. For an exploration of Murdoch's "unselfing" in relation to film as an art form, see Lucy Bolton, *Contemporary Cinema and the Philosophy of Iris Murdoch*, Edinburgh: Edinburgh University Press, 2019.

41. Scarry's sense of fairness is centered on loveliness of aspect but there is a far more pernicious association with fairness in Edmund Burke's work on beauty and the

sublime. Burke describes colors of beautiful bodies as 'clean and fair' not 'dusky and muddy' initiating a hierarchy in skin color that links to race and then blackness as the text progresses. See Edmund Burke, *A Philosophical Inquiry into the Origin of our Ideas of the Sublime and Beautiful,* London: Howlett and Brimmer, 1823 [1757]), 169. For more on the question of race in Burke's and Kant's theories, see Meg Armstrong, "The Effects of Blackness: Gender, Race, and the Sublime in the Aesthetic Theories of Burke and Kant," *The Journal of Aesthetics and Art Criticism 54:3* (Summer 1996), 213-36.

42. Haraway's slogan appears throughout *Staying with the Trouble: Making Kin in the Chthulucene,* Durham, N.C: Duke University Press, 2016.
43. Irigaray, in Irigaray and Marder, "Through Vegetal Being," 38.
44. Irigaray, in Irigaray and Marder, "Through Vegetal Being," 50.
45. Irigaray, in Irigaray and Marder, "Through Vegetal Being", 49-50.
46. Luce Irigaray, "The Invisible of the Flesh: A Reading of Merleau-Ponty, The Visible and the Invisible, 'The Intertwining - The Chiasm'" in *An Ethics of Sexual Difference,* translated by Carolyn Burke and Gillian C. Gill, Ithaca: Cornell University Press, 1993 [1984]), 151-84 (152).

THE BOUQUET NOTEBOOKS

1. *Bouquets 11-20: Notebooks by Rose Lowder,* VSW PRESS, Film Art Book 2018.

ROSE LOWDER, SINGLE FRAME WORKER

1. Henri Chomette made *Cinq minutes de cinéma pur* in 1925.
2. *Film Culture* n° 29, 1963.
3. *Film Culture* n° 29, 1963.
4. Scott MacDonald, *A Critical Cinema 2: Interviews with Independent Filmmakers,* University of California Press, 1992, p. 22.
5. *Robert Breer A to Z,* Ed. Scott Hammen, AFEA Editions, 2016.
6. Rose Lowder, *Poétique de la couleur,* Ed. Nicole Brenez, Miles McKane, Auditorium du Louvre-Institut de l'image, 1995.
7. P. Adams Sitney; *Visionary Film: The American Avant-Garde 1943-1978,* Oxford University Press, Inc., 1974.1979.
8. Scott MacDonald, *A Critical Cinema 5: Interviews with 4 Independent Filmmakers,* University of California Press, 2006.
9. Herman Mhire (editor), Robert Russett; *Robert Russett: A Retrospective Survey,* University Art Museum, University of Southwestern Louisiana, 1989.
10. Gehr, in MacDonald, *A Critical Cinema 5.*
11. Really Red, *Ode to Kurt Kren,* Released by Angry Neighbor, 1992.
12. Peter Tscherkassky (editor); *Film Unframed. A History of Austrian Avant-Garde Cinema;* sixpackfilm, 2012.

FILM AS VISUAL ART

1. Not to mention the pitfalls of the manneristic virtuosity currently in fashion, noted by the Catalan graphic artist Peret: "It is obvious that the computer has radically changed the practice of graphic art. But these splendid images are often hollow, insignificant. Where has the poetry of Cassandra gone, the caustic vision of Cieslewicz? This new mannerism of virtuosity lacks a soul." *Le Monde,* 20 April 2002, p.31.
2. Len Lye, "Film Making. Movement as Language" (1935), pp.39-42 and "The Art That Moves" (1964), pp.78-87 in *Figures of Motion. Selected Writings*, Eds. Wystan Curnow and Roger Horrocks, Auckland University Press/Oxford University Press, 1984.
3. Remarks by Raymond Depardon at L'École des Arts de la Sorbonne (EAS), Université Paris I, 26 March 2002.

ACKNOWLEDGMENTS

The contents of this book were assembled with the help of Rose Lowder and Miguel Armas of Light Cone. It could not have been created without their support.

The contributing authors, Enrico Camporesi, Sarah Cooper, Elena Duque, Scott MacDonald, Tara Nelson, and Michael Sicinski, generously allowed their writing to be published here and Marie-Hélène Hammen patiently reviewed the text for errors. The errors that remain are solely the responsibility of the editor.